THE CRAFT OF
AMERICAN HISTORY

Volume II

THE CRAFT OF AMERICAN HISTORY

Selected Essays

EDITED BY
A. S. Eisenstadt

Volume II

HARPER TORCHBOOKS ❦ The Academy Library
Harper & Row, Publishers, New York

To the Memory of My Mother and Father

THE CRAFT OF AMERICAN HISTORY: VOLUME II

Compilation, Introductions, and Bibliographies copyright ©
1966 by A. S. Eisenstadt.

Printed in the United States of America.

First Edition: HARPER TORCHBOOKS, 1966
Harper & Row, Publishers, Incorporated
New York, N.Y. 10016.

Designed by Audrey Sinclare

Contents

Volume II

PART FIVE

The Varieties of History

Introductory Notes

If Clio's is a mansion of many chambers, it is one that periodically undergoes reconstruction. Each age has its new history. In each new history, further vistas are opened up, while, no less significantly, several are closed. New experiences alter a society and alter too its perspectives on the past, demanding new insights for new relevances and making many old insights irrelevant. No age has been without its historical renovation, and no new history has claimed anything less than a wish to renovate the whole past and nothing but the whole past.

Thus, speaking to the American Historical Association in 1924, Charles M. Andrews, one of our outstanding writers of colonial history, staked out "the entire life of the times" as the historian's proper domain. "He may need to know something about the religious creeds, socialistic theories, systems of land distribution and agronomy, the working of the common law, the influence of money and banking and international exchange, the literature, art, architecture, and philosophy of an age, and even of the laws of nature in the fields of physics, chemistry, biology and psychology—indeed the whole historical complex in peace and war. Any part of the whole record of civilization is the legitimate object of his quest." Before Andrews's pronouncement, James Harvey Robinson had proclaimed a New History, with capital letters, which undertook to make the study of the past useful for the cause of social progress. Robinson decried the prominence accorded political history. "Man is more than a warrior, a subject, or a princely ruler; the State is by no means his sole interest. . . . He has, through the age, made voyages, extended commerce, founded cities, established great universities, written books, built glorious cathedrals, painted pictures, and sought out many inventions." These components of man's adventure also belonged in history books.

Writing almost a century before Robinson and Andrews, Thomas Babington Macaulay was no less intent than they to see the past in a new light and to see it entire. In his famous essay on "History," which appeared in the *Edinburgh Review* in 1828, Macaulay declaimed against the faulty perspective of historians, their mistaken sense of what mattered in history. The progress of the truly important circumstances in man's condition "is rarely indicated by what historians are pleased to call important events. They are not achieved by armies, or enacted by senates. They are sanctioned by no treaties, and recorded in no archives." The perfect historian makes his canvas broad. "He shows us the court, the camp, and the senate. But he shows us also the nation." And was this not indeed akin to what Voltaire had said earlier in the introduction to his *Age of Louis XIV* (1752), in which he said that it was not his purpose to present "the exhaustive details of wars, of towns besieged, taken and retaken by force of arms, given and regained by treaty. . . ." Rejecting contemporary modes of historical writing, seeing the scope of history as considerably broader than biography or diplomacy and war, Voltaire said he would write about "only that which merits the attention of the ages . . . that which depicts the genius and manners of men, or which serves to instruct and inculcate the love of country, of virtue, and of art." Andrews, Robinson, Macaulay, and Voltaire are but examples in a larger and longer succession which reveals not merely the changing scope but also the changing purpose of history. A new age, a new history.

In our own age, the realms of history are being freshly cultivated and widely extended. Older varieties of history are coming under a different perspective, and some indeed are being revived: these include the study of constitutional development, of civil liberties and civil rights, of diplomatic relations, and of religious institutions and movements. Among the new varieties that have been explored in recent years are the study of American ideas and their importance in defining our national experience and character, of the growth of cities and the emergence of an urban civilization, of business development and the role of the entrepreneurial class, of the transformation of society and the aspirations and mobility of different social groups, of American historical writing and the larger significance of its changing form and substance.

If historical study is a form of self-consciousness, the way a society measures the distance it has come along the road it means to go, then some of the reasons for the newer varieties of history are not too difficult to find. They spring from the soil of recent American experience. The basic fact of our history in recent decades has been America's emergence as a world leader in a scene of conflicting power systems and ideologies. The basic question before us has been about the vitality and validity of the American idea. If we have of late, in our historical researches, been concerned with the changing pattern of our society, our business achievement, our urban civilization, the American idea and image, and what is called, indeed, the American experience, the reason has been that these researches are immediately relevant to America's new position among nations. Tocqueville stands large at the writing-desk of American history today, just as Turner and Beard did before him; the prophet of Paris, with his inquiry about America considered from without, has replaced the sons of the middle border, with their inquiry about America considered from within. The question that Tocqueville asked concerning the character and significance of America, because ours was then a newer order in a world that was growing old, we now have come to ask of ourselves, because ours is an older order in a world alive with innovation.

Three of the following essays are concerned with different aspects of the new history of our own age. John Higham, of the University of Michigan, deals with American intellectual history, tracing its earlier forms in the nineteenth-century, in the age of the New History (the generation of James Harvey Robinson, Merle Curti, and Ralph H. Gabriel), and in recent years. Professor Higham, whom we have already spoken of, is himself one of our foremost writers on the history of American ideas. Arthur H. Cole has been one of America's leading business historians. With the aid of Joseph Schumpeter, he organized the Research Center in Entrepreneurial History at Harvard. He has served his interest in economic history in various capacities: as associate editor of *The Journal of Economic History,* as librarian of the Baker Library of Harvard University, above all as professor of business economics in the Harvard Graduate School of Business Administration for well over thirty years. His essay on business history, reprinted below, defines the nature of the subject and sets the study of business history in a broad perspective. Charles N. Glaab, of the University of Wisconsin, has been concentrating his efforts on the expanding field of American urban history. His works include *Kansas City and Railroads: Community Policy in the Growth of a Regional Metropolis* (1962) and *The American City: A Documentary History* (1963). In the article that appears in this section, Professor Glaab makes a valuable contribution to the study of our urban past by indicating its complexities, in general, and by spelling out, in particular, some of the ways we have misconstrued nineteenth-century attitudes to the growth of American cities.

Biography is one of the oldest of the many varieties of history and certainly one of the most popular. The great historians of the nineteenth century—Irving, Prescott, Motley, Parkman—were masters of biography no less than of national history. But with the rise of the historical profession during the post-Civil War decades, the study of the past shifted from individuals to groups. The generation of Channing, Osgood, Andrews, Turner, and Beard wrote a history of institutions, not men. They saw the past as an outworking of forces in which individuals were governed by their times rather than the reverse. Since their day, however, professional historians have returned to biography as a valid and proper vehicle for historical understanding. The generation of Allan Nevins, Samuel Eliot Morison, James G. Randall, and Dumas Malone has restored the great man to significance. And our own generation has seen something more than a restoration, indeed, something of an enthronement. The chefs-d'oeuvre commanding the attention of several of our major younger scholars are biographies: that of Arthur S. Link on Woodrow Wilson, of Frank Freidel on Franklin D. Roosevelt, and of Arthur M. Schlesinger, Jr. on Roosevelt and his age. A distinctive feature of today's cult of biography-writing is that it is more than the story of our great men; it is no less a commentary on our times, on present politics, and the problems and directions of twentieth-century America.

Two of the following essays—those by John A. Garraty and Frederick B. Tolles—deal with the nature and theory of biography. Both essays stress the idea that writing a man's life requires more than verifying and narrating the facts, that in addition to meeting the demands of science the biographer must meet those of art. Professor Garraty, who teaches at Columbia University, is the author of several biographies, including *Silas Wright* (1949), *Henry Cabot Lodge* (1953), *Woodrow Wilson* (1956), and *Right-Hand Man: The Life of George W. Perkins* (1960). His *Nature of Biography* (1957) is a very fine primer on the development, methods, and problems of a form of history of which Professor Garraty is himself a notable practitioner. Professor Tolles of Swarthmore College is a specialist in early American history and particularly in Quaker history. His best-known book, *Meeting House and Counting House* (1948), is an account of one major aspect of the Quakers' Holy Experiment in Pennsylvania during the years 1682–1763. Professor Tolles has also written biographies of James Logan, the secretary and confidential adviser of William Penn and writer of scientific subjects, and of George Logan, his grandson, who achieved fame in early national politics. It is his adventures in writing the life of James Logan that Professor Tolles records in the essay reprinted below.

If it is true that each generation comes to the past with ardor for cultivating new fields, it is also true that the new fields are often cultivated only partially. The new varieties of history are not fully pursued: politics and related subjects remain the most frequently studied. Some of the reasons why this is so suggest themselves readily enough. Primary materials dealing with politics are most easily accessible. And they are, often enough, very easily manufactured into an acceptable monograph. Nothing is so appealing to the Ph.D. candidate as a body of papers left by a politician. It is fair to add that politics and affairs of state command a natural, obvious interest. And students of history are nothing if not *politiques manqués*.

The practice of students of history thus centers on politics. But the preachment of their mentors continues to be about the new areas they should explore. In his presidential address to the American Historical Association in December, 1963, Crane Brinton of Harvard University, while granting that certain traditional types of history would continue to be worked on, urged that more attention be paid to several newer types—comparative history, nomothetic history, and philosophy of history. Indeed, urged Professor Brinton, "there must be an almost infinite variety of historical writing. . . ." In his own metaphor, he was proposing that in Clio's house "certain rather neglected parts deserve more attention and even that we add some new structures which must of necessity—cultural necessity, artistic necessity—be so modern, so functional, that they will contrast with the fine ripe architectural styles of the rest of the building." He was not, as he well knew and as we have seen, the first to propose a renovation of Clio's house. He was proposing yet another new history and, as his address showed, for reasons which were immediately relevant to the world of the 1960s in which he was speaking.

Suggestions for Further Reading

Berthoff, Rowland, "The American Social Order: A Conservative Hypothesis," *American Historical Review*, LXV (April 1960), 495–514.

Brinton, Crane, "Many Mansions," *American Historical Review*, LXIX (January 1964), 309–326.

Goodrich, Carter, "Economic History: One Field of Two?" *Journal of Economic History*, XX (December 1960), 531–538.

Greene, John C., "Objectives and Methods in Intellectual History," *Mississippi Valley Historical Review*, XLIV (June 1957), 58–74.

Lampard, Eric E., "American Historians and the Study of Urbanization," *American Historical Review*, LXVII (October 1961), 49–61.

Malin, James C., "On the Nature of Iocal History," *Wisconsin Magazine of History*, XL (Summer 1957), 227–230.

May, Henry F., "The Recovery of American Religious History," *American Historical Review*, LXX (October 1964), 79–92.

Mead, Sidney, "Church History Explained," *Church History*, XXXII (March 1963), 17–31.

Morton, Louis, "The Historian and the Study of War," *Mississippi Valley Historical Review*, XLVII (March 1962), 599–613.

Murphy, Paul L., "Time to Reclaim: The Current Challenge of American Constitutional History," *American Historical Review*, LXIX (October 1963), 64–79.

Nevins, Allan, "Not Capulets, Not Montagus," *American Historical Review*, LXV (January 1960), 253–270.

Schlesinger, Arthur M., "An Historian Looks at Science and Technology," *Isis*, XXXVI (1946), 162–166.

Washburn, Wilcomb E., "Ethnohistory: History 'in the Round'," *Ethnohistory*, VIII (Winter 1961), 31–48.

Welter, Rush, "The History of Ideas in America: An Essay in Redefinition," *Journal of American History*, LI (March 1965), 599–614.

16. *American Intellectual History: A Critical Appraisal**

John Higham

At a conference last fall on the relations between intellectual history and American Studies,[1] Russell Nye told a story about the famous baseball pitcher, Satchel Paige. In the later years of his career, Paige was asked how he managed to pitch nine sterling innings at his advanced age. He replied: "Ah jes' stays loose." Nye spoke for most of the attendants at the conference in recommending that the study of American culture "stay loose." Scholars should avoid confining definitions and fixed procedures in the interest of youthful flexibility.

The story itself is characteristically American in its feeling for the openness of experience, the plasticity of life, the success of an ongoing enterprise. The story gets much of its force from our

* Reprinted with permission from *American Quarterly*, XIII (Summer, 1961), 219–233.

1 Conference on the Historical Study of American Culture, Arden House, New York, October 13–15, 1960. An earlier version of this paper was discussed at the Conference, and I have taken grateful advantage of the criticisms of the other participants in trying to clarify and correct my remarks for publication. Since the general tenor of my argument is unchanged, it does not reflect any consensus among the participants. I am also indebted to the Princeton Council of the Humanities for engaging me in a larger study of American historical scholarship, from which this paper is an outgrowth.

It is necessary to add that I sought deliberately to be controversial—even somewhat polemical—and could not therefore do full justice to all sides of the questions involved. My quasi-historical sketch takes up only so much of the record as seemed immediately pertinent to the issue at hand; and the tyranny of argument did not permit adequate recognition, or even mention, of many scholars whom I greatly admire.

recognition of Paige as an acknowledged champion. He was still winning so many games that his questioner did not worry about why the pitcher lost some of them. Can we have the same confidence in the game of scholarship?

Certainly the study of American intellectual history has, until recently at least, stayed loose. So have the other cultural inquiries that are called American Studies. A philosophy of looseness has, in fact, determined the methods of these fields (although a paradoxical mystique of "integration" has ordinarily supplied their objective). It is doubtful if the record to date justifies us in sharing Satch's confidence in his own limber form. Possibly, writers of American intellectual history have valued looseness too highly. Great historians, like great pitchers, also need fine control.

A little reflection on the ways in which American intellectual history has been written, and on the scholarly traditions from which it has developed, may suggest why Americanists have puzzled and argued so much in recent decades over the nature of intellectual history, and why their general attitude toward it has been so eclectic. A critical review may also show a quiet trend of late toward the clarification of objectives. If such a trend is under way, sympathetic discussion of its problems and possibilities should serve a useful purpose.

So long as the nature of intellectual history remains in dispute, one has to begin with an attempt at definition. No one can hope, of course, to legislate what a subject of study "really" is; but a good definition can mark out an appropriate sphere of interest and thus prevent us from using words unsuitably. Let us say, then, that intellectual history is first of all a branch of history, one variety of a species, sharing the general characteristics that distinguish historical knowledge. As such, it has an overriding concern with how and why particular human experiences have followed one another through time. However much analysis or evaluation an historian undertakes, movement and continuity are his organizing principles, and his competence is limited to a definite span of time. "What aesthetic writers claim a passionate apprehension of form to be to the painter, a passionate apprehension of process is to the historian." [2]

---

[2] G. M. Young quoted in C. V. Wedgwood, *Truth and Opinion: Historical Essays* (London: Collins, 1960), p. 95.

Intellectual history simply applies this way of looking at things to a distinctive subject matter, centering attention on the experiences of thought rather than external behavior. For the intellectual historian, not culture, politics, society or art, but states of mind make up the foreground of interest and the focus of curiosity. This choice of subject matter imposes additional obligations on the intellectual historian. Since every state of mind contains a belief, the intellectual historian—to be responsive to his material—should care a good deal about the acceptableness of beliefs. He should feel the appeal of an idea, and weigh critically its tenability. In that sense, he is an amateur philosopher.

He also functions to some degree as a philosopher in organizing his material. We must assume that the ideas and feelings present in the mind of an individual or group at any given time constitute an interlocking structure, the parts of which are shaped and defined by their relation to one another. Thus, catchwords like nationalism or humanitarianism acquire varying meanings from the general mental outlook of different periods. To understand ideas historically virtually requires some analysis of the intellectual structure in which they were located. The *process* that the intellectual historian studies is movement in, or of, such a system. His achievement becomes more considerable as the magnitude of the system increases, and as it brings an increasing variety of ideas and feelings into meaningful relation. The largest distinctive aim of the intellectual historian, therefore, is to describe and explain the spirit of an age.[3]

This was also the traditional objective of intellectual historians. The few men who wrote the history of thought in the nineteenth and early twentieth centuries held substantially the above conception of their task. From W. E. H. Lecky and Leslie

---

[3] Some of the participants in the Arden House Conference objected to the overly unified, monistic implications of the term, "spirit of an age." Some preferred the more relativistic phrase, "climate of opinion." I think it desirable—indeed, essential in large-scale operations—for the historian to strive for unity. To speak of a spirit in an age does not mean that a pervasive presence controls it; or that it has an essence; or that diversity and conflict are less important than agreement in a period; or that any symbolic design an historian constructs will prove illuminating for other purposes or true from other points of view. It *does* mean that life and thought are most meaningful when grasped in patterns. I like the term "spirit" because it implies a kind of energy, whereas "climate" suggests merely a vaporous condition.

Stephen to V. L. Parrington and Alfred North Whitehead, intellectual history meant an attempt to trace the development of the inner life of an age or of a people and thereby exhibit the spirit informing its formal philosophies and its practical achievements. This spirit could be discovered by examining a variety of articulate representatives and determining their distinctive "mental habits" or their common "cast of mind." [4] Undertaken in such fashion, intellectual history served as a nineteenth-century substitute for, or supplement to, philosophy. Evolutionary thinkers, unable to find solid ground for their beliefs in any fixed metaphysical system, looked to the course of history for guidance and to intellectual history in particular for a critical understanding of the strengths and weaknesses of the ideas around them.[5]

On the methodological questions that became so troublesome later—questions of what qualifies as thought, and how it interacts with events—the nineteenth-century intellectual historians maintained a serene and deliberate vagueness. These questions did not interest them very much. An organic theory of culture, which they took for granted, decreed that the relations between thought and deed must be intimate; and their own desire to face the great issues of their time in terms of fundamental principles insured that their history would emphasize serious and substantial types of expression, approached from a non-technical point of view. The traditional intellectual historians were usually naïve in their evolutionary assumptions and unrepresentative in their selection of materials,[6] but they did important work on a generous scale with the aid of a clear purpose.

This long established conception of intellectual history broke down after World War I, when the great amateurs who had dominated and defined the subject gave way to men absorbed in particular academic disciplines. Probably the first major change came from the professional historians. They had con-

---

[4] W. E. H. Lecky, *History of the Rise and Influence of the Spirit of Rationalism in Europe* (London: Longmans, Green, 1865), I, vi–ix, xvii–xx; John Theodore Merz, *A History of European Thought in the Nineteenth Century* (Edinburgh: William Blackwood & Sons, 1896), I, 8–14, 25–26.

[5] In addition to the above references, see Sydney E. Ahlstrom's Introduction to Octavius Brooks Frothingham, *Transcendentalism in New England: A History* (New York, Putnam's, 1876; Harper Torchbooks, 1959), pp. xvii–xix.

[6] Nevertheless, the range of materials from which they drew was sometimes surprisingly wide. Barrett Wendell's chapter, "The American Intellect," in *The Cambridge Modern History* (New York, 1903), VII, 723–51, touched on law, philosophy, literature, art, science and education.

spicuously avoided intellectual history. Pledged to a severe conception of scientific "facts," and distrustful of the flux of speculation and opinion, the professionals had thought objectivity compromised it outside the field of material events and political institutions. Intellectual history became a subject of professional interest only after James Harvey Robinson and his followers challenged the narrow positivism of their guild.

Robinson's challenge came under the name "the New History," of which intellectual history was to be an important part. Robinson belligerently proposed to make history not only more all-embracing but also more relevant to the interests of contemporary democracy.[7] His reform program raised the hackles of the conservatives in the profession, and the intellectual historians who followed in Robinson's footsteps had to vindicate their academic respectability to distrustful, sometimes even resentful, colleagues. These intramural pressures probably contributed to the New Historians' cautious, down-to-earth approach to intellectual history. Certainly the general ethos of the profession did not encourage them to generalize as freely, or to rise as far above the level of events, as outsiders like H. O. Taylor or even Parrington were doing. A philosophic view of intellectual history found little favor in professional circles. There, Carl Becker —sustained surely by the influence of Alfred North Whitehead [8] —was almost alone in retaining a traditional conception of intellectual history.

If professional considerations inclined the historians toward concrete events at the expense of philosophic breadth, their own program pushed them in the same direction. The disciples of the New History in the 1920s and 1930s were determined to break down supposedly artificial compartments, to integrate thought and deed at every point. They were, in Morton White's phrase, in revolt against formalism.[9] The history they wrote was so very comprehensive that it permitted little sustained analysis of ideas.

[7] James Harvey Robinson, The New History: Essays Illustrating the Modern Historical Outlook (New York: The Macmillan Co., 1912).

[8] Becker's outstanding achievement, The Heavenly City of the Eighteenth-Century Philosophers (New Haven: Yale University Press, 1932), was much influenced by Alfred North Whitehead's Science and the Modern World (New York: The Macmillan Co., 1925). After Whitehead had shown the rationalism of medieval thought, Becker demonstrated the medievalism of rationalist thought.

[9] Social Thought in America: The Revolt against Formalism (New York: The Viking Press, 1949).

A more or less pragmatic outlook also restrained the New Historians from studying ideas systematically. They took a tough-minded, "realistic" view of beliefs, emphasizing environmental contexts. Yet the New Historian could never rest easy on this point. The relation between ideas and "interests" became an insistent problem, to which his own assumptions foreclosed any satisfactory answer. As a realist, influenced by materialistic interpretations of history, he supposed that ideas are functionally subordinate to interests. He usually concluded, as Richard Hofstadter did of Social Darwinism in 1944, that "changes in the structure of social ideas wait on general changes in economic and political life." [10] On the other hand, the New Historian counted ultimately on the life of reason to remake society. So he kept distinguishing between ideas and interests as compulsively as he mixed them together.

Closely related to this concern, and almost as intense, was the second major question that the professionals brought to the fore. How do ideas circulate through the various levels of society? How, particularly, do they move the inarticulate masses? This problem was largely an extension of the other, and gained in attractiveness as a more promising way of formulating and studying the interplay of thought and action. At the same time, the fascination with popular thought suited the temper of the New History in a crucial particular: it made intellectual history democratic. To write a broad-based kind of intellectual history had the charm of linking intellectuals with the common man. The New Historian had the authority of John Dewey for believing that an undemocratic class structure had kept traditional philosophy aloof from the needs and interests of ordinary people. On the same premise, he might suspect that the older type of intellectual history was aristocratic, and out of tune with the conquering advance of science and democracy.[11]

In spite of the reductionistic character of such views, the joining of high culture with popular thought may turn out, in

[10] *Social Darwinism in American Thought* (Philadelphia: University of Pennsylvania Press, 1944, p. 176.

[11] R. Richard Wohl, "Intellectual History: An Historian's View," *Historian*, XVI (1953), 62–77. Another characteristic statement is Dixon Wecter's "Ideas as Master Switches," *Saturday Review of Literature*, XXXII (August 6, 1949), 64–65. Notice that Wecter's metaphor clearly assigns an instrumental role to ideas: as master switches, they complete an electrical circuit, but the source of energy is presumably elsewhere.

the long run, to be the most considerable achievement of the new intellectual history and one of the most stimulating developments in historical scholarship during the last generation. Led by Merle Curti and Ralph H. Gabriel, historians showed that the intellectual history of a democratic society, where no class lines set natural limits to the circulation of ideas, calls for close attention to the processes of popular diffusion and intellectual crystallization. Many of our leading intellectuals, Franklin and Whitman, for example, and such popular currents at the pro-slavery philosophy and Jacksonian democracy, can not be understood without connecting an earthy accent and an airy creed. It also became gradually apparent that the tensions between "higher" and "lower" levels of thought can be studied as seriously as their affinities: the ambiguous relations between the intellectual and his audience, or the strains between his basic principles and the popular moods and fashions that impinge upon him. The study of popular thought has increasingly distinguished between cross-purposes disguised by slogans, and has taken account of the gap between highbrows, middlebrows and lowbrows.

The more sharply we distinguish between the various levels of thought, the more difficult becomes the task of connecting them in a single historical design. No one has entirely succeeded in doing so—in uniting, that is, the philosophy and the social psychology of an age, in making its original ideas and its conventional opinions equally alive and meaningful.[12] Nonetheless, attempts to relate these levels of thought seem essential if history is to retain its ancient claim to wholeness and its standing as a unifying discipline. We honor the New History because it maintained this claim, and even reinvigorated it; but its zeal for

[12] The most revealing line of inquiry running in this direction in recent years has been the mythic approach of Henry Nash Smith and other writers. This approach has the advantage of dramatizing popular thought by rendering all ideas in pictorial terms. Thus, in Smith's *Virgin Land: The American West as Symbol and Myth* (Cambridge: Harvard University Press, 1950), the image of the "garden of the world" vividly unites Jeffersonian abstractions with crude notions about increased rainfall. The objective is a kind of analysis "that fuses concept and emotion." This fusion brings the emotions into the foreground of intellectual history without destroying the framework of conceptual thought. But the conceptual side of intellectual life becomes largely a vehicle for the affective side. So the problem of relating systematic to popular thought has become in our time a problem of relating rational to irrational ideas.

wholeness outreached its integrative power. The intellectual history born out of the revolt against formalism had the virtue of bringing ideas at various levels into juxtaposition; but the resulting amalgam also incorporated so much else that the distinctive character of intellectual history was overborne. The New History had so sharp a repugnance for compartmentalization, and so strong a desire for comprehensiveness, that many of its disciples did not care greatly about intellectual history as such. They valued it more as an instrument for interpreting the multifarious doings of men—as a means of generalizing political and social phenomena—than as a subject with its own intelligibility and importance. In quest of a pragmatic synthesis, the New History tended to squeeze all ideas into a matrix of events and institutions.

I conclude, then, that an instrumental approach to intellectual history—a desire to *use* it rather than to *possess* it—raised crucial methodological issues but left them unresolved; brought intellectual history into the mainstream of professional historical interests, and into relation to general American history, but dissipated the force and coherence that the older intellectual history had had at its best; inspired an abundance of useful research but a paucity of interpretations of the spirit of an age; made us critical of the functioning of ideas, but deterred us from penetrating to their essence.

Not only in intellectual history, but also in its whole attitude toward the past, the New History prescribed an external view of historical data. Aligning itself with the social sciences, the New History treated human experience as comparable to natural phenomena, from which the observer seeks to detach himself as completely as possible. Ever on guard against subjective entanglement in this supposedly external reality, historians maintained a critical stance toward it. In attempting to objectify the past, they could not participate in it wholeheartedly, identify themselves fully with its inmost feelings through imaginative sympathy, or internalize its thoughts. Their theory was more suitable for "unmasking" ideologies, exposing "rationalizations," or analyzing "propaganda."

Did the study of intellectual history follow a different course outside the ranks of professional historians? During the twenties, thirties and forties, men in several disciplines, with a variety of scholarly commitments, were discovering intellectual history and adapting it to their own purposes. Because of their professional background, teachers of literature, religion and philosophy, and general cultural critics like Lewis Mumford, could be expected to have a deeper interest in ideas and values than the traditions of the historical guild permitted. One might expect, therefore, that these nonprofessionals would uphold—against the New History—the older view of intellectual history as a subject of intrinsic importance.

To some extent, this happened. One thinks, for example, of Parrington's sense of the sweep and range of ideas, and perhaps of his vivid intellectual portraiture too. In another discipline, Ralph Barton Perry wrote the older type of intellectual history; so did Perry Miller.[13] In view of the enormous proliferation of humanistic scholarship during these decades, however, it is remarkable how few Americans wrote broadly and effectively about the movement of ideas through time.

Two obstacles stood especially in the way. For one, the pragmatic, anti-formalist attitude characteristic of the New History also influenced many scholars in other disciplines. Many historians of literature, religion and other subjects felt the same distrust of abstractions, the same desire to bind ideas closely to practical life, the same subordination of thought to action. Another obstacle was the particular criteria built in to each of the academic disciplines concerned with the history of thought. Scholars wearing various academic allegiances were trying, with the aid of intellectual history, to overcome compartmentalization, but the standards and objectives of their own disciplines could not be given up. Consequently, the history they wrote was usually more technical and less truly historical than the work of the great nineteenth-century amateurs. In many cases both obstacles interfered simultaneously with a coherent view of intellectual history: authors who superimposed the pragmatic, comprehensive spirit of the New History upon an underlying commitment to a particular discipline were perhaps trying to realize too many objectives at once. Consider, for example, Joseph Dorfman's *Economic Mind in American Civilization* (5 vols., 1946–59) and Herbert Schneider's *History of American Philosophy* (1946). These were major achievements; but their attempt to deal comprehensively with ideas

---

13 See Perry's *Puritanism and Democracy* (New York: The Vanguard Press, 1944), and Miller's *The New England Mind: The Seventeenth Century* (New York: The Macmillan Co., 1939).

in social context, combined with their commitment to the technical criteria of a single discipline, prevented the attainment of a meaningful synthesis.

In radical opposition to the New History was the school of Arthur O. Lovejoy. This school had a genuinely historical interest in the intrinsic character of ideas, a sublime disregard of instrumental considerations, and a determination to approach intellectual history without respect to the limits of individual disciplines. Yet here too we can observe the loss of a large view of intellectual history under the pressure of a particular academic commitment. A technical philosopher, fascinated by the method of logical analysis, Lovejoy taught a scholastic, mechanical kind of intellectual history, largely detached from a living culture. As one critic has remarked, Lovejoy spoke constantly of cutting into, breaking up and isolating ideas: [14] operations more appropriate to a post mortem than to a parturition. Lovejoy brought an unprecedented precision to intellectual history, but he did so at the expense of a unifying vision. In lesser hands, his method of fine discriminations became a purely academic exercise, and his influence on the whole probably worked to atomize intellectual history at a time when other forces were also blurring its outlines.

Lovejoy's impact on the study of American thought was, however, peripheral. Very few professional philosophers since World War I have had much interest in American intellectual history; and none of them has illuminated it as brilliantly as Santayana and Dewey did in their early essays on the Genteel Tradition (1911) and the influence of Darwinism (1909).[15] American sociology has had no Max Weber; American political theory has had no formidable historian.[16] Undoubtedly this is due in some measure to the antihistorical turn that much

[14] R. W. B. Lewis, "Spectroscope for Ideas," *Kenyon Review*, XVI (1954), 313–22.

[15] "The Genteel Tradition in American Philosophy," in *Winds of Doctrine* (New York: Charles Scribner's Sons, 1912), pp. 186–215; *The Influence of Darwin on Philosophy* (New York: Henry Holt & Co., 1910).

[16] Eighteen years ago a student of American political theory pointed out the sterility and poverty of his colleagues' historical labors. Making allowances for some recent distinguished exceptions, the indictment has remained largely true. Benjamin F. Wright, "Research in American Political Theory," *Research in Political Science*, ed. Ernest S. Griffith (Chapel Hill: University of North Carolina Press, 1948), pp. 178–81.

contemporary thought has taken since World War I.[17] At any rate, history in general and American intellectual history in particular aroused only sporadic interest outside of two disciplines most directly concerned: history and literature. We must, therefore, look closely at the field of literary scholarship to understand how intellectual history has fared outside of the historical guild.

In dealing with American intellectual history, literary scholars since the 1930s have been guided by the American Studies movement. It has enjoyed an influence comparable to that which the New History had on professional historians. Indeed, the two movements were strikingly similar. Each of them represented a protest against narrowly specialized horizons. Just as the New Historians wanted to go beyond the orthodox kind of political history, so the professors of American literature who were usually the prime movers in establishing American Studies programs [18] were trying to break out of the orthodox kind of literary history. One group appealed for integration of ideas and events in a comprehensive view of the past; the other called for integrated study of art and society in a comprehensive view of "culture" or national character. Both hoped to link that past to the present—one in pursuit of reform, the other in search of identity. Both groups turned to intellectual history not because it was a natural focus of their respective endeavors but because it seemed an appropriate way of synthesizing heterogeneous materials. Thus the New Historians readily joined hands with their literary colleagues in sponsoring American Studies.

One result of American Studies, therefore, was to perpetuate the loose, indefinite conception of intellectual history that came out of the earlier revolt against formalism. Whereas the New History encouraged a pragmatic attitude toward ideas,

---

17 In the nineteenth century, historical theories and knowledge were opening new horizons in every field of humane learning; and until the 1920s men of the stature of Santayana, Whitehead and Parrington wrote intellectual history with the object of clarifying current issues. In recent decades, however, original thinking in the social sciences, philosophy and literary criticism has gone more largely into analytical problems abstracted from the dimension of time. Whether an increasingly vigorous engagement with intellectual history may help to reverse the decline of historical consciousness in American culture remains to be seen.

18 Richard H. Shryock, "The Nature and Implications of Programs in American Civilization," *American Heritage*, III (April, 1949), 36.

American Studies was eclectic and experimental. In both cases the study of intellectual history gained in popularity and diversity, somewhat at the cost of coherence. Hostile toward compartmentalized knowledge and too diffuse in aim to maintain a consistent interest in ideas, most American Studies enthusiasts levied upon intellectual history for every purpose except its own.

In spite of the similarities between the New History and the American Studies movement, the latter brought a different emphasis into the writing of intellectual history. American Studies derived from its origins in literary scholarship a humanistic emphasis that was foreign to the New History. Robinson, Beard and their followers looked primarily to the social sciences rather than the humanities for support and cooperation. Their principal effort in respect to intellectual history was relating it to the history of politics and society. On the other hand, the stress in American Studies has lain more upon literature and values, particularly artistic ones. This has been an important contribution, offsetting the rather matter-of-fact approach of the early New Historians. Literary scholars were trained to make the close textual analysis so often essential in grasping a man's thought. The methods of modern literary criticism enabled them to reach the ambiguous feelings and symbolic references that lurk beneath the surface of an historical document. When literary scholars began to apply such methods to materials other than conventional literary sources, they were in fact writing a new kind of intellectual history. This penetration in depth, first fully displayed in Henry Nash Smith's *Virgin Land* (1950), deserves as much credit as we give to the New History for extending the range of intellectual history.

Yet, in spite of the effort to be interdisciplinary, the demands of a particular discipline exacted their price. Although teachers of American literature produced a tremendous number of books and articles on what American intellectuals have thought and said, the results with rare exceptions were too specifically literary in interest to qualify fully as historical.

In distinguishing between literary and historical interests, I am not endorsing Bernard DeVoto's supercilious definition of the literary mind as the mind least adapted to the utilization of fact.[19] But historians and literary scholars do tend, I think,

[19] Bernard DeVoto, *Forays and Rebuttals* (New York, 1936), p. 185.

to select and handle their facts differently. The student of literature, characteristically, chooses data that will get us, as directly as seems practicable, to an act of evaluation. The object under evaluation persists independently, in that we can read it ourselves without the literary scholar's evaluative assistance. The historian, however, constructs his object. Whereas the art of the past exists in its original form, the life of the past is accessible only in the form in which the historian casts it. The historian scores by arranging his facts into a self-explanatory whole; the literary scholar triumphs by enriching his facts, embroidering upon them the speculative insights and poetic images they evoke but do not wholly contain.

Literary criticism, therefore, and even literary history, are fundamentally unhistorical. Since an independent object controls the range of inquiry, the literary scholar is not impelled to give a complete account of how things were, to feel the density of a milieu or to appraise the relative weight of diverse factors in a situation. His explorations of intellectual history sacrifice wholeness for the sake of expressive power. He makes use of a world of ideas selectively, to illuminate a particular text or literary category; but the true historian makes use of texts selectively, to illuminate a world of ideas. Even in a work so authentically historical as *Virgin Land,* an interest in literary forms sometimes dominates the story of the ideas flowing through them. More often, the avid pursuers of symbols and myths lose sight of any firm historical structure. One can conclude, therefore, that literary scholars made intellectual history functional to art, as professional historians made it functional to action; and like a lady of easy virtue, it slept wherever it had shelter.

So far I have dwelt largely on the period from the 1920s through the 1940s in order to show how the increasing popularity of intellectual history brought a new attention to methods and a confusion over ends. None of the difficulties that appeared then has disappeared in the last decade. A certain amount of confusion is probably inevitable and stimulating. Nevertheless, after the vigorous dispersal of the thirties and forties, intellectual history seems to be renewing its central purpose. If, as I think, a period of experimentation and controversy is passing, intellectual history may be returning—with far greater sophistication—to its traditional aim of discovering and explaining the spirit of an age. Surely the teaching as well as the writing of American intellectual history is more systematic and selective, more sharply focused on general beliefs and major thinkers, than it was a few years ago. None of the leading colleges or universities still offers the shapeless course that used to be called "Social and Intellectual History"; the disorder that Professor H. L. Swint discovered as recently as 1953 [20] has markedly diminished.

Probably, one of the most important reasons for this clarification of goals is a more favorable attitude toward intellectual history in the historical profession at large. The pioneering is over; the historical guild has accepted the intellectual historian and respects his work. The old fogeyism that used to breathe distrust of ideas, unless they were treated as so many inert facts, no longer weighs heavily upon us. One still meets commonly the prejudice that intellectual history is "unreal" unless continuously linked to behavior, as if the movement of thought is somehow less free, or less capable of separate treatment, than the movement of other historical structures. But the insights of intellectual history have become so widely accepted into the corpus of American historiography, and so frequently drawn upon by historians primarily interested in other segments of experience, that the intellectual historian can tend his own garden if he wishes.

Another circumstance that is making for a more manageable and definite conception of intellectual history is the revival of American social history, unhappily eclipsed in the thirties and forties. Social history enjoyed a brilliant development in the 1920s through the sectional and economic interpretations that Arthur M. Schlesinger, J. Franklin Jameson, Dixon Ryan Fox and Thomas J. Wertenbaker applied, under the influence of Beard and Turner, to its miscellaneous data. But the publication of the thirteen-volume *History of American Life* (1927–48) demonstrated that no adequate analytical scheme had yet been found. In the ideological thirties, social history as such fell into the background, and the livelier young minds turned to an extended kind of intellectual history, confident that an understanding of social history could best be attained in this more inclusive medium. Only recently has social history begun to escape from the embrace of ideology on the one hand and encyclopedism on the other, and to acquire a shape of its own

[20] H. L. Swint, "Trends in the Teaching of Social and Intellectual History," *Social Studies*, XLVI (1955), 243–49.

from the quantitative methods and the structural interests of contemporary sociology. This development relieves the intellectual historian from over-extended commitments. It also engenders a healthy tension between two different but equally revealing types of historical patterns: the arrangement of ideas into a working system, and the arrangement of people into a functioning society. It is significant that a senior intellectual historian, Merle Curti, should move with fresh vigor into the newer social history, and that a young general historian, writing about slavery, should separate clearly its institutional from its intellectual setting.[21]

These alterations in the scholarly environment have been occurring under the favoring influence of a much larger change in contemporary thought. Since the 1940s pragmatism, and indeed the whole revolt against formalism, have lost their freshness and charm. When Carl Becker in his old age concluded ruefully that there were generalities that still glitter,[22] when awesome destruction taught other intellectuals not to trust the course of history to vindicate their values, when the intractable dilemmas and the narrow range of alternatives in the postwar world came fully home, the disposition to appraise ideas chiefly from the point of view of their practical consequences received a decisive check. The activist temper of the New History, with its emphasis on direct, continual interchange between ideas and interests, fell out of fashion. Now it began to seem important to take stock of our intellectual assets and liabilities, instead of rushing them pell-mell to market.

The decline of a pragmatic approach to thought made for a greater interest in first principles, in values that have some ultimate claim and not a merely instrumental role. The celebrated "return to religion" may have failed in other respects, but it certainly roused the secular intellectual to a sympathetic scrutiny of religious ideas. Accordingly, the history of religious thought constitutes one of the outstanding cumulative achievements of American Intellectual history in recent years. Just as the modern theological renaissance began before World

---

21 Merle Curti, *The Making of An American Community* (Stanford: Stanford University Press, 1959); Stanley Elkins, *Slavery: A Problem in American Institutional and Intellectual Life* (Chicago: University of Chicago Press, 1960).

22 Carl Becker, "Some Generalities That Still Glitter," in *New Liberties for Old* (New Haven, 1941).

War II, so the beginnings of a new kind of American intellectual history go back to Perry Miller's Puritan studies in the 1930s and, most explicitly, to H. Richard Niebuhr's *The Kingdom of God in America* (1937). In that book the author confessed that his earlier sociological approach had failed to explain either the underlying unity or the distinctive force of American Christianity. Since World War II the history of religious ideas has almost entirely superseded the old "church history." Moreover, intellectual history is taking on a more integrated character as the search for first principles bridges conventional distinctions between the pious and the profane. R. W. B. Lewis' *The American Adam* (1955), for example, gives a powerful rendering of social ideas by sounding their religious depths.

If all these changes do mean a renewal of the traditional aims of intellectual history, they do not cancel the efforts of the last generation. Literary scholars will undoubtedly continue to explore the relations between ideas and art. Most historians will continue to emphasize the relations between ideas and action. And rightly so. From one point of view, intellectual history must remain contributory to an appreciation and understanding of cultural achievements; from another point of view, intellectual history must remain contributory to that general history in which the whole of an age is dimly perceived. These perspectives still leave room and need, however, for a third point of view, in which neither art nor action, but feelings and ideas, stand in the center of vision.

This is not to say that any intellectual historian can afford to ignore concrete events and institutions. Even the most austere kind of intellectual history should, if it is fully historical, take account of the circumstances in which ideas arise and terminate. But most writers of American intellectual history have, I think, broken loose from the compulsion to refer ideas at every point to a structure of social action. Surely a better understanding of the problem is available if we stand far enough back to see a complex structure of opinion, bearing upon events at certain strategic points or in certain general directions. To understand the encounter of ideas with action in a massive way, we need a systematic view of the ideas.

To get such a view we seem to be moving, in one sense, toward greater specialization than has been customary. To restore, in the light of modern knowledge, the traditional aim of intellectual history calls for a paradoxical concentration of effort and rigorous training. The "pure" intellectual historian may have to leave the task of synthesis to the general historian, who moves between topical fields without final commitment to any one.

In another sense, however, the writing of intellectual history should become less specialized as scholars work out the complex patterns of thought that stamp a period, a movement or a major thinker. The comprehensive aspirations of the New History and of American Studies encouraged in practice a good deal of fragmentary work. The historians often fragmented ideas to fit them within events, while the literary scholars experimented with fragmentary perspectives. During the decade of the 1940s, 159 articles and 26 books about Herman Melville came out,[23] and perhaps for this reason we still do not have, so far as I know, a good over-all account of his intellectual life. Three years ago Stow Persons ventured the first serious attempt to periodize American intellectual history in terms of a sequence of dominant ideas. Even more recently, Henry May published the first detailed and integrated account, on a national scale, of a single period.[24] The specialized task of intellectual history today is one of constructing general designs.[25]

What part in all of this will the American Studies movement have? Will it too become less experimental and more systematic? In what direction is this possible? Only a rash prophet would hazard an answer to such questions. It seems likely, however, that the unequal partnership between intellectual history and a presumably inclusive interest in American civilization will not endure unless—contrary to my argument—intellectual history stays very loose indeed.

23 M. L. A. American Literature Group, *Report of the Committee on Trends in Research in American Literature, 1940–1950* (Baton Rouge, 1951), p. 69.

24 Stow Persons, *American Minds: A History of Ideas* (New York: Henry Holt & Co., 1958); Henry F. May, *The End of American Innocence: A Study of the First Years of Our Own Time, 1912–1917* (New York: Alfred A. Knopf, 1959).

25 But see a recent statement about intellectual history that is antithetical to mine: Daniel J. Boorstin, *America and the Image of Europe* (New York: Meridian Books, 1960), pp. 43–78, which argues for an unstructured historiography that will reflect the formless homogeneity of American life.

17. What Is Business History?*

ARTHUR H. COLE

As one grows old, he becomes increasingly annoyed at confusion of almost any variety; and that which continues to surround the concept of "business history" chances to impinge frequently enough upon my attention to impel me to try to reduce the disparities in concepts still existent among individuals interested in the field. Diversity of concepts was evident even among men interested enough in the area to come—in some cases, goodly distances—to attend a two-day meeting at the Harvard Business School on the teaching of the subject. Perhaps because I was already teaching economic history before business history was born, because I have known the chief actors in the world created by Professor N. S. B. Gras, and because I have had to give thought to the nature of entrepreneurial history, I may in this connection pretend to pose as a sort of academic *amicus curiae*. And I think that I have made manifest my interest in the field.

The Nature of Business

Too often young folk start talking about business history without first stopping to secure a clear concept of business itself. They may carry the notion that business is merely buying and selling, huckstering, the hurly-burly of the traditional bazaar of the Middle East; others may hold the image of business as an arena populated by giants of great wealth and great power who buy politicians and generally are up to no good; and the novelists or muchrakers or others have created other impres-

* Reprinted with permission from *Business History Review*, **XXXVI** (Spring, 1962), 98–106.

sions. Actually business is much more complex than the concepts which any of these notions convey. It can be visualized on at least three levels or in three patterns.

One level or pattern is the ideational. It is constituted of all the knowledge by aid of which the wheels of production, distribution, advisory service, etc., are established and maintained: how to secure a corporate charter, how to manage a shoe factory, how best to compensate salesmen, etc.—millions and millions of "bits" of knowledge, accumulated over centuries of experience, and daily being added to. It is the presence or lack of this body of knowledge that really distinguishes the developed from the underdeveloped countries, and it is the slow manner in which such knowledge can be absorbed into an industrial order that spells the slowness with which such underdeveloped countries can rise toward equality with the older business nations.

A facet of this ideational world—ideas transmuted into modes of behavior—was spoken of recently by Professor Solomon Fabricant: [1]

> Underdeveloped countries are learning that in their rush to reach desired levels of economic efficiency time must be taken to develop the kind of business ethics, respect for the law, and treatment of strangers that keep a modern industrial society productive. Widening of the concept of family loyalty and tribal brotherhood to include love of man "in general" is a necessary part of the process of economic development.

Another facet is made a significant portion of Mrs. Edith Penrose's theory of the growth of "the firm" when she specifies experience of men working together in individual enterprises as conditioning greatly the manner in which those concerns would be expected to perform in the future. A firm uses two types of knowledge, she writes, one that may be looked upon as objective and available to everyone, and, the other, knowledge which is born of experience within the particular enterprise. Moreover, "increased experience," she asserts, "shows itself in two ways—changes in knowledge acquired and changes in the ability to use knowledge." [2]

[1] Solomon Fabricant, "An Economist's View of Philanthropy," in *Proceedings of the American Philosophical Society*, vol. 105 (April 21, 1961), p. 163.

[2] Edith T. Penrose, *The Theory of the Growth of the Firm* (New York and Oxford, 1959), p. 53.

Again, the importance given to decision-making in some descriptions of primary business processes—even in some definitions of business—is related to this level or feature of business life. Thought processes do precede and condition the decisions of businessmen; and those who participate in the decision-making process are surely important cogs in the business machinery. It is a question merely whether decision-making constitutes a full description of business—surely not.

At all events, it scarcely behooves those of us who have been or are now connected with schools of business to look askance at the notion of business possessing a prime basis in knowledge. Such institutions of learning are founded on the faith that business experience can be observed and generalized into assertions of wider or narrower pertinence to future business action, and that these acquired truths can by oral communication or the perusal of books be somehow made to lodge in the brains of students to a degree adequate to guide them in their own efforts to manage business enterprises or help in that management.

Stemming in large part from this ideational level is the world of institutions—the production enterprises, the construction companies, the banks, the department stores, and a myriad of other forms of organization—through which business operations are carried out. Traditionally such institutions have been viewed as a multitude of independent units—*a* candy factory, *a* hardware wholesaler, *a* bank, *a* railroad, etc.—with the only connection among them being competition of units concerned with the same or overlapping areas of activity. I would propose a different image, that of an interconnected, mutually supporting congeries of business units. For purposes of exposition, the extractive, manufacturing, and construction industries may be conceived to constitute the central core of this business system, while, outside of this primary citadel, one can specify a series of concentric circles in which other business institutions may be held to lie—the complement in each successive circle being perhaps those ancillary or service institutions closely and then less closely connected with the performance of the institutions located in the central region. Purveyors of productive equipment, providers of short-term capital, transporters of raw materials and finished goods, etc., might lie in an inner circle, the publishers of trade periodicals, public accountants, etc., perhaps in a more removed circle, while still further away might lie the interior decorators of executive offices, schools that trained workmen or clerks for the establishments, etc. Perhaps the major industries of steel, rubber, textiles, and the like could be envisaged as possessing to some extent separate and distinct institutional worlds—like Innis' "staples," perhaps Rostow's "sectors," or the Swedes' "development blocks"—but, inasmuch as some of the ancillary and service institutions—such as railroads, commercial banks, etc.—serve many industries, a good deal of overlapping would need to be envisioned.

Incidentally, attention may be drawn to the circumstance that such a business construct differs essentially from that usually employed by economists. The latter seem content to line institutions up in industries and go no further, except perhaps as required by the modern ideas of monopolistic competition —a rather specialized instance of business interconnections.

Actually, it is somewhat difficult to draw a limit to the series of concentric circles that I have proposed. Out some distance would lie perhaps management advisory concerns, commodity exchanges, and the publishers of trade journals; possibly still farther, schools of business, architects specializing in industrial buildings, or counsel specializing in antitrust matters; and it might be questioned whether the Federal Bureau of Standards, the Census Bureau, the Securities and Exchange Commission, and other governmental agencies should not be added, since the government is by no means merely regulatory; it also provides much information useful to the managers of individual enterprises.[3]

In fact, one may wish to conceive of the outermost ring of the business circles as merging closely with much that we are inclined to call "society." There are surely many connections between the business world and the publication of both newspapers and general periodicals; there are portions of the world of art which affect business and, in turn, are affected by the latter; there are connections between business affairs and liter-

3 In reality, of course, the domain of business has really quite ragged edges. For example, there are cooperative enterprises; there are central banks, sometimes privately owned but devoted to a public function; there are stock, bond, and commodity exchanges; there are professions not much removed from businesses; there are privately endowed colleges and universities—with Harvard College the American business institution with the record of longest continuous existence; and there are business functions evident in governmental agencies, e.g., budgeting, accounting control, purchasing, etc. "Business" trails off into foundations, hospitals, and other eleemosynary institutions.

ature, the drama, and sometimes even poetry. It was actually a consequence of this line of reasoning that led me to envisage three areas of social action—the individual business unit, the business system, and the contacts with the total society—when I ventured to write about the "business enterprise in its social setting." [4]

The third level or pattern of business is that of performance —bales of cotton goods produced, shares traded on the New York Stock Exchange, ton-miles of freight carried, and the like. To many businessmen, this aspect of the business world would seem the most important; and surely it is the most obvious. I would hold, however, that this is an area of minor interest to the business historian. When there is a question of the value of the whole business system, he would undoubtedly desire to indicate the increase in the output of goods and services which has occurred over the centuries and decades under the exertions of the private enterprise system; and, for the short run, he may be concerned with "volume" as a factor in the determination of diminishing prices. But it seems to me that, by and large, this counting of output is more properly the domain of the economic historian. When goods are really produced or distributed, the work of the businessman is finished.

The Practical Spread of the System

That the world of business spreads out geographically from border to border of most countries—with perhaps only small enclaves of even modestly self-sufficient farmers—needs hardly be stated. Less common, I believe, is an appreciation of the variety of economic activity—the provision of goods and services—which has come under the domain of business action. That the world of business extends over divers extractive, manufacturing, construction, distributive, financial, and transportation activities is obvious. However, surely commercial or market-oriented farmers should be embraced, likewise many entertainment and recreational facilities from theatres to bowling alleys, baseball teams to the producers of ski wax, while many of the basic human activities or experiences do not escape the advantages (or disadvantages) of response to business man-

[4] Arthur H. Cole, *Business Enterprise in its Social Setting* (Cambridge, 1959).

agement: materials for the control of pregnancy, presentations of young ladies to society, commercial administrators of weddings, and both funeral homes and huge mausoleums to wind up one's stay on earth.

It is also to be noted that, with the increase of the professional quality in business management personnel, the divergence of business and the professions seems to have become narrowed—at least vis-à-vis some of the professions such as actors and actresses of screen or television, lawyers, architects, and even college professors, thanks to the inroads of foundation funds and the increased opportunity for employment in government service. Our "business civilization" has lately become even more inclusive than ever before of events in the total society.

Corollaries of the Foregoing

It is obvious that the earlier identification of "business history" with company history is grossly inappropriate. No doubt company history is business history; but the reverse gives an erroneous view of conditions, as if one identified any one architectural style and "architecture." The preparation and publication of company histories seem not far different from the drafting and issuance of personal biographies in the area of political history. They are surely of much value, but they can hardly be viewed as pre-empting the whole field.

Secondly, it becomes desirable to look at the forces and instrumentalities which make viable the business system of a nation. Some of the so-called "business virtues" may be worth noting, such as reliability, promptness, rectitude in business dealings, and the like. Also, one should observe the importance of such instrumentalities as stock certificates, bills of lading, promissory notes, time-payment contracts, and the like.

Since the paths taken by the evolution of the business system will almost inevitably differ from country to country, perhaps even among regions in so large a nation as our own, and since the timing of such developments would surely differ in the several areas, there would appear to be many opportunities for comparative studies. Professor Karl Deutsch used to propose a study of the relative speeds in the adoption of particular technological advances—such as the adding machine or the Linotype apparatus—in various countries as likely to make manifest variations in entrepreneurial character; but surely a comparison of the course, speed, and extent of achievement in the development of a complex business system would prove even more revealing of variant national business characters. This would seem a sort of symphonic form for business history writing.

However, I am tempted to add two lines of thought pertinent to economico-business performance. The first is that when one brings down to earth or—to change the figure—puts flesh on the bare bones of such economistic phrases as "capital formation" or the "international movement of the productive factors," one is coming closer to a consideration of realities and, if one wishes to make use of historical inquiries, one is better equipped to propose public policies appropriate to the circumstances of the real world. Governments and public censors cannot deal effectively with abstractions; indeed, in policy administration governments must deal with business institutions and businessmen. I am particularly annoyed when I read of the "British export of capital" to the United States or other countries. One receives the idea unconsciously that British lenders stood on the street corners of America or Australia or other "undeveloped" countries, and tried to press pounds, shillings, and pence upon unhappy borrowers. The whole point of the activity seems to me to be obscured by this particular phrase—this abstraction.

In the second place, I believe it worthwhile to suggest that, relative to economic growth of nations, the world of business is not without distinct and separate importance. It seems to me by no means clear that the innovational activities of businessmen, their attention to operational improvements—not merely technological developments—and the internal drives toward at least keeping up with one's competitors may not constitute a force productive of economic advance quite apart from the economists' "supply of the productive factors." Businessmen's intellectual efforts, no less than those of the inventor, the scholar, or the statesman can be creative.

The Themes of a Rejuvenated Business History

From the perspective of the foregoing comments, it is possible to visualize a marked expansion of the area of business history —"history as written":

Surely the histories of individual enterprises should be specified —and I would suggest the use of the term "enterprise history" to designate this branch of composition.

Businessmen's biographies would still remain worthwhile.

Now would be included the history of the evolution of business instrumentalities: the bill of exchange, the mortgage bond, the through bill of lading, etc. Here business history would rub elbows with legal history.

Efforts can also be made to trace the evolution of business thought —as, for example, relative to accounting, scientific management, budgeting, etc.—and the development of business literature.

Sketches of the development of the business system relative to particular branches of industry or particular geographical areas would become appropriate, and comparative histories of national developments could be attempted.

Last but not least, changes could be investigated as to the attitudes of specific groups in society toward the business world as a whole, to the traits of character perceived in representative figures within that world, to the economic performance of the whole system or specific parts of it, and the like. Contrariwise, so to speak, studies could be promoted of the changing public censors of business, the reasons for the latter's approvals or disapprovals, the competence of their observations, etc.

In point of fact, the individual scholars now interested in the area of business history (as now broadly defined) appear to fall into three groups. One takes a professional point of view —the lessons of past experience in business are valuable for the enlightenment of current business executives and perhaps the training of future executives. In turn this interest can be seen to be two-pronged. One prong tends to relate the developments of the past to continuing business problems. Indeed, a casebook might be compounded for these teachers and scholars along the line perhaps of classic examples of bad and good judgment, or good or bad fortune in the face of uncontrollable circumstances. Cases of beginning business operations at the wrong phase of the business cycle, of excessive optimism, of too great reliance on a single large purchaser of one's products, etc., could be brought together, with all useful historical detail and a knowledge of what actually did happen after the decisions were made.

The second prong in the interest of this group concerns the changing place of business in the whole society. Here the term "business" is taken as synonymous with the private enterprise system, and the whole process of public appraisal above noted is involved. The business historian is, in fact, not necessarily well qualified to deal with this facet of his field any more perhaps—to take an extreme case—than an obstetrician should be an authority on the population problem. An adequate handling of the inquiry calls for competence in social history and the history of ideas, and familiarity with sociological concepts. However, if this line of analytical history is properly developed, the business executive or the student in the school of business will secure a notion of his position relative to a changing scheme of thought and emotion and will be in a better position, on his own initiative, to influence the future course of such ideas and feelings, or to adjust to them.

This latter approach to business history seems to hold a considerable interest for scholars and teachers outside the schools of business. Students and instructors of college courses on comparative economic systems would have concern with the materials; and so also perhaps scholars and students in the area of ethics, at least if the latter subject were examined in historical perspective. In some measure, likewise, scholars and courses dealing with the changes in social and political thought would have use for these data. Here business history overlaps with general or social history; but I believe that there would be value in the devotion by the business historian of attention to this area. Surely he could place the actions and thoughts of businessmen more fully in their historical setting than a sociologist or general historian unfamiliar with the arena in which the actions or thoughts took place.

Finally, there is a body of scholars who are concerned with business history as an adjunct to their examination of economic growth. It is interesting, for example, that Professor Conrad in his recently compounded sketch of the evolution of the American economy—generally in quantitative terms—finds it useful or necessary to call upon the activities of investment bankers to explain satisfactorily to himself the course of economic change in the post-Civil War decades.[5] (The business historian might be inclined to put to Professor Conrad the question: why were these particular alterations in the business structure important in explanation of economic change and not many others of our colonial, pre-Civil War, or even twentieth-century

[5] Alfred H. Conrad, "Income Growth and Structural Change," in *American Economic History*, edited by Seymour E. Harris (New York, 1961), pp. 46–54.

periods?) Customarily, indeed, economists and economic historians have called upon facts and changes in conditions of the business world to provide explication of events which chance to interest them; and those recently concerning themselves with economic growth are likely to do the same. I believe that the historian of business change can make a real contribution to discussion in this new area of speculation—not the less because I believe changes in the structure of business to effect alterations in economic productivity independent of other conditions and circumstances in the economy and society.

Conclusion

In sum, I believe the business historians of the past have been given to intellectual myopia, and to have been thus unfortunate in no inconsiderable part by reason of the identification of the term "business history" with company history. Since the withdrawal of Professor Gras from the scene, business historians seem much too modest and timid in viewing the potentials of their territory. Perhaps they could be compared with the sort of person whom Philip D. Bradley used to hold to be common in Latin America—a man who would sit on a mountain of iron ore and do nothing creative about it. It appears to me that business history, if properly developed, holds numerous enticing opportunities for research and writing—in a rather diverse rainbow of relationships and themes. Business historians need not abandon enterprise histories, but they can add on other fields of inquiry more fruitful for both the improvement of professional training in the schools of business and for enlightenment of scholars and students engrossed in social history. The future of the area seems exceptionally bright, if these opportunities are grasped by the present and rising generations of scholars working in the field.

18. The Historian and The American Urban Tradition*†

CHARLES N. GLAAB

The writing of history is a most conservative craft; for the historian, whether he likes it or not, is charged with perpetuating traditional common-sense ways of looking at collective experience. If he refuses this responsibility and tries to look at society from outside the existing framework of social traditions, then he becomes something else—a behavioral scientist, perhaps—and few historians are willing to follow that path.

The historian is, in a sense, a secular theologian, who justifies society, rather than the universe, to man. As storyteller, he portrays the heroes of the past in their archetypal social roles as chieftains, warriors, builders, or prophets. (It is comforting to find them thus in the texts; the difficult psychological complexities of public behavior and leadership simply become irrelevant.) When he puts on the mortarboard of the interpreter —and no respectable history can be without "interpretation"— he constructs "forces" or "movements" to explain change. But these, too, more often provide justification than explanation.

* Reprinted with permission from the *Wisconsin Magazine of History,* XLVI (Autumn, 1963), 13–25.

† AUTHOR'S NOTE: This paper is based on informal lectures delivered October 14, 1960, and October 26, 1962, to the Second and Fourth Annual Institute for Teachers of High School History, sponsored by the State Historical Society of Wisconsin. In rewriting these, no attempt has been made to provide the detailed qualification and amplification of extreme statements that proper scholarship requires. The lectures were originally intended to stimulate discussion of questions in American historiography, not to answer them. Portions of the research on which this article is based were supported by the University of Wisconsin (Ford) Urban Program.

Whether he chooses to pit liberal against conservative, section against section, class against class, or those within the consensus against those without, the past devised by the American historian is shaped by struggle. And viewed by society's lights, it is moral struggle, for in the end that which is "progressive" and in accord with American traditions always triumphs over that which is not. But in this system, "progressive" is little more than what society concedes has happened and acquiesces in (*i.e.*, social good) and the "unprogressive" little more than the opposite (*i.e.*, social evil). Still, it is probably this element of righteous conflict in their dialectic that leads historians arrogantly to proclaim: "No, history does not have to be dull!"

Traditional national history may be popular, but there are certain subjects involving fundamental social change that are difficult to examine by its canons. The urbanization of the United States supplies a good example. This would seem, on the face of it, to be a development of enormous consequence, and we are assured that it is every time we pick up a magazine or newspaper. Since American cities have been growing by leaps and bounds for over 150 years, the topic would appear to demand historical treatment. But the story of large numbers of people moving about in time and space does not provide very promising material for dramatic treatment; it is difficult to infuse the process with conflict and value. At least partly because of this difficulty, national historians in the past largely ignored the growth of cities, and American urban history, which is formally concerned with the subject, is still in its infancy.

Only very recently, in fact, has the urban historian been accorded a limited degree of recognition in the establishments of American history. Formerly, anyone who labeled himself as such was usually considered an antiquarian in disguise, who might have the proper academic credentials but who debased the craft by searching for ancestors in a favorite city. Lately, he has been regarded more as an enemy agent from the camp of the social sciences who comes to history armed with secret weapons of precise definition and statistics, seeking to undermine the authority of a tried and true humanistic discipline. The urban historian himself has never been sure if either of these views is accurate, nor has he been sure of what role he ought to be playing in the community of scholarship. Still, the city is very much with us; it has become intellectually fashionable to defend something termed "the urban way of life." The writing of history reflects cultural imperatives, and historians, in rather uncertain fashion to be sure, have been forced to incorporate urban themes into their interpretations. And urban history, even in its undeveloped state, is at least important enough to provide a long footnote in any history of American historical scholarship to this point.

American historians have never, of course, neglected the city completely. Among the great nineteenth-century historians, even James Ford Rhodes, for all his allegiance to the tenets of conventional political history, considered some aspects of urban development in the years after the Civil War, and John Bach McMaster, in his multi-volume account of the life of the people in the ante-bellum period, occasionally provided descriptions of the growth of individual towns and cities. The fifth volume of Edward Channing's *History of the United States,* published in 1921, contained an excellent assessment of "The Urban Migration" of the years 1815–1848. A formal interest in the history of American cities really dates, however, from the early 1930's with the start of publication of volumes in the famous *History of American Life* series. This series represented an ambitious attempt to write the social history of the United States, and in shaping the design of the study the editors fixed on urban life as one of the important dimensions of the American social experience. Arthur M. Schlesinger, one of the editors, entitled his own volume on the years from 1878 to 1898, *The Rise of the City.* Although only a portion of his work was actually devoted to the subject of urbanization, Schlesinger found the growth of cities to be the unifying theme of the period. From a variety of original sources he provided an account of population movement during the twenty-year period and described in rich detail the pattern of life in the rapidly growing American cities.[1] His volume proved the most influential in the series in generating further research.

In the bibliographical essay for his work, Schlesinger noted explicitly the lack of historical interest in urban topics. "The American city has not yet been studied generically," he wrote, "nor do there exist any adequate social histories of particular

---

[1] (New York, 1933). For sections of Schlesinger's work dealing with urban themes, see particularly "The Lure of the City," 53–77, and "The Urban World," 78–120.

cities." [2] In the next few years, scholars began to fill this gap. By the late 1930's a number of studies of individual cities had appeared: Holyoke, Memphis, portions of New York's history, and the beginning of Bessie L. Pierce's multi-volume history of Chicago. As a result of this interest Blake McKelvey, in a 1952 bibliographical article which still provides the only general survey of scholarly writing in urban history, could cite the publication after 1930 of forty volumes of urban biography (the standard term to describe a scholarly history of an individual city) and another "dozen good books of urban history on a broader scope." [3]

During the same period, general American historians began to take some account of the developments described in urban histories, but these were rather artificially woven into an established synthesis. The leaders of the movement for a "New History"—among them Charles A. Beard, James Harvey Robinson, and Frederick Jackson Turner—had earlier focused attention on history as an instrument of social reform, on the clash of economic interests in the past, and, most influentially perhaps, on the creative force of the Great West—Turner's "Frontier"—in shaping the unique qualities of American civilization.

As the study of American history became a part of graduate instruction, conflict between classes, between interest groups, or between geographic sections became fundamental dichotomies absorbed by students as readily as they acquired a respect for evidence and the exact procedures of the German seminar method. Urbanization was fitted to this fixed scheme of interpretation. In the texts, a dramatic post-Civil War rise of the city became an aspect of the triumph of industrialism over agriculture. A commercial-urban East threatened the values of an older America represented by an agrarian-rural West. The city had created new social and political problems—the slum, the political machine, the boss, the downtrodden immigrant. Economically, the rise of the city exemplified the growing power of a class of exploitative capitalists, dealing in traction franchises, corrupting city governments, and oppressing workers and immigrants. These problems aroused the populace to support a vast body of desirable social and regulatory legislation. A generation of reformers, the leaders of the Progressive Move-

2 *Ibid.*, 448.
3 Blake McKelvey, "American Urban History Today," in the *American Historical Review*, LVII: 919–929 (July, 1952).

ment, were thus able to preserve old values through new methods; in the cities particularly, to employ the cliché, Hamiltonian means proved necessary to preserve Jeffersonian ends. But then urbanization drops from the story, not to return again until Americans are described fleeing the city for the suburbs in the years after World War II. As Eric E. Lampard observes in a recent searching critique of urban history, an "urban-industrial tranformation" has now become "part of the furniture displayed in every up-to-date textbook of United States history." [4] There is little evidence, however, that the substantial body of writing in urban history has influenced in any significant way the general historian's interpretation of the American past.

Nor can one really be quite sure what urban history is. Unlike the urban branches of the social sciences, neither its method nor its subject matter has been well defined. There are no textbooks to provide a framework for inquiry. Only a handful of university courses in the subject are taught under a variety of names, "The History of the American City," "American Urban History," or "The History of Urban Society in the United States." The contents of these courses vary more than the labels. Is urban history the history of cities, the history of urbanization as a process, or the history of anything that takes place in an urban setting? The question has not yet been answered. Many studies seem customarily to be classified as urban history simply because they have something to do with cities and can not conveniently be fitted into one of the more formally established categories of American history.

Traditionally, the urban historian has confined himself rather narrowly to the history of one city, to the history of a few cities treated comparatively for a limited period of time—usually in regard to commercial or transportation rivalry—or to specialized aspects of urban development, particularly urban politics and reform. Critics have frequently enjoined him to broaden his horizons, to try to use urbanization as the basis for a new synthesis of American history, or to indicate more precisely what he is attempting to contribute. But this has had little effect. Historians in general are little inclined to fret about weaknesses in their method, and the urban historian is no exception. Although a number of urban biographies and comparative city histories represent the tradition of local history at its very best, the urban

[4] Eric E. Lampard, "American Historians and the Study of Urbanization," in the *American Historical Review*, LXVII: 52 (October, 1961).

historian admittedly has seldom been moved to examine broader themes that might reasonably be considered a part of his subject.

One theme embedded in our historiography which probably bothers anyone who looks into the history of American cities is the alleged anti-urban bias of nineteenth-century American culture. The texts tell us that the American of that era hated the city, that he grew up a good agrarian committed to the mythology of the yeoman in the garden. Yet, if one reads urban biographies or looks into the local sections of a nineteenth-century newspaper—even one from a town or city located in the heart of the agricultural hinterland—he is confronted by exuberant pronouncements extolling the city as the exemplar of American growth and progress. If he goes a bit further and examines the census returns for the century, he can find evidence to support the view that Americans rushed to the cities as fast as they could get there. The contradiction represented here merits much more attention than it has received.[5]

This is not to say that there is any shortage of writing on the question of the American attitude toward the city. In recent years, a school of writers has developed which stridently advances the view of the city as a positive good.[6] According to its doctrines, mostly directed against certain varieties of urban planning, the city is the center of diversity and vitality in a culture. Congested streets are colorful and organically self-policing. Those who propose renewal schemes with high-rise residential buildings and space for grass and trees are in effect trying to destroy great cities and must be considered anti-urbanists. These schemes succeed because Americans hold to an outmoded agrarian tradition; we should, we are told, abandon the myth of the evil city and get on with building a better world in an era in which the super-city has become reality.

This argument has been given scholarly substance in a recent study by a distinguished philosopher and his wife. They find that intellectuals from Jefferson to Frank Lloyd Wright have been opposed to the city, and assert that the city planner and urban reformer of today have accordingly been left without a

5 Although lacking in historical depth, Anselm Strauss, *Images of the American City* (New York, 1961), is a significant attempt to examine this topic through the use of techniques of social psychology.

6 For a prominent recent book in this vein, see Jane Jacobs, *The Death and Life of Great American Cities* (New York, 1961).

mythology or a mystique to sustain their efforts.[7] A recent article, based on an examination of some 6,000 volumes of verse published between 1876 and 1905, comes to a similar conclusion about the attitude toward the city of an important segment of the intellectual community. American poets of the period, the author writes, were nearly united in their opposition to the city. They "constructed a myth of the city formidable in its detail and frightening in its intensity. . . . Pealing the great knell of doom, the poets pointed out the city's materialistic greed and assigned it to everlasting damnation." [8]

Historians of American scholarship have long emphasized that much of the early study of the city—particularly by the pioneer urban sociologists—rested on the assumption that the city represented an abnormality in society, a deviation from a normal order of life. Similarly, it has been argued that the appeal of Frederick Jackson Turner's "Frontier Hypothesis" lay not in the originality of his conception but in the fact that he succinctly and poetically crystallized a generally held nineteenth-century American prejudice against the urban-industrial society we had become. The more extreme examples of the recent revisionist historical writing concerned with political reform in the twentieth century appear to be designed to root out and destroy any alleged anti-urban bias in past scholarship. The rather shrill efforts to refurbish the city political boss and to give proper credit to the urban immigrant masses and their leaders for their support of reform often read more like pro-city tracts than dispassionate pieces of scholarship. In short, the urban tradition and conceptions of this tradition radically influence the way we formally regard our national experience.[9]

There is little difficulty in finding everyday examples of anti-urban attitudes in our culture. In politics, of course, the rhetoric

[7] Morton White and Lucia White, *The Intellectual Versus the City* (Cambridge, 1962), especially 231–239.

[8] Robert H. Walker, "The Poet and the Rise of the City" in the *Mississippi Valley Historical Review*, XLIX: 98–99 (June, 1962).

[9] An excellent summary of the development of scholarly study of the city is provided by William Diamond, "On the Dangers of an Urban interpretation of History," in Eric F. Goldman, ed., *Historiography and Urbanization* (Baltimore, 1941), 67–108. For the relation of the Turner hypothesis to nineteenth-century thought, see Henry Nash Smith, *Virgin Land* (Vintage ed., New York, 1957), particularly 291–305. J. Joseph Huthmacher, "Urban Liberalism and the Age of Reform," in the *Mississippi Valley Historical Review*, XLIX: 231–241 (September, 1962) is an example of the attempt to supply an urban reinterpretation of the Progressive Era.

of agrarianism persisted long after we had become a nation of cities. Recent politicians as diverse as the Columbia University-trained North Dakota Senator, William Langer; the Kansas Citian, Harry Truman; and that model of urbanity, Dean Acheson, have all, on one occasion or another, declared themselves to be just simple country boys.[10] Although this type of appeal seems finally to be disappearing, still very much with us is an anti-urban celebration of the bucolic to be found in magazine and newspaper writing. There is a need, these pieces argue, for everyone to escape from the frenzy of the city, at least occasionally, in order to seek serenity in the country. In a recent article on the West, Eric Sevareid, the journalist and television commentator, writes of the possibility of self-renewal in the empty spaces of the mountains and prairies: "It's crowds and close quarters that make most of us feel lost and little; you can't increase the density of human beings without increasing the individual sense of anonymity. . . . There must be millions of us who can't sit still for an hour in the city, even on a holiday, even in the park, without getting jumpy, but who can sit beside a Hunter Creek unaware of minutes or hours until the evening chill catches us by surprise." [11]

It seems clear, then, that a body of sentiments which could be termed anti-urban supplies at least a veneer overlaying our essentially urban culture. Yet even a casual effort to disentangle these sentiments and to look at their development historically reveals serious difficulties in trying to sustain the prevailing simple view that Americans have always been opposed to the city. From the writings of Americans about their cities emerges nothing as formal as a doctrine of anti-urbanism, but rather a number of ambiguous, contradictory notions that vary through time and from place to place.

Before one can even begin to delineate the nature of these sentiments, several fairly obvious things, often ignored in the glib pronouncements on the subject, should be pointed out. First, it is necessary to distinguish between the sharply varying sentiments about the city to be found in formal literature, popular fiction, and promotional writing. Which of these types of materials more accurately reflects the "national mind" in-

10 See R. Richard Wohl, "Urbanism, Urbanity, and the Historian," in the *University of Kansas City Review*, XXII: 55 (Autumn, 1951) for an incisive statement on the presence of rural anachronisms in our present-day culture.
11 *The Saturday Review*, XLV: 45, 91 (October 20, 1962).

volves the kind of interesting epistemological question that intellectual historians like to wrestle with but can not resolve. Secondly, much writing that seems on the surface to be anti-urban in tone does not assert a contrary agrarian position or even necessarily an anti-urban position. It may represent a protest against aspects of the social scene that are associated in a general way with the city—Catholicism, the New Immigrant of the late nineteenth century, materialism, the power of business, the devolution of democracy—but not, if carefully read, against the city itself or what might be termed urban ideals and values. Thirdly (and this point is closely related), historians have tended to read works dealing with the city from only one period—the late nineteenth century—when reformers of varied persuasion were grinding out vast quantities of material on these subjects. Much of this writing was polemical, even inflammatory, in tone, since it was designed to bring about major social changes. The reformers lashed out at the evil city, to be sure, but only in relationship to other problems they saw in American society. They seldom proposed doing away with the city; they only proposed to reform it along lines not inconsistent with the classical ideal of the city in Western civilization. Moreover, literature from a time of crisis is not always the best gauge with which to measure fundamental attitudes that underlie a society.

Finally, what is one to make of the vast body of writing in defense of the city—especially promotional material in which the city served as a principal indicator of material growth and general American progress? If one were to judge only by quantity—taking into account newspapers, gazetteers, local history, promotional tracts, and the like—then writing in praise of the American city would outweigh writing that condemned it. With little more distortion than is involved in some of the learned discussions of Americans and their myths, it would be possible to show the existence of an "urban myth" in our past and to construct a learned monograph focussed on the question: "Why did a people, planted in a wilderness with the possibility of organizing a workable civilization based on the freehold and an agricultural economy, so quickly embrace an ideology which had at its heart a belief in the growth of cities?"

The question is absurd and is intended only to point up the danger of talking readily about national traditions and mythologies after examining too few sources or only one kind of source. Nevertheless, it may be worthwhile to sort out a few themes running through the writing about cities in the early and mid-nineteenth century—a period when people began to become aware of their influence in American life—as a means of suggesting some of the lines along which inquiry into the nature of the American urban tradition might proceed.

Much of the nineteenth-century writing that could be termed anti-urban stems from a formal literary convention at least as old as Vergil's *Georgics*. This is the view, which most everyone expresses from time to time but usually not too seriously, that the city is unnatural and corrupts man, that one must get close to nature occasionally to restore his inner resources. Benjamin Rush, the great scientist and physician, expressed an enduring sentiment when he wrote in 1801 of the pleasure he received from cultivating twelve acres of ground a few miles from Philadelphia. There he could retire two or three afternoons a week to "forget for a few hours the bustle, the sickness, the selfishness, and scandal of Philadelphia." He could listen to the "songs of the little feathered tribes who jump from twig to twig over my head and sometimes peck their food at my feet." He could enjoy the fragrant flowers and fruit trees that he had planted and cultivated. "My care of them," Rush continued, "will not be repaid with persecution, for they have *never grown in the city of Philadelphia*." [12]

Nineteenth-century novelists—Charles Brockden Brown, Hawthorne, Melville, James—utilized the city as a symbol of restraint, knowledge of evil, and corruption opposed to the innocence, freedom, and expansiveness of the American forest or garden. The anti-urban tones in the writings of the Transcendentalists were based on this kind of conception of the polarity of nature and society; the city often provided the most convenient example of man's denial of nature. It should be noted, however, that the prevalence of these anti-urban sentiments in literature and philosophy has little relation to how people reacted to the developments taking place in the early and mid-nineteenth century. We read Thoreau today and are moved by the power of his protest against the machine and the city. But in his time his was figuratively as well as literally a voice in the wilderness. His contemporaries did not read *Walden*, but rather the enthusiastic paeans to the telegraph, the iron horse, the growing cities, and

[12] L. H. Butterfield, ed., *Letters of Benjamin Rush* (Princeton, 1951), II: 836.

the expanding factories to be found in *Hunt's Merchants' Magazine* or their local newspapers.

A second basic strain in writings about the cities—the credo of agrarianism—is in some respects equally formalistic. Thomas Jefferson provided its main elements. "I think our governments will remain virtuous for many centuries," he characteristically wrote to James Madison in 1787, "as long as they are chiefly agricultural; and this will be as long as there shall be vacant lands in any part of America. When they get piled upon one another in large cities, as in Europe, they will become corrupt as in Europe." [13] But in Jefferson and his colleagues this view was often somewhat casual. Jefferson, practical man that he was, came to terms with cities. It was only as the position of the farmer weakened in the nineteenth century that agrarian sentiments hardened into a doctrine of agricultural fundamentalism. The more agriculture declined, the more vigorously was opposition to the city expressed. Agricultural newspapers of the nineteenth century are filled with warnings to country boys about the fate awaiting them in the city largely because migration from the farm was one of the principal reasons for the deteriorating position of the farmer. By the 1850's, to question in a farm journal that the city was anything but absolute evil was to expound heresy. The pursuits of agriculture, wrote a correspondent to the *Prairie Farmer* of Chicago in 1850, "are so connected with every thing around us which tends to enlighten and ennoble the mind, improve the condition of society, and promote the common welfare—and its influences have so direct a bearing in all its ramifications, upon individual and national felicity, that it would seem as if a man must come from some other planet who could find any thing to say in its disparagement." City life, he went on, "*crushes, enslaves,* and *ruins so many thousands of our young men,* who are insensibly made the victims of *dissipation,* of *reckless speculation,* and of *ultimate crime. . . .*" [14]

Anti-urban sentiments were a fundamental part of the rationale sustaining the great farmer movements of the late nineteenth century. "The great cities·rest upon our broad and fertile prairies," said William Jennings Bryan in his famous 1896 Cross of Gold speech. "Burn down your cities and leave our farms, and your cities will spring up again as if by magic; but destroy

---

[13] Paul L. Ford, ed., *The Writings of Thomas Jefferson* (New York, 1894), IV: 479–480.
[14] *The Prairie Farmer*, X: 18–19 (January, 1850).

our farms, and the grass will grow in the streets of every city in the country." [15] But, after all, the agrarian crusade failed. So to what extent can anti-urbanism in the agrarian sense really be said to reflect national sentiment when it had no effect on the fundamental course of national development? An argument which evolves in defense of a declining economic interest in society does not necessarily constitute community ideology.

Both the romantic and the agrarian sides of anti-urbanism found expression in the books about city problems written by well-known late-nineteenth-century religious critics such as Josiah Strong, William A. Stead, Samuel L. Loomis, and Charles L. Brace. They disliked one or another aspect of existing urban life—the Jew, the Catholic, the extremes of wealth and poverty, the irreligion and materialism, or the way children were treated. Still, they often recognized that large cities were here to stay and were concerned with making them better places in which to live. To call their position either pro-urban or anti-urban says very little. Amory D. Mayo in *Symbols of the Capital,* one of the first and one of the more obscure of these clerical examinations of urban life, attacked the city in formal agrarian terms: "The majority of successful dwellers in town are scarred in body and twisted in mind by their prolonged stimulation of all the powers of life, and in grasping the prize of ambition have lost their own best resources of enjoyment. . . . All dangers of the town may be summed up in this: that here, withdrawn from the blessed influences of Nature, and set face to face against humanity, man loses his own nature and becomes a new and artificial creature—an inhuman cog in a social machinery that works like a fate, and cheats him of his true culture as a soul. The most unnatural fashions and habits, the strangest eccentricities of intellect, the wildest and most pernicious theories in social morals, and the most appalling and incurable barbarism, are the legitimate growth of city life." Yet Mayo understood the appeal and the reality of the city. He saw young people flocking there and being challenged by the experience. If they survived the ordeal, he thought their faith and character would unquestionably be strengthened. Moreover, an ideal city, a monument to Christian principles, was conceivable if there were only a way of removing the poor and the exploiters of the poor. "But," he wrote in a

15 For a discussion of the agrarian myth in American culture, see Richard Hofstadter, *The Age of Reform* (Vintage ed., New York, 1960), 23–59.

more realistic vein, "we cannot build cities 'to order'; they are and will be the huge receptacles for all varieties of humanity, and represent the worst as surely as the best in our American character. All the teacher of Christianity can do is to take men and women in towns as he finds them, and, spite of disheartening influences, keep on forever warning, instructing and inspiring to virtue." [16]

There is a substantial body of nineteenth-century writing which argues not that the city itself is evil but that the Amercian city, with its extremes of wealth and poverty, its materialism, and its exploitation, represented a denial of Christian principles. This point of view received thorough exploration in a philosophical prelude to an 1857 governmental report of the results of a systematic investigation of the slums of New York. The writers argued that man was a gregarious creature who yearned for neighborhood. Theorists of all ages had conceived of noble cities. Even the Bible had "coupled the forms of earthly splendor with the more spiritual excellences of a New Jerusalem." The city could be the site of "intellectual and moral beatitude." If desolate nature was "symbolical of savage or barbarous life," then its polar opposite ought to be found where art, luxury, and industry existed in profusion. "Yet here," the writers continued, "in reality, where pleasure wreathes perennial flowers, and magnificence runs wild with varied forms; here, in sad refutation of utopian speculation, the leper crouches in dumb despair, the beggar crawls in abject misery, the toiler starves, the robber prowls, and the tenant-house—home of all those outcast beings —rises in squalid deformity, to mock civilization with its foul malaria, its poison-breeding influences, its death-dealing associations." [17]

The metaphor of the American city as New Jerusalem was a favorite. If Americans were God's chosen people—and this was a vital part of nineteenth-century assertions of doctrines of progress—the prophetic vision could include a spiritual capital. "While the beginning of things was a garden in the paradise of Eden," said the Reverend James Cooper in describing the American experience as Christian saga, "the end of things, as prophe-

[16] Amory D. Mayo, *Symbols of the Capital; or, Civilization in New York* (New York, 1859), 50–51, 55.

[17] State of New York, *Report of the Select Committee appointed To Examine Into the Condition of Tenant Houses in New-York and Brooklyn* (Assembly Document 205, March 9, 1857), 9–10.

sied in the Book of Revelation, is a city, magnificent and populous, the New Jerusalem." [18]

As the various investigations of urban life in the period indicated, the nineteenth-century American city was a monstrously unhealthy place in which to live. Insufficiently emphasized in speculations about the urban tradition is the fact that much of the protest against the city rested precisely on this point. When one-third of the children in New York tenements in the 1860's died before they were a year old and one-half before the fifth year,[19] is it any wonder that men of good will lashed out at the evil city? This was humanitarianism, not anti-urbanism. Moreover, it was largely city dwellers who were struck down by the dreaded nineteenth-century epidemics of cholera and yellow fever. Ebenezer Hazard, who had survived the Philadelphia yellow fever epidemic of 1793 in spite of the massive bloodletting prescribed by his physician Benjamin Rush, was expressing ecological not agrarian doctrines when he observed that the plague ought to check "the prevailing taste for enlarging Philadelphia, and crowding so many human beings together on so small a part of earth." Perhaps, he wrote, all Americans would learn to reject the "fashions of the Old World in building great cities." [20]

These sentiments related closely to prevailing scientific conceptions of the nature of disease. Not until the 1880's was the germ theory of disease generally accepted in the United States. Before that time many diseases, particularly those that were epidemic in nature, were regarded not as entities but as dynamic conditions whose manifestations varied in terms of a range of moral, climatic, and environmental factors.[21] Those who advanced this type of etiology generally argued that the city provided an unwholesome, unnatural atmosphere for human life. Miasmas which induced both physical and moral disease (and the two were not rigorously demarcated) were inextricably asso-

18 Quoted in F. J. Kingsbury, "The Tendency of Men to Live in Cities," in the *Journal of Social Science*, XXXIII: 12 (November, 1895).

19 Gordon Atkins, *Health, Housing and Poverty in New York City, 1865–1898* (Ann Arbor, 1947), 30.

20 Quoted in John H. Powell, *Bring Out Your Dead* (Philadelphia, 1949), 276.

21 For an imaginative exploration of the relationship between social attitudes and theories of disease in the nineteenth century, see Charles E. Rosenberg, *The Cholera Years* (Chicago, 1952).

ciated with an urban environment; their effects could be alleviated through introducing the purity of the country to the city. When Jefferson spoke of cities as "pestilential" or as "sores" he was only in part employing metaphor and in a sense was reflecting the best scientific opinion of his day. In this instance, as in others, his statements have too frequently been interpreted outside the context of his times. Benjamin Rush, a firm believer in miasmatic theories of disease, made this point about cities explicit in a letter to Jefferson: "I consider them in the same light that I do abscesses on the human body, viz., as reservoirs of all the impurities of a community." [22] As President, Jefferson devised a plan to remove disease-causing vapors from New Orleans: "Such a constitution of atmosphere being requisite to originate [yellow fever] as is generated only in low, close, and ill-cleansed parts of town, I have supposed it practicable to prevent its generation by building our cities on a more open plan. Take, for instance, the chequer board for a plan. Let the black squares only be building squares, and the white ones be left open, in turf and trees. Every square of houses will be surrounded by four open squares, and every house will front an open square. The atmosphere of such a town would be like that of the country, insusceptible of the miasmata which produce yellow fever. I have accordingly proposed that the enlargements of the city of New Orleans, which must immediately take place, shall be on this plan. But it is only in case of enlargements to be made, or of cities to be built, that this means of prevention can be employed." [23]

Until the 1860's, by which time it was recognized that an epidemic was not necessarily a scourge of God and that cholera, at least, could be checked through proper sanitary practices, each year of plague produced warnings to abandon the unhealthy cities. A physician wrote, for example, that the 1849 siege of cholera could be considered one of the "greatest *reforms* the world has ever known," for it might teach Americans "to forsake large cities . . . and to choose the country's wholesome air, with its quietude and competence." [24] The first investigations of urban life in America reflected this view that the atmosphere of the city sapped the moral and physical vigor of its residents.

[22] Butterfield, ed., *Rush Letters,* II: 824.
[23] Andrew A. Lipscomb and Albert E. Bergh, eds., *The Writings of Thomas Jefferson* (Washington, 1904), XI: 66.
[24] *The Spirit of the Age* (August 11, 1849), 91–92.

The famous 1845 report of John H. Griscom, a pioneer in the public health movement, argued that the foul air of New York caused an individual's blood to become burdened with impurities, preventing it from imparting to the "system the qualities demanded by nature for the due maintenance of health and strength." All that was necessary to demonstrate this was a stroll in the country. The contrast between an atmosphere filled with "animal and vegetable exhalations" and the air of grassy plains, rivers, and mountains needed "no epicurean lungs to detect it." The "superior corporeal activity" and the mental stimulation imparted by these latter surroundings provided "prima facie proofs" of the country's superiority.[25]

It is usually argued that the effort to introduce trees and parks to the city in the nineteenth century was an outgrowth of the romantic enthusiasm for nature aroused by the writings of John Ruskin, William Cullen Bryant, Andrew Jackson Downing, and others. This is probably true in part. But the movement was also based, as the writings of the most famous of nineteenth-century planners, Frederick Law Olmsted, clearly demonstrate, on the belief that parks and trees would be a means of improving the health of the city. Parks would serve as "lungs" or "ventilators," absorbing or dispelling the impurities of the urban environment. A physician who wrote about the 1849 cholera epidemic speculated that the principal cause of the disease was insufficient electricity in the air, a result of the unnatural congestion of cities. Accordingly, the answer to epidemics was clear: "If cities must exist let many and large spaces be devoted to parks, and let all the streets on each side of the way be lined with trees, with two or three trees to every building, so that the people may be supplied with electricity and oxygen in abundance from Nature's own laboratory." [26] Regardless of the particular environmental theory of disease advanced, parks were considered an urban public health measure of fundamental importance.

Another little-examined aspect of the nineteenth-century urban tradition is the influence of sectional considerations in shaping views expressed about cities. Writers in the American West frequently argued in good Jeffersonian terms that the cities of the East were corrupt, sinful, and dangerous to republican

25 John H. Griscom, *The Sanitary Condition of the Laboring Population of New York* (New York, 1845), 12.
26 *The Spirit of the Age* (August 4, 1849), 71.

virtue. They were the counterparts of the evil cities of Europe, which Americans had rejected. But the Western city set in space was another matter: it was the potential center of a great new civilization, the modern successor to the metropolises of the ancient world, the symbol of a thriving society. Even in the South, the traditional bastion of agrarianism, there was continual demand before the Civil War that the region develop its own great cities in order to avoid further exploitation by the business interests of the North. This damning of cities elsewhere while defending those closer to home sometimes took an odd turn. A Southern writer in 1866 published a long poem in *De Bow's Review,* the famous New Orleans magazine, attacking the city for its filth and noise, its knavery, its materialism, its fraud, its licentiousness:

> Athwart the glare of theatre or ball,
> The shadowy forms of vice and misery fall,
> To drunken orgies, gay saloons entice,
> Grey-headed seniors leer at flaunting vice . . .
> Riot and drunken rowdies haunt the street,
> Mob matched with mob in brutal conflict meet,
> Then in the coarse debauch of midnight crown
> The day's exploits, and care and conscience drown.

But he or his editors must have been aware that these many stanzas of diatribe might offend the numerous readers of the magazine who lived in cities, for appended to the poem was the following formal footnote: "The description of city life, here given, applies to the *great cities only* of the United States and Europe."[27]

Ironically, it was the great interior garden of America, whose existence sustained the hopes of those who wished the United States to remain an agrarian republic, that produced the most elaborate visions of an urban future for the nation.[28] A group of promoter-intellectuals, including Daniel Drake, Jesup W. Scott, Robert T. Van Horn, and William Gilpin, who borrowed ideas freely from one another, shaped a rationale in support of Western cities that permeated the newspapers, gazet-

[27] *De Bow's Review,* Series 2, I: 502–504 (May, 1866).
[28] For a more detailed discussion of this theme, see Charles N. Glaab, "Visions of Metropolis: William Gilpin and Theories of City Growth in the American West," in the *Wisconsin Magazine of History* XLV: 21–31 (Autumn, 1961).

teers, and commercial journals of Cincinnati, St. Louis, Chicago, Kansas City, and other aspiring interior cities. The view that the cities of the West would inevitably become larger and greater than those of the Atlantic Coast was defended with two somewhat contradictory economic notions—first, that internal commerce provided the only sound means of sustaining population growth and hence large cities would inevitably be concentrated in the interior of a nation and, secondly, that Western cities, because of their strategic location along the natural paths of world commerce, could expect to become the future great international trading capitals. Western writers also relied heavily on the German geographer Alexander von Humboldt, whose geopolitical theories emphasized the continual westward movement of world population along an isothermal zodiac and the formation of cities where yearly temperature conditions were most favorable for civilization. In developing these themes, prophets employed a rich imagery which portrayed the cities of the West as the successors of the great cities of the ancient world. Thomas Hart Benton in his advocacy of a transcontinental railroad spoke of the "Tyres, Sidons, Balbecs, Palmyras, Alexandrias" destined to spring up along his proposed route to the west, and a Kansas City promoter predicted that cities "greater than Babylon, Nineveh, or Thebes" would tower above the green hills along the line of his projected mid-continental railroad to run from Galveston Bay to Lake Superior.[29]

However, if the cities of the American West were to be the successors of the existing great cities of the world, this raised a problem—recognized by many of the promotional writers—of the inevitable decline of these new metropolises. Many simply dismissed this possibility as too far in the future to be worthy of serious consideration, but an ingenious writer in *De Bow's Review,* by tying his theory to prevailing conceptions of epidemics, even supplied a plausible answer to this prophetic dilemma. In the past, Peking, Canton, Constantinople, Naples, Vienna, Madrid, London, and Paris had succeeded Babylon, Nineveh, Memphis, Tyre, and Carthage. But the fate of ancient cities was now being prepared for these present world capitals. "Most of these great cities are," he wrote, "in their oldest portions, at the heart, exhibiting evident signs of decay. Like

29 *Ibid.,* 27, 30.

ancient trees, while at the heart they are wasting away, they add circle to circle of outward growth; now gaining in progress of growth on the measure of interior decay, and again failing to increase outwardly as fast as the interior portions waste away." This decay was chiefly the result of the impure exhalations of a great city caused by the accumulation of filth at its interior. But the metropolises of the American West would not face this problem. Because of the pattern of the magnificent Mississippi River system, these natural impurities could be continually and safely carried away, and a long life could thus be predicted for the future great cities of the world.[30]

Any final word from the West should be left to the most flamboyant and exuberant of the Western city prophets, Logan U. Reavis of St. Louis. Reavis combined the views of Humboldt, Scott, Gilpin, and anyone else who had anything to say on cities into an involved defense of the future of St. Louis and dedicated the better part of a journalistic career in the 1860's and 1870's to trying to get the national capital moved there. Reavis in today's terms was a dedicated "urbanist"; he castigated those who saw more beauty in the quiet of the country than in the energy and vitality of the city. And his was a nineteenth-century vision of megalopolis: "Thus have I written a new word—a new prophecy of a city central to a continent of resources, whose productive energies are greater than those possessed by all the world besides, and upon which is destined to reside a population greater than now exists on the globe . . . a city destined to become the all-directing head and the central moving heart of the great family of man—a city from out whose throbbing life and comprehensive brain will go forth new laws and new principles of civilization for the better government of states and nations—a city destined to control the commerce of more than one hundred thousand miles of railway, reaching with equal facility to every extremity of the continent, to gather the surplus products of more than one hundred populous states, and to whose central life more than one hundred continental cities, populous and powerful, as all the present existing cities of the globe, will contribute prosperity and greatness—a city which . . . will flash upon the mind of the human race, and the world will behold in America the city of prophecy—the Apocalyptic City—

[30] *De Bow's Review,* XXX: 20–25 (January, 1861).

'The New Jerusalem, the ancient seer
Of Patmos saw.' " [31]

A few gleanings from nineteenth-century writings about cities do not really permit any elaborate conclusions about the nature of the American urban tradition—in spite of the tendency of historians of late to generalize about the character of a movement or an aspect of thought on the basis of one or two literary products. They do suggest, however, that the concepts of "city" and "urban" are sufficiently vague to have lent themselves to a variety of uses in our past, and certainly these uses ought to be explored more fully than they have been before one speaks authoritatively of either the prevalence of urbanism or anti-urbanism in our culture. Historians of the past, reflecting little more in our national consciousness perhaps than a vague nostalgia over a lost opportunity to create a better civilization in a new world, undoubtedly exaggerated the importance of the "agrarian myth" and fixed it in our historiography. There would be no difficulty in assembling the evidence to show that nineteenth-century Americans passionately embraced their urban destiny.

However, historians prefer to re-examine and reinterpret well-established sources and to ponder again old questions within a received framework. Frederick Jackson Turner, who did so much to shape this framework, was bolder than this. He recognized that there was another side to his hypothesis, and late in his career suggested the need for an "urban reinterpretation of our history." [32] The urban historian wisely has not attempted to design this kind of new strait jacket for fashionable scholars to wear, but instead has confined himself to limited subjects—one city's biography or the history of a few cities treated comparatively for a short period of time. Because his work has lacked ostentatious "interpretation," his substantial contributions, particularly in adding another dimension of understanding to the confining national synthesis, have been generally ignored.

But the United States is now the land of the city and the super-city and since the historian is as much concerned with

[31] Logan U. Reavis, *Saint Louis: The Future Great City of the World* (3rd ed., St. Louis, 1871), 215.
[32] Quoted in Arthur M. Schlesinger, "The City in American Civilization," *Paths to the Present* (New York, 1949), 210.

finding a "usable past" as a real one, we shall undoubtedly see more in our future general histories about the urban side of the American experience. One can hope that our national historians in developing these urban themes will at least read the solid works in urban history that have been written and be guided by their spirit of caution and dispassion. It would be unfortunate if urban history were merely to become a means of arguing the other side of a supposed urban-rural dialogue, which earlier historians artificially imposed on our past. Any such simple conception reflects only slightly the complexity of the historical reactions of Americans to the growth of their cities.

19. The Nature of Biography*

JOHN A. GARRATY

I

Biography, to begin with a very simple definition, is the record of a life. It is thus a branch of history, a small segment of a bigger pattern, just as the story of the development of a town, a state, or a nation may be thought of as an element in a larger whole. The word "biography" has often been used loosely. Marquis James has called his history of a great insurance company *The Biography of a Business*. George Gamow has written a *Biography of the Earth* from the time it "was born from the Sun, its mother, as the result of a brief but violent encounter with a passing star" to its "violent thermal death in the far-distant future." Others have written "biographies" of buildings, books, even of ideas. But such works are biographies only by analogy, and perhaps the simplest accurate definition of biography should read: "the story of a human life."

Since all biographies must say something of the times in which their subjects lived, the form is tied even more closely to history. There have been great variations in the amount of this "background material" in biography. At one extreme, for instance, are the "psychographs" of Gamaliel Bradford, in which the protagonists float like disembodied spirits in a vacuum. At the other pole is such a massive, multi-volumed "life and times" as Douglas Southall Freeman's *George Washington*. In any life the author must of sheer necessity provide a certain amount of "background" if his hero is to be made intelligible to the reader. But how important and how con-

* Reprinted with permission from *The Centennial Review*, I (Spring, 1957), 123–141.

scious and conspicuous a role ought "history" to play in a biography?

Some writers have gone so far as to argue that individual men are significant only because the times in which they live make them so. A sociologist, Joseph Schneider, after an elaborate study of the lives of English botanists from 1700 to the present, concluded that certain periods of history had proved favorable to the development of many plant specialists, whereas in other times (in the early 19th century, for example) few important ones had appeared. "It is the cultural situation which produces famous men," he concluded. V. F. Calverton, writing in the 1920's, also denied the importance of the individual. "The idea of looking upon greatness as a mystery or an accident is . . . absurd," Calverton wrote in *The Newer Spirit;* the "peculiar manifestations" of "circumstances" provided the opportunity which "made it possible for certain men to become great." Shakespeare, according to Calverton, was great only because he "came in contact with those stimuli . . . that, reacting on his nature, could but inevitably make him the man and author he was," while a proper study of George Washington would show "not how Washington rose above conditions to success, but how conditions . . . rode him to success." In the same vein, Stephen Vincent Benét once wrote a short story, "The Curfew Tolls," describing what a nonentity Napoleon would have been if he had been born a few years before his time and thus too old for the role he actually played in the denouement of the French Revolution.

Even a "great man" like Goethe spoke of the individual as a reflection of the times, intimating that any man born a decade earlier or later than in fact he was, would "become quite a different being." And Professor Edward P. Cheyney, in his presidential address to the American Historical Association in 1923, without denying to man a limited freedom of action, concluded that every person "is controlled at every turn by the natural laws of the world in which he dwells."

But other writers have insisted that forceful individuals can often change the trend of events. Thomas Carlyle, of course, carried this theory to its logical extreme. Carlyle was a "hero worshipper"; he insisted that history was no more than the sum of innumerable biographies. The biographer Sidney Lee emphasized "those aspects of men's lives which affect the movements of the crowd." And William Roscoe Thayer urged his fellow historians to "try to discover how the human will—that force more mysterious than electricity—shapes and directs the deeds of men."

A third group has argued that neither the man nor the times in which he lives really controls what happens in history. "In the queer mess of human destiny," wrote one of Washington's biographers, "the determining factor is Luck. For every important place in life there are many men of fairly equal capacities. Among them Luck decides who shall accomplish the great work . . . and who shall fall back into obscurity and silence." Oscar Handlin wrote an entire book, *Chance or Destiny?*, in which he examined a series of critical events in American history and concluded that in each case the fate of the individuals concerned and of the nation as a whole was determined by pure chance. Whether this force be called luck, chance, or fate, those who stress it are in essential agreement that neither men nor great social forces control historical development.

It would be difficult to write a biography without having a definite opinion on the importance of the "hero" in history, and whatever one's theory, it must inevitably influence the kind of book one writes. The extreme position of Carlyle, though challenging, is certainly exaggerated. For history deals with societies as well as individuals, and any society is far more than the sum of its parts. Vast economic, social, and cultural forces, which obviously transcend the lives of individuals, are basic elements in history. And luck too plays a part.

But the biographer had better avoid any oversimplified theory of historical development. The individual makes history; so does chance; so do social forces. One need not look beyond his daily experience to observe the operation of all three elements. Each of us makes decisions that influence the lives of others; each is controlled and limited by the world we live in; each is affected by the caprice of fortune. It is the biographer's job to determine the relative importance of each factor throughout his subject's career. Thus Gilbert Chinard wrote in *Thomas Jefferson: The Apostle of Americanism:* "Jefferson . . . could have followed the line of least resistance and enjoyed the good things of life. . . . Such would have been Jefferson's destiny, had he been born in the Old World." In this way he illustrates the role of determinism and of chance in life. But Chinard added: "Had he been made of weaker stuff he would have become one of the fox-hunters, horse-racers and card-players of the Virginia gentry." Here the subject is seen overriding both fate and his environment. Taken as a whole, the passage shows that Chinard considered all the possibilities and arrived at his own judgment of their relative importance in a particular case. Whether one deals with small incidents or entire careers, the three major points of view should be always be always kept in mind—for they are all persistently operative.

But aside from this essentially philosophical question, the biographer must decide how to place his subject in his precise environment. Even the confirmed hero-worshipper must describe the world his protagonist is shaping.

David S. Muzzey put the problem well when he compared the individual to the waist of an hour-glass, standing "at the apex of a pyramid whose base broadens downward through descendants and at the apex of a pyramid whose base broadens upward through ancestors." In Muzzey's image every historically significant man is "focal," gathering the experience of the past into himself and sending forth "widening rays of influence" into the future. "The task of the biographer," he concluded, is "to calculate the resultant of the forces" furnished by the personality of the subject and "the problems of the times in which he lived."

In his own biographical work, Muzzey never applied this idea fully. But the English scientist Angus Armitage did so in his life of Copernicus, *Sun, Stand Thou Still*. Armitage was handicapped in writing a biography of Copernicus, for almost nothing is known of the great astronomer's personal life. He overcame this difficulty by stressing the development of the science of astronomy and Copernicus's contributions to it. His book has three parts, corresponding to the waist and the two pyramids of Muzzey's hourglass. "Astronomy before Copernicus" traces the history of man's knowledge of the stars down to the last quarter of the 15th century; "The Man and his Work" explains the subject's contributions, and details the limited knowledge of his life which has survived; and "The Triumph of the Copernican Theory" describes the "widening rays of influence" (to use Muzzey's term) of Copernicus on the later development of astronomy.

II

The biographer, however, must deal not only with the facts of the subject's career, with what he did, why he did it, and how he influenced his times and was in turn affected by them. He must also describe the man himself—his personality and character, his individuality. This aspect of biography is of fundamental importance; indeed it explains the enduring popularity of the biographical form. For people are interested primarily in people. They have never had to be convinced that "the proper study of mankind is man." And the convincing description of personality involves problems distinct from the accurate description of facts. It is this which makes the writing of biography a technique apart from that of history.

Biographical writing, therefore, concerns itself with two separate yet related tasks. This is not to say that the historical part of a biography is "scientific," or that the personal part is "artistic." A purely "scientific" biography can be deeply concerned with personality, as the examination of any psychiatrist's notebook would make clear, while who would deny the artistic merit of many of the great histories from Herodotus and Thucydides to Macaulay and Parkman?

Nevertheless it is true that the *portrayal* as distinct from the understanding of personality involves an extremely difficult problem which is chiefly artistic in nature. Allan Nevins, long both a champion and practitioner of the artistic expression of historical information, once said that the ability to describe character "is primarily a literary gift; it has little to do with erudite grubbing . . . in tons of manuscripts." Psychologists themselves have found this to be true. In a paper entitled "Personality: A Problem for Science or a Problem for Art?" Gordon W. Allport wrote: "It *is* true that the giants of literature make psychologists, who undertake to represent and to explain personality, seem ineffectual and sometimes a bit foolish in comparison. Only a pedant could prefer the dry collections of facts that psychology can offer regarding an individual mental life to the glorious and unforgettable portraits that the gifted novelist, dramatist, or biographer can give." Dr. Henry A. Murray, attempting to present the results of his exhaustive psychological study of fifty men of college age, was also made aware of the futility of all his work unless it could be effectively presented. He solved the dilemma by partially sacrificing science to art, frankly seeking to utilize the techniques of the novelists in the effort to make his characterizations "real." "A psychologist who believes that he can tell the truth without being 'literary' has only to try writing a case history or biography, and then compare what he has done to a character sketch by any novelist of the first order," Murray concluded.

The best novelists have excelled and indeed outdistanced nearly all biographers in describing personality, setting a standard almost impossible of attainment for writers of lives. Naturally, therefore, the novel has had great influence upon biography and has made the average biographer possibly more aware of the role of art in his field than the historian is in his.

The secret of the novelist's success lies in his unrestricted imagination. He may create what seems to be a very complicated character, but the character is never more complicated than the creator wishes to make it. He is never confronted with the need to select the typical from a maze of trivial or contradictory actions, nor is he bothered by the absence of evidence: his imagination can supply whatever detail his artistic sensibilities require.

The biographer, however, has at once more and less to draw upon. He has mountains of evidence from which to extract the essence of his subject. He has also the advantage of reality —he need not convince his readers that he is dealing with an actual person. And his imagination is constantly stimulated as each new fact falls into place. On the other hand, his "facts" do not always yield their meanings easily, and he must choose among them with discernment. Also, no matter how much evidence he has, he never has it all, and often lacks the most vital elements in the edifice he is trying to reconstruct. Yet he is bound by what he has. He can bring great artistry to the selection and interpretation of his evidence, but if he is to perform his proper function, the sources must be there, and all the relevant sources must be considered.

At the heart of the matter is the fact that in describing personality, the biographer is dealing with qualities that defy absolute analysis. Somerset Maugham was probably exaggerating the complexity and inconsistency of man when he wrote: "We know very little even of the persons we know most intimately; we do not know them enough to transfer them to the pages of a book and make human beings of them." But it remains true that the picture of a personality can be no more than convincing. Absolute certainty in interpreting character is something that even the psychologist does not claim to achieve. As T. S. Eliot wrote in *The Confidential Clerk:*

> There's always something one's ignorant of
> About anyone, however well one knows them;
> And that may be something of the greatest importance.

The infinite complexity of the mind of man gives the biographer a tremendous power, but it also burdens him with a great responsibility. When he describes a personality, no one can be certain that he is right, but it is almost equally difficult to prove that he is wrong. If he says that his hero wrote a particular letter or was at a certain place at a specific time, his accuracy can be checked. But when he says that his hero was shy, or selfish, or self-satisfied, he is dealing, essentially, with matters of opinion. The average man is so contradictory and complicated that by selecting evidence carefully, a biographer can "prove" that his subject is almost anything. "A little reflection," a writer in the *Southern Literary Messenger* remarked in 1856, "will show that half a dozen different narratives of the same life may be constructed, each of which shall contain facts and facts only, while none of them shall furnish . . . a true account."

Even when he is dealing with directly observable actions, the biographer's ability to select from among many different facts gives him a tremendous power. Suppose one were writing a life of Harry S. Truman. One might emphasize Truman's failure as a haberdasher, his connection with the corrupt Pendergast machine in Missouri, the devious circumstances of his selection as Roosevelt's running-mate in 1944, his early fumblings with the complexities of his job after Roosevelt's death, his overdependence upon certain unsavory cronies, his temper (as expressed, for example, in a letter to a certain music critic), the failure of his China policy, his "softness" toward Communism in his administration, and many similar aspects of his career. On the other hand, one might play down or ignore all these things and stress Truman's fine service as an artillery officer in World War I, his liberal record as Senator from Missouri during the New Deal era, the way he championed civil-rights legislation as President, the high calibre of so many of his appointees in the foreign policy field, his courageous stand in the Korean crisis, and other incidents that show him in a friendly light. All the *facts* used in either of these approaches might be accurate, but the resultant stories would be very different. Anyone who considers these accounts impossibly exaggerated should look into two lives of Andrew Jackson, one published by his friend Amos Kendall, the other by Davy Crockett.

Even when the biographer is scrupulously fair in his selection of evidence, he can still alter the impression he leaves by the way he interprets the evidence. In his life of Andrew Carnegie, John C. Winkler attempted to portray the great steel baron as an avaricious, selfish man. He did not ignore the fact that Carnegie had given millions to charity. Instead he pointed out the fact that Carnegie had no sons. "Could he have resisted the temptation to place *his* son among the world's super-rich and super-powerful? One doubts. For Andrew Carnegie came of a tribe clannish and jealous of its privileges, eager for glory, and with both eyes peeled for the main chance." Of course, Carnegie did have a daughter. This, to Winkler, was beside the point!

Most interpretations are more honest than this but not necessarily more correct. Consider the myriad ways that biographers have interpreted a simple fact in the life of Abraham Lincoln. In the years before the Civil War, while he was speaking out strongly against the extension of slavery, Lincoln was strangely reluctant to join the new Republican Party, though it embodied the principles he believed in. To explain why involves not discovering new facts but interpreting the known facts. And almost every conceivable interpretation has been offered by one or another of Lincoln's biographers:

Ward Hill Lamon, *Recollections of Abraham Lincoln:* Lamon simply ignores the whole question.

Emil Ludwig, *Lincoln:* Ludwig denies that Lincoln hesitated. "Lincoln was naturally in the fore in the foundation of the new party."

N. W. Stephenson, *Abraham Lincoln:* Stephenson says that Lincoln's delay was an example of his "natural deliberation."

A. J. Beveridge, *Abraham Lincoln:* Beveridge attributes the hesitation to Lincoln's "obstinate mind."

Edgar Lee Masters, *Lincoln, the Man:* Masters claims that Lincoln was too stupid to make up his mind. "He did not know what to do; and there was no fire in him to burn up and light the way."

Some authors, striving for objectivity, have tried to avoid all interpretation by confining themselves entirely to "the facts," but this is neither possible nor desirable. The reader wants to know not only what the facts are, but what the author thinks they mean. Admittedly the accuracy of most important interpretations, especially those concerned with personality, is beyond positive demonstration. But the biographer must do his best, using his knowledge and his imagination. Instead of steering clear of interpretations, instead of stifling his imagination, instead of attempting the impossible task of refusing to select the important from the trivial in the interest of an unattainable objectivity, the biographer must interpret, imagine, and select constantly if he is to approach the reality he seeks. But he must remember that it is *reality* that is his object, not a mirage. He is, as the critic Desmond MacCarthy once said, "an artist who is on oath."

Scrutinize these excerpts from two widely-read biographies. The first, from Lytton Strachey's sketch of Florence Nightingale (in *Eminent Victorians*), seems completely straightforward and factual:

> Why, as a child in the nursery, when her sister had shown a healthy pleasure in tearing her dolls to pieces, had *she* shown an almost morbid pleasure in sewing them up again? Why was she driven now to minister to the poor in their cottages, to watch by sick-beds, to put her dog's wounded paw into elaborate splints as if it was a human being?

The second, from Benjamin P. Thomas's *Abraham Lincoln*, seems much less solidly grounded upon fact:

> The lonely man in the White House had time for meditation while he waited for news night after night. With his strong sense of fatalism, he felt a Power beyond himself shaping the nation's destiny, and in an hour of anxiety he solemnly penned his thoughts.

Strachey's obvious purpose in the first passage was to show that in childhood Florence Nightingale exhibited almost as an obsession the passion for nursing that was to become her chief interest in life. But his statements, "based on" Sir Edward Cook's *Life of Florence Nightingale,* are distortions and outright perversions of the facts as Cook reported them. The dog, for example, was not hers, its leg was not "put into elaborate splints," and Florence merely assisted the local parson in the first aid that was actually administered. The source that Strachey "translated" into the sister's "tearing her dolls to pieces," actually reads: "[Florence] used to nurse and bandage the dolls which her elder sister damaged," a remark that clearly indicates no more than ordinary childish wear and tear. Further, the whole passage ignores Cook's explicit warning that most stories about Florence's early interest in nursing are unauthenticated, probably representing no more than an *ex post facto* exaggeration of traits common to most little girls. "Florence Nightingale is not the only little girl who was fond of nursing sick dolls or mending them when broken," Cook wrote. "Other children have tended wounded animals." Strachey interpreted the evidence; he used his imagination; but he violated his "oath" as a biographer.

Thomas's description of Lincoln, however, while more imaginative, is truthful. Fortunately, he has described the reasoning behind his reconstruction of Lincoln's thoughts and feelings:

> Sometime during the late summer of 1862, when Lee and his army were thrusting into Maryland, Lincoln wrote a memorandum. . . . "The will of God prevails. In great contests each party claims to act in accordance with the will of God. Both *may* be, and one *must* be wrong. God cannot be *for,* and *against,* the same thing at the same time." Then he goes on, wondering why God, who, by his mere quiet power over the minds of men, could stop the war at any time, allows it to continue; trying to find out what God's purpose is. Those are all the facts we have. But here is where the imagination comes in. Lincoln must have been alone. He couldn't have thought out and penned such a memorandum except in solitude. But he was an extremely busy man. If he was alone, he must have written it late at night. Why was he up late and not working? He must have been waiting for news. What was his mood? Solemn, obviously, from the nature of the memorandum. Anxious, inevitably, with the enemy on Northern soil and a great battle impending.

As a result of this reasoning, Thomas wrote the above-quoted lines. "These sentences are largely imaginative," he admitted, "yet I am convinced that they portray the situation accurately, and that something would have been lost in the telling without the use of imagination.

The novelist can use imagination the way Strachey used it,

for the truths he seeks to describe are universal and non-specific. The biographer's imagination must be *controlled,* for his truth is individual and specific. Marchette Chute, who has managed to write biographies of men like Chaucer and Shakespeare (whose personal lives can only be reconstructed imaginatively) without violating the canons of her profession, has put it this way: "There is no fun in a thing unless you play the game according to the rules. . . . The basic restriction upon any biographer is that he must be trying to tell the truth."

But the dangers involved in the over-free use of imagination and the reckless misuse of selection and interpretation are scarcely more serious than those resulting from the attempt to suppress these devices completely, Lytton Strachey must be forgiven many of his failings, if only for the lively attack which he aimed, in his *Eminent Victorians,* at all dull and uninspired biographical compilations: "Those two fat volumes, with which it is our custom to commemorate the dead—who does not know them, with their ill-digested masses of material, their slipshod style, their tones of tedious panegyric, their lamentable lack of selection, of detachment, of design? They are as familiar as the *cortège* of the undertaker, and wear the same air of slow, funereal barbarism. One is tempted to suppose, of some of them, that they were composed by that functionary, as the final item of his job."

Actually, in his assault upon such books Strachey in one sense went too far, and in another not far enough. He was complaining of the inordinate length and artlessness of so many Victorian biographies. His own works were brief and compact —and malicious. Yet he conveniently forgot works like John Morley's life of Voltaire, Lord Bryce's biographical sketches, James Parton's *Famous Americans of Recent Times,* and many other examples of 19th- and early 20th-century biography that were brief, lively, and far more honest than his own.

But Strachey also failed to stress the weakness of so many biographies which, though unbiased in judgment and well-expressed in form, showed a lack of understanding of the dual nature of biography. Since the publication of *Eminent Victorians* in 1918, the bulky "commemorative" biography which Strachey scorned has generally disappeared, victim of the increasing cost of bookmaking and (it may be hoped) an improvement in public taste. But the majority of present-day works, particularly those that represent the greatest investments of time and scholarly effort, those whose authors may be best trained professionally for the task at hand, have failed to deal with the problem of personality in any coherent, organized way. Too often the writer, an academic person trained in history, say, or literature, has been interested only in describing minutely the significance of X's role in the fight over the Tariff of Abominations, or in advancing some new interpretation of the poetry of Y. The result is poor biography, and perhaps it is not even good history or good criticism.

In 1750 Doctor Johnson complained that "biography has often been allotted to writers who seem very little acquainted with the nature of their task." This continues to be true. On the one hand there have been the glib and careless popularizers, those whom Addison called the "Grub-street biographers, who watch for the death of a great man, like so many undertakers, on purpose to make a penny of him." On the other hand there have been the plodding collectors of facts, to whom the need for artistry or even technique has never occurred. As Edmund Gosse once complained: "The popular idea seems to be that no one is too great a fool, or too complete an amateur, or too thoroughly ignorant of the modes of composition, to undertake the 'life' of an eminent person." Occasionally (but only occasionally) a biographer has appeared who appreciated the nature of his task. When this happens, first-rate biography may be the result.

III

If biography is to be compounded of career and character, what is the recipe, what the balance? According to Gosse, "there should be some relation between the size of [a subject's] portrait and the effect which he produced in public life." But there must be room for different tastes and purposes. A satisfactory study may be very short, in which case career is probably subordinated to personality, or it may just as logically run to several volumes with greater stress laid upon the historical setting and a detailed record of the subject's activities. The danger is that the former will be long on unsupported generalizations, and that the latter will lose its subject in a maze of detail. This is not to disparage longer works, which, from John Morley's *Gladstone* and Albert Bigelow Paine's *Mark Twain* to such modern behemoths as Freeman's four volumes on *R. E. Lee* and the still uncompleted works of Arthur S. Link on Wilson, Frank Freidel on Franklin D. Roosevelt, and Dumas Malone on Jefferson, have served a useful purpose. It does often seem, however, that all of these books and others of the type are closer akin to history than biography. In his mammoth *George Washington,* Freeman devoted 110 pages to a description of the Virginia society in which Washington grew up, scarcely mentioning his subject's name in the process. He even covered a full page with a description of the state of the world during the months Washington spent in his mother's womb—a passage which included a select list of important figures recently deceased and soon to be born, and the ages and contemporary status of George II, Sir Robert Walpole, Montesquieu, Handel, Bach, Frederick of Prussia, Kant, William Pitt, and half a dozen others.

In truth, for a literary form with a long history, biography has produced fewer recognized masterpieces than any other type of writing, and many of these gems have been special cases, lucky accidents rather than the result of the application of sound principles of biographical writing. Nearly all our outstanding biographies, from Einhard's *Charlemagne,* to Vasari's *Lives of the Painters,* to Boswell's *Life of Samuel Johnson,* and down to such recent classics as Robert E. Sherwood's *Roosevelt and Hopkins,* have been written by men who have known their subjects personally.

Most of the authorities on biography have believed that intimate acquaintance with the subject is a prerequisite of great biography. Doctor Johnson certainly thought so, and Boswell's experience in writing *his* life seems to bear his judgment out. So did Voltaire, who wrote: "'Tis a monstrous piece of charlatanry to pretend to paint a personage with whom you have never lived." Waldo H. Dunn, in his important history of English biography, came to the same conclusion. The German scholar, Georg Misch, wrote that "great works of biographical art . . . are always made possible only by a living relationship between the biographer and his subject." More recently, Harold Nicolson pointed out the advantage of personal acquaintance in providing "a system of triangulation enabling the author to fix the position of his hero with greater accuracy than would ever be possible were he writing about people whom he had never personally known."

But there have been dissenting opinions. The merit of such lives lies chiefly in the pictures they present of their subjects' personalities, which not only look "real," but, because of the special circumstances, may be presumed to be so. They are not likely to excel in descriptions and evaluations of their subjects' careers or in estimations of their subjects' place in history. Since both career and character are vital in biography, most biographies by contemporaries have serious defects, however interesting they may be. Even Boswell's *Johnson*, certainly the most universally admired biography in any language, suffers from grave faults when judged as a biography. Boswell has been justly praised for his brilliant use of anecdote and conversation, for his subtle synthesis of materials, and for his masterly presentation of character. But his book is all out of proportion, with its heavy emphasis on the last years of Johnson's life, and it is dependent for that period chiefly on the observations of one man, the author. Where Boswell was forced to make use of sources other than his own keen eye and acute ear for dialogue, his book is hardly more than pedestrian in quality. It may be the world's best biography, but it is not a model biography.

Indeed the great virtues of all the classic biographies written by authors who were intimates of their heroes have really been autobiographical rather than biographical. And despite superficial similarities, the two forms are intrinsically quite separate. Autobiography results from remembrance, biography from reconstruction. Boswell's *Johnson* is essentially one man's recollections of another. (Or at least its lasting interest depends upon the personal relationship that existed between the two men, and Boswell's ability to describe that relationship vividly and honestly.) It is not that books like the *Life of Johnson* are unimportant. Of course they are far superior to the general run of biography. But to discuss them in a consideration of the nature of biography is not very profitable. They have been unique personal successes.

Admittedly there is no reason why Boswell, for instance, could not have written a biography of someone he had not known. He was a close student of the form. If he had, it might have been a great book—but it would have been quite unlike his *Johnson*. Johnson's own biography of the unfortunate friend of his youth, Richard Savage, is a much sharper portrait than most of the later *Lives of the English Poets* to which it was eventually appended. So is Carlyle's brilliant sketch of his friend John Sterling (as portraiture) to his mammoth lives of Cromwell and Frederick the Great. But few would argue that Johnson's estimate of Savage as a poet, or even Carlyle's judgment of Sterling's *career*, are comparable either to similar judgments in these authors' other biographical works, or to the critical evaluations of Savage and Sterling made by later students.

In short, those who stress the importance of personal knowledge are thinking in terms of character rather than career. If, by its nature, biography must encompass both, the life written by a contemporary is not likely to be perfectly balanced. Further, if great biography must await the chance congruence of a worthy subject and a talented observer, it has only a limited future, and many important individuals can never hope to be chronicled adequtely after they have passed on.

Perhaps the nature of biography places perfection beyond attainment. To describe the *man* one really ought to know him intimately; to evaluate his *work* one needs perspective, and access to records seldom available to contemporaries. But fortunately for the practicing biographer, who deals chiefly with figures out of the past, it is at least possible to overcome the absence of personal acquaintance, whereas perspective by definition) can come only with time. The problem of recreating a personality one has never known is great, but should not be insurmountable. The serious biographer, baffled by the imponderables of personality, may be tempted to limit his activities to describing and explaining his subject's career, which is concrete and definable. But he should resist this temptation. He may never be able to know his man as Boswell knew Johnson. But he must try to do so. The end is understanding; the means are sympathy, scholarship, and sensitivity.

In sum, biography is the reconstruction of a human life. It attempts to describe and evaluate one individual's career and also to reproduce the image of his living personality, analyzing its impact upon his actions and the world in which he lived. All biographies must be historical and scientific in that they aim at truth and depend upon verifiable evidence. At the same time they must be imaginative and artistic, because insight and felicity of expression are essential if the full three-dimensional truth is to be transferred to the flat surface of a printed page. The biographer's responsibility is large. He assays the role of a god, for in his hands the dead can be brought to life and granted a measure of immortality. He should at least, then, seek to emulate the more reliable divinities in his zeal for truth, his tolerance of human frailty, and his love for mankind.

20. The Biographer's Craft*

FREDERICK B. TOLLES

Whatever else it is, biography is an art. It is, of course, other things too. First of all, it is an exercise in historical research, requiring great industry, great ingenuity, great integrity. As a fact-finder, the biographer faces many problems, some of them peculiar to biography. These I shall not discuss except incidentally. I am concerned here with the biographer's problems as a writer—the problems he faces when, his research completed, he sits down at his desk or his typewriter with a blank piece of paper before him.

Perhaps a fragment of autobiography will serve to get us started. Nearly four years ago I sat down to write a biography. I thought I knew how to do it. I had written a volume of "straight" history in which I had followed a fairly standard pattern: a topical arrangement of material within a general chronological framework. I realized, of course, that in doing a biography I had to pay more attention to chronology. But still I tended to do what came naturally; I set down my material by subjects: childhood, education, marriage and family life, scientific farming, political activities, and so on. That was the way my notes were arranged in the shoebox, and that was the way it seemed reasonable to transfer their contents to the page. If as a scientific farmer my man carried on experiments with plaster of Paris as a fertilizer in 1786 and tried marl in 1791, why not discuss them together, in adjacent paragraphs? It made sense to do it that way. It was also easy to do it that way.

What I had when my first draft was done was a series of ac-

*Reprinted with permission from *The South Atlantic Quarterly*, LIII (October, 1954), 508–520.

ceptable articles tied together by the fact that they were about the same man and arranged more or less chronologically. I say they were acceptable, because a couple of them were published in learned journals. It was scholarly as all get-out, this book of mine. It contained everything or nearly everything it was possible to know about George Logan (there's no use concealing his name, by the time this essay appears, the book—and my secret—will be out). Everything, that is, but George Logan. Somehow he had escaped me.

A kind friend read the manuscript and told me what a good job of embalming I had done. Politely, he raised the question whether that was what I had really wanted to do. Only then did I realize that if I wanted to write the *life* of George Logan I should have to start over again, and I should have to write as a biographer, not as a historian. For a biographer, it finally dawned on me, is something different. Bradford Smith has put the matter succinctly and vividly:

> The biographer is a queer duck. Neither historian nor novelist, he tries to be both. He uses the techniques of the historian to get his man and get him right, yet he must use the art of the novelist to bring him back alive. For he will not be worth bringing if he comes stuffed. The biographer is a hunter, not a taxidermist. No one would buy a circus ticket to see a stuffed lion. No one wants to read a biography that is stuffed with scholarship rather than with blood, brains, and guts.

I should not have expressed myself in quite this way, but in principle I accept Mr. Smith's view of the biographer and his job, including the part about "the art of the novelist." At the mention of these words I expect a shuddering to overcome any historian who reads this. Before his mind the words will conjure up something called "fictional biography" or "biographical fiction." Let me make it clear that I am not talking about either of these bastard genres. What I am saying—and what I take Mr. Smith to be saying—is that one of the biographer's essential tools is imagination, a disciplined historical imagination.

This belated awakening called for some basic and painful decisions. The first and most far-reaching was one which would have been elementary for any novelist: my book must be strictly narrative in method. In other words, its development must parallel, must be George Logan's development. I had no business reaching ahead five years to bring in what farmer Logan would presently learn about fertilizers. However messy it might seem to my orderly, pigeonhole mind, however much reshuffling of those four-by-six cards it might require, I must unfold events as they unfolded to George Logan's consciousness. I simply could not irresponsibly jump forward and backward in time. That would be false to the life I was writing and would only confuse and annoy the reader.

I have lately come across a flagrant example of this sin of playing fast and loose with time in an otherwise admirable book by Jeannette Mirsky and Allan Nevins, *The World of Eli Whitney*. Phineas Miller, Whitney's partner in getting the cotton gin into production, dies on page 163. Suddenly on page 204, he turns up again discussing with Eli the marriageability of his daughter. I blinked; my hair started to rise. It was like seeing a ghost. No author outside the field of horror fiction, I think, has the right to shatter his reader's sensibilities this way.

It is not easy to write straight narrative, as I quickly found out. George Logan was in the United States Senate for six years during the Presidency of Thomas Jefferson. During the session of 1805–1806 he was a kind of floor leader for the administration in domestic affairs; at the same time, he was at outs with the President and Cabinet over their foreign policies. Thus he was busy steering through the Senate laws to establish a national university and give federal aid to an important canal project while he was fighting Jefferson's aggressive policy toward Spanish Florida, his truckling to Napoleon in Santo Domingo, his provocative stance against Great Britain. The point I am making is that he was doing all these things at the same time. All five subjects were debated off and on all winter long. Telling the story of that winter in the Senate, I felt like an amateur juggler trying to keep five balls in the air at once. It would have been much easier, more orderly, to sort them out, to take up each subject separately and polish it off. But things didn't happen that way. And I could not tell the story right, I decided, unless I told it the way it happened. After all, I was writing the life of George Logan, and in life things don't arrange themselves in neat, logical patterns. I am not exclusively a parent for a week, then a writer for a week, then a teacher for a week, and then a Quaker for a week. I am all these things at once, and sometimes conflicts arise, which are an essential part of life. The conflicts belong in a biography. They make the book real, and, incidentally, they make it interesting.

The biographer, then, must learn to write narrative. So, incidentally, must the historian. It is just here that G. M. Trevelyan finds the "spinal weakness" in modern historical writing. But the biographer needs the skill even more than the historian. And he can learn much from the masters of narrative in the novel. He can learn from the dramatist too. He can learn to compose wherever possible in scenes, to build his chapters around scenes, scenes in which the character of his subject will stand revealed as if a spotlight were on him. The same kind friend who told me my George Logan was stiff with *rigor mortis* (or perhaps it was *rigor eruditionis*) gave me a maxim to inscribe over the lintel of my doorposts: *Don't tell me; show me.* Don't tell me George Logan was benevolent, he said; show him being benevolent. Don't tell me that he and Jefferson disagreed over foreign policy; show them disagreeing. One doesn't have to make up such scenes. It is only necessary to read the sources with an eye for them.

To take an example, again from my own book: George Logan, though normally a serene, gentle soul, occasionally flew off the handle. Even his wife, who idolized him, spoke of his "quickness of temper," and a younger contemporary, who also revered him, delicately hinted that Logan was "not always amiable in his domesticity." Now I could quote these observations, and I could say in half a dozen different ways that Logan was subject to fits of wrath. But one scene which showed George Logan losing his temper, I decided, was worth any number of quotations or comments. I found the material in my sources.

In 1787, for example, George Washington, temporarily in Philadelphia for the Constitutional Convention, drove out to Stenton, Logan's mansion just outside the city, for dinner. Knowing her husband's insistence on simple "republican fare," Deborah Logan ordered a Spartan meal of beef, potatoes, and small beer. With such a great man coming to dinner, however, she could not resist the temptation to prepare with her own hands an elaborate and tasty dessert. When the dessert appeared —so the story ran when it passed into gossip—Logan "got up in a passion," declared that "he never suffered them things, such trumpery, on his table," and, to Debby's bitter mortification, ordered the lovely confection away. Admittedly, the story is based on gossip—set down years later by a British diplomat in a manuscript now reposing in the Huntington Library. Still, it has the ring of authenticity, it is consistent with everything else

I know about Logan, and it throws a strong beam of light on one facet of Logan's personality.

The figure of the spotlight is a good one for the biographer to keep in mind. He should never let his main character wander off into the circumambient darkness, nor, if he can help it, should he focus his light for too long on the other actors or on the stage set. Here the biographer as artist has to keep strict rein on the biographer as historian. Of course he must sketch in the historical "background," but he must never let it swallow up the man in the foreground. The old "life and times" technique, I think, is no longer useful, especially when handled mechanically. Modern readers will not swallow—nor should they be expected to—a book in which slices of biography alternate, as in a club sandwich, with large chunks of general history.

The fourth chapter of the late Douglas S. Freeman's *Young Washington* shows how Homer can nod. Entitled "Virginia in the Youth of Washington," it runs to 120 pages; it contains 941 footnotes, and George Washington scarcely puts in a single appearance. This fantastic chapter can only be regarded as the aberration of a great biographer. Anyone who writes about Washington, mind you, must know all that about Virginia in the 1740's, all 941 footnotes' worth. But most of it he mustn't use; at least, he mustn't use it so obviously. He must insinuate it into his narrative slyly, subtly, indirectly, unobstrusively, in an adjective or a phrase here, a sentence or possibly a paragraph there.

Personally, I am bored stiff when, reading biographies of Jefferson's contemporaries, I come repeatedly upon the same half-digested "background" material on, say, the Louisiana Purchase —the same tired quotations ("We must marry ourselves to the British fleet and nation"), the same overworked incidents (Napoleon in his bath silencing Joseph's objections by splashing him with water). I feel like Lord Asquith, who once irritably asked: was it really necessary for every biographer of the late-Victorian statesmen to tell the whole story of the fight for Irish Home Rule and tell it in the same way? "Background" material in a biography should be kept down, I think, to the barest minimum necessary to set the stage and place the central figure in context. Contemporary events, no matter how stirring or how important, must never crowd the main actor into the wings.

The central figure in a biography must, in a word, be central. And though he may cut a figure, he must never merely be one.

That is to say, he must never be merely a "public figure," or a "significant figure," or what is usually comes to—a marble figure. In his own time he was a human being—not a writer, a scientist, a politician, or a statesman, but a man writing, a man in a laboratory, a man in politics or statecraft. This means that the biographer in his research must constantly be on the watch for revealing details of personality and personal life. When he finds them he must cherish them, use them to the utmost, to convey his subject's looks, his gestures, his habits, his manners—his and those of the people with whom he comes face-to-face in the biography. It is possible, of course, to overdo this sort of thing, as the "debunkers" and other popular biographers of the 1920's did. They were sometimes so preoccupied with the trivial, intimate detail—especially when it revealed a public idol's feet of clay—that they usually overlooked or denied the importance of larger issues, thus falsifying history and revealing the essential smallness of their own minds. But on the other hand, it is quite possible by leaving out these personal habits and idiosyncrasies, these lesser human traits, to create a marble statue, imposing and grand, but cold to the touch.

I was perhaps more fortunate than some biographers in that I had among my sources a brief memoir and a number of personal letters written by George Logan's wife. Though she was sometimes inaccurate and though she consistently idealized her husband, she sometimes unconsciously let drop some petty but revealing detail about him, about the family at Stenton, about the famous people who came to visit. From these and other sources I learned that Logan in his leisure moments played the flute; that, whereas he dressed as a matter of principle in homespun clothes, his good wife (who did the spinning) did not share this enthusiasm and "dressed like other folks"; that Thomas Jefferson, when he first came to Stenton, fresh from the court of Louis XVI, was decked out like a dandy in silks and ruffles, wearing "an elegant topaz ring," but that he too soon adopted a plain "republican" costume. These details, trifling in themselves, give life to a biography.

But nothing, I think, gives reality and a sense of immediacy to a scene between two or more people so much as reading their very words—eavesdropping, as it were, on their conversation. Before the historians start to shudder again, let me state flatly that I do not approve of inventing dialogue. (An involuntary quaking overcame me too when, in a book on the singing Hutchinsons, a kind of crusading American Trapp family of a century ago, I found one of the boys saying, anent the annexation of Texas: "Andy Jackson is fer it, and what Andy sez is good enough fer me.") One of my grievances against the writers of "fictional biography" is their propensity to put words into the mouths of their characters—and usually to do it rather ineptly, thus spoiling rather than heightening the illusion of reality. For my own part, I do not even hold with the practice of putting indirect into direct discourse and surrounding it with quotation marks, though some reputable historians of my acquaintance think nothing of it. But when one has the words, the *ipsissima verba* in one's sources, it is foolish, I conceive, not to use them.

I hope I shall be excused if I draw another example from my own book on George Logan. In 1798, in a period of international tension following the "XYZ affair"—there was a "cold war" on with France—Logan returned from an unofficial mission to Paris with evidence that French policy had shifted, that the war which the Federalist administration regarded as inevitable could be avoided and with honor. He promptly waited on the Secretary of State, Timothy Pickering, who received him coldly, refusing to credit the report he brought from France. An invasion was imminent, Pickering insisted; preparedness was of the essence. Logan allowed that it would do no harm to have the militia in order. "The militia, sir," sputtered the Secretary of State, "the militia never did any good to this country except in the single affair of Bunker Hill. We must have a standing army of fifty thousand men." As he showed his unwelcome visitor to the door, the Secretary could not resist a final withering remark. "Sir," he said, "it is my duty to inform you that the government does not thank you for what you have done."

Now there are extant four nearly contemporary accounts of this interview—one by Pickering himself, one by Thomas Jefferson, one by Tom Paine, and one—the latest in date—by Deborah Logan. Naturally they are not identical, but they are sufficiently consistent with each other so that I felt justified in drawing details from all four. Both Jefferson and Paine quote Pickering's remark about the militia in slightly variant forms; both Paine and Deborah Logan quote the Secretary's parting shot, again with minor variations. My reputation, if any, as a scholar may be at stake, but I am perfectly willing, in fact delighted, to use this kind of material.

My decision to write a narrative biography, keeping George

Logan always downstage, center, caused me some headaches when I came to his writings. For this Logan was, among other things, an author, a pamphleteer, what used to be called a publicist until the advertising men took the word over. How should I tell the story of a man of ideas without shifting the focus from the man to the ideas, without slowing down the narrative with long quotations and analyses of his pamphlets? One solution would be to ignore the writings or simply to discuss their composition and publication as events in the man's life. This was Ola Winslow's solution in her Pulitzer-prize-winning *Jonathan Edwards*, and to a degree it was Leon Howard's in his fine biography of Herman Melville. But Jonathan Edwards, it seems to me, was nothing if he was not a man of ideas, and a biography of Melville in which the novels themselves—the myth of the white whale and the tragedy of Billy Budd—are not central events strikes me as a biography manqué. Still, in each of these instances a good case can be made for deliberately focusing on the man to the virtual exclusion of the books; after all, others have written and will continue to write about *The Freedom of the Will* and *Moby Dick*. But George Logan was not an Edwards or a Melville; his writings, though interesting and important, are not well known. I could not justify leaving them out or playing them down. So I wove them into the narrative, endeavoring to set out his ideas briefly by paraphrase and quotation, always keeping George Logan, the man writing, in the picture. No doubt the reviewers will tell me how successful I have been.

In one or two instances my task was made easier by the fact that Logan set forth his ideas in rather unusual circumstances. He spoke, for example, before the Tammany Society of Philadelphia in May, 1798, in the midst of an atmosphere of public hysteria. McCarthyism and McCarranism—not yet so named, of course—were rampant. A fearful Congress was debating the Alien and Sedition Acts. Logan chose this moment to deliver an address openly critical of the government, and he delivered it before an audience of radical Irishmen—just such supposedly subversive aliens as Congress was bent on harrying out of the land. The conditions, in other words, were tense and exciting, and to have discussed the speech in a calm, "scholarly" way would, I am convinced, have been false to the historical realities. So I tried to re-create the scene in Tammany's Columbian Wigwam—the audience of pipe-smoking, whisky-reeking Irishmen, the slight, austere, aristocratic figure of Dr. Logan, the tumult that must have greeted his incendiary utterances. I may have overwritten this scene. I am not sure whether, as it stands, it is history or not. But I am sure that it would not have been history, that it would have borne no relationship to the way things actually were, had I written coolly, dispassionately, objectively, as if I were describing William Wordsworth placidly composing *The Prelude* at Dove Cottage in the Lake District.

This raises the large question of the biographer's relation to his story, his part, if any, in it. It is the problem every novelist faces—the problem of the narrator, the point of view. Shall the storyteller be an Olympian who sees all, knows all? Shall he be a Greek chorus, commenting on the action as it unfolds? Shall he be a critical intelligence, interrupting the narrative from time to time with judgments, evaluations, analyses, interpretations? There is, I think, no one answer to this question, no one solution that is exclusively right. The critical or interpretative biography is a legitimate, indeed a necessary type of book. I chose, however, in dealing with George Logan, to write a narrative biography and to keep myself, so far as possible, out of it. Like the Manager of the Performance in *Vanity Fair,* I decided to appear before the curtain at the beginning (in the Introduction) and then bow out. It was hard, but most of the time I resisted the temptation to step on the stage to explain what was going on, to award praise and blame, to speculate about what might have happened if. . . . Not that I think the biographer can sidestep the responsibility to pass judgments. I said my say about George Logan in the Introduction, though I now think it would have been better to have done it at the end.

Speculation in particular does not belong in a narrative biography. *Perhaps, probably, no doubt, it would be interesting to know whether*—these words and phrases should be banished from the narrative biographer's lexicon or at most admitted only to his footnotes. The statement that "Ambrose Bierce may have met Kipling in 1899 in a barroom on San Francisco's Barbary Coast" adds nothing to our knowledge of either Bierce or Kipling. If they met, the fact is of interest and belongs in their biographies; if the biographer merely fancies that they might have met, he had best save the speculation for dinner-table conversation.

Again, the biographer must remember to write about his man, not his sources. If he has to discuss textual problems, disputed attributions, questions about the reliability of evidence, let him do it in an appendix or a footnote, in a learned article or in the circle of his learned friends, but let him not intrude qua textual critic or bibliographical detective or historical researcher between the reader and Ambrose Bierce, or George Logan or, for that matter, George Washington.

If biography is an art, it must have shape, it must have form, like a sonnet or a sonata or a piece of sculpture. This is the biographer's knottiest problem as an artist. For his materials— the stubborn facts with which he must work—are not notably plastic, and the biographer, if he is a conscientious scholar, cannot take liberties with them. The best analogy, I suppose, is the art of the portrait-painter. The subject matter—the sitter— is given. The painting must first of all be a faithful likeness— warts, as Cromwell said, and all. But if it is to have any superiority over a photograph, it must have something more. I assume that Leonardo's portrait of Signora del Giocondo is a good likeness, that Gainsborough really caught the features of Jonathan Buttall. But that is not why I go out of my way to see the Mona Lisa or the Blue Boy. It's that something more—something added by the shaping spirit of the artist—that draws me.

The biographer has a problem that Leonardo and Gainsborough never had. After all, Lisa and Jonathan were there— all of them. The biographer has to create his portrait from fragmentary sources—sources that have probably been preserved capriciously, more or less by accident. Shall he let the quantity and distribution of his sources determine the shape of his biography? If he does, he will almost certainly have a queer, even a grotesque portrait, as if his subject were reflected in a distorting mirror—tremendous head, narrow shoulders, enormous hips, infinitesimal feet. Sometimes, to be sure, a painter like El Greco will use distortion—but he will use it deliberately, for its effect, not because he ran out of white paint for the shoulders and had a lot of red to use up on the trousers. But we have all read biographies that are distorted in just this fashion and for just this reason. Perhaps there will be two or three chapters on a single year, where the sources are exceptionally full, then a ten-year period will be passed over in silence because the documents are missing.

Sometimes this change of pace or change of scale is justified. Perhaps, if the subject was an author, he had an *annus mirabilis*, like Charles Brockden Brown, who produced his four best novels in the short space of a single twelvemonth. Perhaps, if he was a politician, he had the fortune to be President of the United States, like Abraham Lincoln, to whose last six years James G. Randall devoted several sizable volumes after a mere preliminary glance at his first fifty. In the case of my book on George Logan, I devoted three chapters to the last six months of 1798, the period of his private diplomatic mission to France and its sequel. The material was suddenly plentiful—but for a good reason. The reason was that Logan became overnight a national figure. The newspapers were full of him; Congress debated his actions at length; he himself, aware that something big was happening, kept a diary; others, sensing that this was his great hour, preserved the document. In other words, the documentation was copious in part because the incident was important. But sometimes there will be almost no sources for the most crucial transactions of a man's life.

And what about the years of childhood and adolescence? We recognize them as critical, formative years; we know that in the living each year had 365 days; but in most cases we have hardly any sources. For George Logan's first twenty-two years, for instance, I had the following: *item,* the record of his birth; *item,* the record of his enrollment in the Friends Public School in Philadelphia; *item,* one letter written in his own schoolboy scrawl at the age of fourteen; *item,* one passing reference to him in a letter to his father; *item,* three pages in his widow's memoir of him—in which some of the facts were demonstrably wrong. That was all. What to do? Dismiss these all-important years with two pages and start Logan's story in full scale at the age of twenty-three? I could not do this and still claim to have written Logan's life *wie es eigentlich gewesen ist.* Invent a boyhood for him? I could not do that and still keep my self-respect as a scholar. How, then, to reconstruct his early years so that they would be real?

I found, when I put my mind on the problem, that I did know something about Logan's boyhood. For one thing, I had prowled around Stenton, his family home, which is still standing. I knew something of his father and grandfather, of his two teachers, of the merchant to whom he was apprenticed. I knew something of the schools he attended, of the Philadelphia Quaker milieu in which he grew up. And I had a seven-year-old boy of my own. I hope I did not make the mistake of writing about Jimmy Tolles instead of young George Logan. But one cannot write about a seven-year-old boy without knowing how they act and react—and there are some actions and reactions which are characteristic of all seven-year-old boys. So I wrote a chapter of nearly eighteen pages about George Logan's childhood and adolescence. Imagination? Yes, I had to use a good deal of that; but it was imagination, I really think, disciplined, restrained, given direction by solid historical knowledge. And I think the book is better biography—yes, and better history too—because of that chapter.

Twenty-five, fifty years ago, no scholar would have accepted that chapter; probably no one who called himself a scholar would have written it. (Maybe no scholar will accept it today, maybe I was no scholar when I wrote it; but if so, then nearly everything I have said up to now is wrong.) I venture to suggest that our ideas about biography have changed over the last half-century. At the risk of sounding pretentious—and perhaps of suggesting more than I mean to suggest—I would submit that a kind of Hegelian dialectic has been at work in this field. At the beginning of the century the standard biography was a ponderous "life and times," usually written by a historian, usually concentrating on the outward, public life of the subject to the exclusion of his true inwardness, his qualities as a human being.

In the twenties the pendulum swung in the other direction, and we had a spate of popular or debunking biographies by Lytton Strachey, André Maurois, Emil Ludwig, Rupert Hughes, W. E. Woodward. Their books have not stood up well—not as well as the oldstyle academic biographies. They were too sensational, tiresomely preoccupied with sex, with dirt and scandal, with titillating but unimportant details of personal life. They were apt to be written too glibly, with too facile a pen: Strachey's style, said Sir Charles Firth, was "a very bad style in which to tell the truth." They were often presented to the public—to borrow Carl Becker's phrase—"without fear and without research."

Dumas Malone quotes Havelock Ellis back in 1896 bemoaning the fact that "most men had come to the piano of biography from the organ of history." Embroidering the metaphor, Malone suggests that during the twenties "a new group of performers tickled the ears of the public with new instruments, rendering old tunes in a modern tempo, while an occasional historian-biographer was playing organ music decorously in an empty church." These new performers, he goes on, "were aware of an audience which most of the scholars forgot, and the form that they followed, consciously or unconsciously, was not that of heavily annotated history, but that of the novel." In other words, the biographies of the twenties had one characteristic that was not to be sniffed at: they were readable—and they were read. People said, when they put one of these books down: "Why, it reads like a novel." One more comment from Dumas Malone:

> When we say that a book that isn't a novel reads like one, probably the main thing we mean is that it is interesting, that it is a good tale. Not even a professor can rightly object if a biography turns out to be a corking story. One of the essentials of a good biography, indeed, is that it be a good narrative. Whether it be in the realm of action or of ideas it ought to move. If the new biographers reminded us of this, they rendered us a distinct service.

I make bold to suggest that out of this Hegelian interaction of thesis and antithesis—the solemn, plodding, respectful Victorian "life" followed by the bright, fast moving, debunker's portrait—has come a synthesis, a new conception of biography, combining the research and scholarly integrity of the first type with the imaginative, artistic qualities and readability of the second. I select only a few examples at random from my own shelves: Fawn Brodie's Joseph Smith (*No Man Knows My History,* 1945), Roland Bainton's Martin Luther (*Here I stand,* 1950), Benjamin Thomas's *Lincoln* (1952), Samuel Eliot Morison's Columbus (*Admiral of the Ocean Sea,* 1942), Dumas Malone's Jefferson (*Jefferson and His Time,* 1948 and 1951).

The mention of these names will, I hope, reassure anyone who may fear that I mean to minimize or slur over the importance of sound, painstaking, accurate scholarship. In this essay, I have deliberately chosen to discuss problems of wriitng, not of research. I am concerned that scholars re-establish communication with the general reading public—the kind of communication that existed in the days of Macaulay and Parkman. I think it can only be done as those writers did it—by giving conscious attention to artistic as well as to scholarly problems. The biographer, I believe, must practice an art that conceals scholarship —certainly not an art that conceals *lack* of scholarship, but an art that goes hand in hand with scholarship, and makes just as rigorous demands on its practitioners as the best scholarship does.

PART SIX

History and Other Disciplines

Introductory Notes

In 1954, the Committee on Historiography of the Social Science Research Council published its famous Bulletin 64, entitled *The Social Sciences in Historical Study*. The report undertook to present contemporary social science methods and concepts, in the belief that learning is a cooperative enterprise and in the hope that historians would make a greater use of these concepts and methods. The report dealt with several important themes: current concepts and viewpoints in the social sciences, the problem of historical causation, analyzing the whole process of change in history, and the theory and practice of methods that can be used in historical study. "The use of knowledge is the purpose of scholarship," said the report; "scholarship exists for the sake of life. . . ."

The words, indeed, reflected upon the larger meaning of the report. They signified that the new historians of our day, conscious of having to do more than renovate Clio's mansion, understood that Clio must live in a world of other new mansions. The words reflected too the sense that historical knowledge, no less than other kinds, is a function of social purpose, and that the substance and varieties of knowledge change with the changing directions and purposes of society. Every age, indeed, seeks to establish a science of man, to explain the goals and institutions of society or to argue that they ought to be reformed. Historical writing, no less than that of social science and creative literature, expresses society's concern to know itself. More devoted to the theme of continuities in social experience than they, it is less susceptible to change, less adaptive to new ideas and methods. The inquiry of historians regularly reveals this difference between the world they inhabit and the world they wish to reconstruct. Each new history is thus a somewhat belated expression of the need to eliminate the difference.

Historians are living in an age that is teeming with new methods and ideas. There have been major transformations in various related disciplines: in the study of literature, in the particular amalgam known as American Studies, and, most significant for history, in the social sciences, particularly those known as the behavioral sciences (which include central aspects of anthropology, psychology, and sociology). Literary studies, from having centered for some time on the esthetic and formal elements of creative writing, have paid increasing attention to social and historical elements. Interest has also been rapidly increasing in American Studies, which seek to understand the culture of the United States through its history and literature. This growth of interest has reflected, above all, America's need to take its place in the international community after World War II and to define its identity and purpose. Very notable, too, has been the wider dissemination of Freudian ideas and their increasing impact on literature and social science. The principal features of the new social sciences are their concern with insuring that the premises of inquiry are valid; their rigorous methodology—particularly their emphasis on quantification and on open, self-conscious, and objective techniques of investigation; and their interest in the transforming values and institutions of contemporary society.

If social change is the source of the new scholarship, it is not too difficult to ascertain the factors in the one which have produced the interest in the other. The central problems of our society—the aspirations and mobility of different social groups, the quest of individuals for status and security, the under-education of the underprivileged, voting preferences and habits in urban, suburban, and rural areas, shifting patterns of industrial enterprise and employment, the emotional trials of adolescence and indeed of the whole process of growing up in America, the role and identity of minority groups, to name some of the more obvious ones—have also been among the central themes of social science. The quantitative methods of social science are the methods of a mass society, in which meeting the needs of the society depends on knowing the mentality and resources of the masses. They are the methods, among others, of advertising, which is central to an economy that must sell its goods; of political parties, which wish to find out the disposition and predilections of the electorate; and of government, which has to ascertain the needs of its citizens no less than their ability to man the state's armies and to pay the state's costs.

The following essays will afford the student of the past some significant suggestions about history's relation to other disciplines. In "History and the Social Sciences," Professor Thomas C. Cochran of the University of Pennsylvania, drawing from his own rich experience, shows how the study of the past can be enriched by using the methods and insights of modern social science. One of the principal proponents of an interdisciplinary approach to the past, Professor Cochran has practiced what he has been preaching in his many writings, which include *The Age of Enterprise* (with William Miller: 1942, revised 1961), *Railroad Leaders, 1845–1890: The Business Mind in Action* (1953), and *The American Business System: A Historical Perspective, 1900–1950* (1957). My own essay, "American History and Social Science," attempts to explain why writers of American history have, in the main, not embraced the teachings of social science.

In "History as Human Behavior," Professor Samuel P. Hays of the University of Pittsburgh, by using the example of politics, shows how a new perspective of the past might be gained by examining it in terms of the behavior of different groups of individuals in their daily lives. In his own researches, Professor Hays has displayed a healthy willingness to challenge traditional interpretations with fresh questions and to put old subjects in a new and broader frame of reference. His writings include *The Response to Industrialism, 1885–1914* (1957) and *Conservation and the Gospel of Efficiency: The Progressive Conservation Movement, 1890–1920* (1959). Before his recent retirement, William L. Langer was for many years Coolidge Professor of History at Harvard University and one of America's foremost writers of diplomatic history. His many publications include *The Challenge to Isolation, 1937–1940* (1952) and *The Undeclared War, 1940–1941* (1953); he has also edited The Rise of Modern Europe

Series. In "The Next Assignment," which he delivered as his presidential address to the American Historical Association in December 1957, Professor Langer urged his fellow historians to expand their horizons and deepen their understanding by exploiting the concepts of psycho-analysis.

Professor Henry Nash Smith of the University of California at Berkeley is the author of *Virgin Land: The West as Symbol and Myth* (1950), one of the most famous and important books in the recent literature of the history of American ideas; for it he received the John H. Dunning award in American history from the American Historical Association and the Bancroft award from Columbia University. Professor Smith has been much concerned with the problems and practice of American Studies and his essay, "Can 'American Studies' Develop a Method?" grows out of a long-standing interest in the discipline. Construing American Studies as the study of American culture, Professor Smith faces the dilemma of finding a method which encompasses both social facts and esthetic values. Because he regards American Studies "as a collaboration among men working from within existing academic disciplines but attempting to widen the boundaries imposed by conventional methods of inquiry," his essay is full of important suggestions for the student of history.

C. Vann Woodward, of Yale University, is one of America's finest historians. Fresh research, excellent writing, and profound insight make him a master of the historian's craft. To these he has added a sympathetic exploration into the forces shaping human history, one which recognizes that history is a condition of human beings no less than of forces. These qualities are reflected in his principal writings: *Tom Watson, Agrarian Rebel* (1938), *Reunion and Reaction* (1951), *Origins of the New South, 1877–1913* (1951), and *The Burden of Southern History* (1960). They are also reflected in the following essay, in which Professor Woodward suggests that literature has a meaning for the historian, and that the historical dimension in recent Southern creative writing is closely related to the dimension the historian himself is trying to attain.

In their suggestions that historians master other disciplines to achieve a greater mastery of their own, the following essays reflect the kind of history our own age fashions and fancies. They remind us again that each new history is an intelligence about past society that expresses the social intelligence of the present. They are reminiscent surely of the words of James Harvey Robinson, who was, some fifty years ago, propagating the new history of his own day. At that time, Robinson urged historians to expand their knowledge and learn about the teachings of prehistoric archaeology, anthropology, and social psychology:

> These newer social sciences . . . have entirely changed the meaning of many terms which the historian has been accustomed to use in senses now discredited. . . . The kind of thought suggested by the new allies of history should serve . . . greatly to strengthen and deepen the whole range of historical study and render its results far more valuable than they have hitherto been.

The student of history today faces no less a challenge than that to which Robinson summoned his predecessor half a century ago. Bulletin 64 of the Social Science Research Council puts the challenge in modern terms. It spells out the terms of the new history. The essays that follow reflect and discuss the problem of writing that history. The problem, as the essays well indicate, is both formidable and inviting. It calls the student to re-think the American past in terms of contemporary American thought, and it prescribes that his history should begin at home, among the fields of knowledge of his own day.

Suggestions for Further Reading

Degler, Carl N., "The Sociologist as Historian: Riesman's *The Lonely Crowd*," *American Quarterly*, XV (Winter 1963), 483–497.

Garraty, John A., "The Interrelations of Psychology and Biography," *Psychological Bulletin*, LI (November 1954), 569–582.

Hughes, H. Stuart, "The Historian and the Social Scientist," *American Historical Review*, LXVI (October 1960), 20–46.

Mead, Margaret, "Anthropologist and Historian: Their Common Problems," *American Quarterly*, III (Spring 1951), 3–13.

Pargellis, Stanley, "Clio in a Straight Jacket," *American Quarterly*, XI (Summer 1959), 225–231.

Saveth, Edward N., "The American Patrician Class: A Field for Research," *American Quarterly*, XV (Summer 1963), 235–252.

Schlesinger, Jr., Arthur M., "The Humanist Looks at Empirical Social Research," *American Sociological Review*, XXVII (December 1962), 768–771.

Sykes, Richard E., "American Studies and the Concept of Culture: A Theory and a Method," *American Quarterly*, XV (Summer 1963), 253–270.

21. History and The Social Sciences[*]

Thomas C. Cochran

The inclusion of history as a full-fledged cooperating member of the social science group has not appealed to most historians in the United States.[1] They see difficulties in the way of such a union that range from philosophic doubt regarding the possibility of a "social" science, to objections to new terminology. Possibly there is feeling of loss in exchanging the free creativity of the artist for the more restricted methods of science. A Gibbon in his study casting a past society in his own mold, and judging it accordingly was an individual master of the universe he surveyed. While the historian trying to be a social scientist is largely the slave of other people's knowledge and hypotheses, a lowly feeder-in of data to test against theoretical models. Perhaps the younger generation of historians in the United States, somewhat uncertain as to their values, are more favorably inclined to this role than their elders, but the evidence is still inconclusive.

United States graduate training in history, stressing neither philosophical attitudes nor social science concepts, has generally proceeded on the basis of an undefined "common sense." Resistance to a more intensive study of the social sciences has been based on indifference, on a feeling that common sense is good enough, as much as on strongly held opposing views. Many historians incline to see no necessity for insisting on a single

[*] Reprinted with permission from *Metodologia, Problemi Generali*, Vol. I of *Relazioni del X Congresso Internazionale di Scienze Storiche* (Florence, 1956), 481–504.

[1] For indifference or objections of historians to defining a propositional or scientific basis for their methods see: *Theory and Practice in Historical Study: A Report of the Committee on Historiography*, "Bulletin," 54, New York; Social Science Research Council (1946), pp. vii–viii.

orientation. Choice of method may be dictated by purpose. History written to inspire a popular audience with respect for continuing traditions may rest on the aesthetic appeal of the presentation, and history, designed consciously or not, to document a point of view may have value as persuasive rhetoric. But history used as an effort to find repetitive or probable relationships between past events demands some type of systematic method.[2]

Unfortunately the social sciences are in their infancy. Aside from economics and political science the specialized disciplines are scarcely seventy-five years old. A large part of the basic concepts now being tested in anthropology, sociology, and social psychology are the creation of the present generation of scholars. As a consequence all social science knowledge is in flux, and conclusions lack the relative permanence of scientific laws. Robert K. Merton says of his own discipline:

> The growing contributions of sociologcial theory to its sister-disciplines lie more in the realm of general sociological orientations than in that of specific confirmed hypotheses . . . Despite the many volumes dealing with the history of sociological theory and despite the plethora of empirical investigations, sociologists (including the writer) may discuss the logical criteria of sociological laws without citing a single instance which fully satisfied these criteria.[3]

The question, therefore, is not a philosophical one of what some ideal, mature social sciences could contribute to historical understanding, but an immediate practical one of what can today's social science contribute? It is this pragmatic aspect that leads me to stress personal experience in proposing answers to the question. Furthermore, any general survey of social science knowledge useful to historians within the scope of a single paper would be too brief to be convincing.[4] A few specific

[2] In this connection, it should be noted that writers such as R. G. Collingwood claim that historical understanding is of a unique and immediate character. History is held to be made up of human thoughts and experience, and the historian is able to relive these experiences in his imagination. A brief statement and refutation of this theory may be seen in W. H. Walsh, *An Introduction to Philosophy of History*, London, Hutchinson's University Library, 1951, pp. 48–71.

[3] R. K. Merton, *Social Theory and Social Structure: Toward the Codification of Theory and Research*, Glencoe, Ill., Free Press, 1949, pp. 86, 92.

[4] For a more extended attempt, see *The Social Sciences in Historical Study: A Report of the Committee on Historiography*, "Bulletin," 64, New York: Social Science Research Council (1954).

instances illustrating how social science knowledge or methods have proved useful in various types of situations seem more likely to carry weight.

Before turning to such examples, however, it should be noted that experience has indicated some general difficulties in the way of a merger between history and the social sciences. The relationship of advance conceptualization to historical source materials is one of the chief areas of misunderstanding. Purely deductive theory has value in stimulating the historian's imagination, but is seldom directly applicable to his material. The type of concepts or hypotheses being argued for here are those that have arisen from other empirical data. To this extent the argument does not deny that the materials come first. But they do not need to be the specific letters or reports that the historian is about to use. Just as a broad knowledge of the secondary historical writing on his problem enables the historian to take advantage of the investigations of others, a knowledge of what social scientists have thought allows him to take advantage of their inductions from the study of comparable situations. These ideas will doubtless direct the historian's attention to aspects of his material that he might otherwise miss, and allow him in turn to suggest changes in the social science concepts.

There are also practical problems in bringing together these fields of knowledge. Many of the areas of research suggested by the social sciences demand close collaboration between the historian and some specialist. This is often difficult to arrange and carry out. Social scientists are inclined to regard historians as primarily gatherers of facts, as scholars without lively theoretical interests, and are skeptical regarding the applicability of historical materials to present problems. Historians, on the other hand, are likely to see many social scientists as too specialized, and uninterested in broad syntheses. When one adds these mutual doubts to the difficulties always inherent in group activity and to university and professional disciplinary barriers, it is not surprising that relatively little interdisciplinary research is undertaken.

It is not always necessary, however, to undertake the hazards of interdisciplinary research. The historian may learn the social sciences for himself and apply them in his own work. Some conferences with colleagues in the particular social science field involved are desirable, to avoid the kind of misinterpretations that may arise from the printed page, but the historian must in any case readapt existing techniques to his kind of material.

I

The first examples of the value of the social sciences to the historian are selected to illustrate the use of advance conceptual plans. Before beginning the history of the Pabst Brewing Company we asked Professor Arthur H. Cole of Harvard University to draw up a list of questions that an economist would ask of business records.[5] The questions suggested a number of problems not generally dealt with by historians. From having attention called to such matters in a formal theoretical way, emerged some of the most interesting aspects of the history. For example questions regarding locational factors and marketing brought out the following relationships:

While the Milwaukee location was excellent, the specific location of the brewery within the city of Milwaukee deteriorated in value. This was due, ironically enough, to the success of the Pabst company in helping to change the character of the Milwaukee brewing business. Presumably to ensure dry storage cellars, the plant was built on a low hill instead of on the banks of a near-by navigable river. As long as business was local the extra haul up and down the hill was relatively unimportant, but when the company started shipping beer by boat and railroad, a location inaccessible to either of these forms of transportation was a distinct disadvantage. Furthermore, artificial refrigeration eliminated by 1880 the need for deep storage cellars. Pursuing this factor down to the present day, however, we see that the bad specific location in Milwaukee has led to the development of Pabst plants in other cities, and this may ultimately be a great advantage to the company.

The most compelling locational advantage of Milwaukee over Chicago, Cincinnati, and St. Louis was, ironically again, the smallness of population which restricted the company's home market. With all other factors favorable to large production and the growth of a shipping business, the Milwaukee brewers were forced into a

[5] A. H. Cole, *Business History and Economic History,* in "The Journal of Economic History," Supplement V (December 1945), pp. 51–53; Th. C. Cochran, *The Pabst Brewing Company, The History of a Business,* New York, New York University Press, 1948. "We" is used not as an affectation, but because in all the research noted in this paper I have been assisted by other scholars.

contest for the national market in order to sell their surplus product at a time when their future rivals in the larger western cities were still content to sell at home.[6]

The historical reader may object at this point that the above illustration represents merely the application of informed common sense to the data. To this objection there can be no sweeping rebuttal. The difference between the application of a well structured group of related concepts, and the intuitive use of common sense is often subtle. The gain resulting from the more systematic procedures may appear mainly in the orderly presentation of the evidence and the explicitness of the conclusions. But granting the staggering problems of the historian, even this gain would seem sufficient to justify the method. Researchers unequipped with the concepts of location theory might have seen clearly the paradox of the Pabst brewery location, but then again they might not.

The same procedure of collecting categories of interest to scholars in other disciplines was pursued in the case of a study of the ideas and attitudes of railroad leaders from 1845 to 1890.[7] For this purpose we consulted economists, sociologists, political scientists, and social psychologists. Since the material to be studied was business office correspondence, and research assistance was used, it was doubly important to have explicit reminders of what to look for. Apparent gains from the use of this method in the study will be discussed presently.

The research for both the above books was done by professional historians using conventional sources. A social science approach, however, may suggest the use of materials not generally used by historians. Chief among these are: additional statistical aids such as birth, death, school and tax records, manuscript census reports, and city directories; business, hospital and other institutional records; questionnaires given to carefully chosen samples, and controlled interviews of many different types. In the use of these latter materials it is obvious the historian must decide in advance what he is after. Adjustments may be made as research progresses, but these, in general, will involve repeating the earlier part of the work.

[6] Th. C. Cochran, *The Economics in a Business History,* in "The Journal of Economic History," Supplement V (December 1945), p. 60.

[7] Th. C. Cochran, *Railroad Leaders 1845 to 1890. The Business Mind In Action,* Cambridge, Mass., Harvard University Press, 1953, pp. 5–7.

The following illustration of the value of additional types of material in broadening the scope of history involves inter-disciplinary team research by representatives of all the social sciences. The history of technological change and social adjust-ment in Norristown, Pennsylvania, from 1900 to 1950 has been undertaken at the University of Pennsylvania by a continuing graduate seminar under directors from anthropology, history, and sociology.[8] As ultimately interpreted by the staff, "techno-logical change and social adjustment" included all the subjects that historians could normally expect to explore from the available material. Our interest here is in the additional aspects of the data that traditionally oriented historians might have overlooked.

Let us take the matter of population. The historians were not unaware of the importance of population change in any area study, but they would no doubt have been content with use of Federal censuses. The sociologists, however, being trained demographers, went much further. To begin with they included in- and out-migration among the prescribed topics for research. Dr. Sidney Goldstein, then a graduate student in sociology, later Field Director of the Project, undertook the study of migration. Working with Professor Dorothy S. Thomas, he introduced the group to the problems involved in selecting true random samples, and the use of business directories, school records, and vital statistics as aids to historical population re-search.

The business directories, issued every two years and purport-ing to list all inhabitants over 18 years old were checked against the decennial censuses and found to be substantially accurate.[9] Then random samples of five per cent of the males resident in Norristown were drawn from directories ten years apart for the period 1910 to 1950. From each sample Dr. Goldstein found who had entered the Borough during the previous decade, and who left during the ensuing one. The factor that differentiated this study from any carried out previously for other commun-ities was that by use of school records and vital statistics he

[8] At one time or another, Professors Edward P. Hutchinson, Dorothy S. Thomas, Anthony F. C. Wallace, and the author have acted as faculty directors of the seminar.

[9] For a more detailed description see: S. Goldstein, *Patterns of Internal Migration in Norristown, Pennsylvania, 1910–1950*, 2 volumes (Ph. D. Thesis, multigraphed), University of Pennsylvania, 1953.

could tell with a high degree of accuracy where the members of the sample originated, whether by growing up in Norristown or by inmigration, and for those who disappeared during the following decade, whether they migrated or died.

When Dr. Goldstein examined the results of his research he made an interesting discovery. Of those people in the samples who had been resident in Norristown ten or more years only about 25 per cent left the borough during the following decade, whereas of those who had entered the city during the previous decade more than 50 per cent left during the following one. The city, that is, had two populations living side by side. Fairly permanent residents, many of whom had been born there, and a migrating group that continually came and went.

Judged from crude statistics of population turnover for other cities the Norristown situation was apparently representative. This suggests that United States culture has been divided not only into regional sub-cultures such as northeast or southwest, or rural or urban, but also into migratory and non-migratory categories. If this is the case, the non-migratory group should have been the perpetuators of the regional sub-culture, and the migratory group the spreaders of a standardized national culture. The idea further suggests that there may be ascertainable differences in personality types between the two groups.

From this apparently physical, statistical research, therefore, there emerged an important cultural problem that historians using their conventional methods and materials would presumably have overlooked, one that may have important implications for the study of industrial societies, and might also be applied to cultural permanence and change in the American westward movement.

II

Another value of the social sciences for historical study comes from their emphasis on norms, types and averages that will permit the erection of what many scholars call models and what historians would probably refer to as well-founded propositions or generalizations. Related propositions depending upon orders of magnitude inevitably lead to efforts to measure and quantify historical data.

Economists and sociologists turning to historical study appear to have differed most from historically trained scholars in their greater interest in quantification. Statistical theory offers many helpful techniques. One of the recurrent problems of historical evidence is the mathematical significance of small numbers of cases. If only four Congressmen out of eighty-four for which information could be secured at a certain date had fathers who were farmers, how reliable is this as a guide to the occupation of the fathers of Congressmen in general at this period? Substitution in a simple formula known as the Chi Square Test will provide a mathematical answer.

Yet the other social scientists have not communicated much of this enthusiasm for measurement to American historians. So slight has been the interest of the latter in finding and using norms and averages, even when they are available from government statistics, that some of the most obvious needs have not been met. Educational statistics are usually treated in the most haphazard manner, if at all. Misconceptions regarding industrial growth are perpetuated through failure to examine relevant production series. Crude data regarding national productivity, income, and so forth at different dates are frequently used without adjustment for price and population changes. There are no definitions of classes of urban communities at varying dates. The effect of election issues has been discussed by leading historians without proper statistical analysis of the actual votes.

But many social norms or types are not matters to be handled statistically. The desired knowledge may be seen empirically as a tendency, a probability, or as probably representative of a broader group. A type may also be deduced as a research tool in order to emphasize variations from this "ideal" norm in the real data.[10] Historians tend to use this method, but frequently in an inexact uncritical fashion. Westerner, southerner, businessman, the frontier and other ideal types are employed without the kind of definition that would make them into tools for separating the abnormal from the usual.

III

The social sciences tend to emphasize the uniform characteristics of social processes rather than the unique elements of

[10] A. Spiethoff, *Pure Theory and Economic Gestalt Theory Ideal Types and Real Types,* in F. C. Lane and J. C. Riemersma, eds., *Enterprise and Social Change,* London, George Allen and Unwin, 1953, pp. 451 ff.

each situation. This calls attention to the importance of long-run mass phenomena or trends rather than individual events. But both approaches get at aspects of reality, and shifting from one to the other may have a valuable corrective effect.

For example, the historian records the hardships, economic, social and political caused by the long depression of the eighteen-seventies in the United States. Even the business cycle theorist using selected series will see the decade as one of less than average prosperity. But if the focus is shifted from these business events to the economy as a whole a radically different picture is presented. The westward movement of people and railroads in the early part of the decade brought great new farming areas into production. As a consequence the supposedly depressed decade of the seventies shows a high rate of increase in gross national product per worker or real national income.[11]

A more striking contrast between basic economic development and the apparent trend of immediate events occurs in relation to the Civil War. American historians have been inclined to regard the Civil War as a great stimulating force in industrialization, in fact some disregard industrial activity in pre-war decades and by inference make the war periodize the coming of the "industrial revolution." The Census figures on "value added by manufacture" do not support this generalization. From 1849 to 1859 the figure increased some 84 per cent, and from 1859 to 1869 only 63 per cent.[12] While these early census figures on manufacturing are of questionable accuracy, series on major elements of production tell the same story. Coal, iron, and railroads were the basis of nineteenth century industrial progress. Coal production continued at approximately the same rate of increase as during the decade of the fifties. Pig iron production and railroad construction both levelled off during the war and then by 1870 rose to a point about on the extension of the curve for the decade of the fifties. That cotton manufacture, immigration, foreign trade and ship building all languished between 1860 and 1870 is not surprising in view of the nature of the war, but that according to the official figures the value of machinery and equipment on farms, ad-

11 D. S. Thomas, *Some Aspects of a Study of Population. Distribution and Economic Growth in the United States 1870–1950*, Paper Presented at World Population Conference, Rome, September 1954, (Mimeographed), p. 25.

12 The census figures are adjusted to a gold rather than a currency base.

justed for price changes, fell challenges the widely held idea that the Civil War began the rapid mechanization of agriculture.[13] The Woolen industry is one of the minority that progressed with unusual speed during the war years, but Arthur H. Cole writes: "Expansion in the industry as a whole, however, proceeded at great rapidity and quite independently of the direct war needs." [14]

Recourse to quantitative data suggests the conclusion that if the Civil War had a major stimulating effect on American industrialism it must have been delayed in action, and not susceptible to measurement in terms of contemporary statistics. This may have been the case, but the long-run quantitative series pose questions that must modify the conclusions of the historian engrossed in apparently revolutionary events.

IV

The historian turning to quantification or typification of past phenomena often finds that the particular trends whose amplitudes he would record were not measured by contemporaries, and cannot be directly recovered from existing statistics. The relative economic welfare of various groups in society, the efficiency of marketing arrangements or transportation are representative of present interests that cannot be followed by direct statistics much back of the twentieth century. To estimate these and other unrecorded relationships in earlier society, resort must be had to indices. From this standpoint an index is a datum that manifests the co-existence of some other datum. If a relationship may be inferred between the known data and the unrecorded movement under investigation, the index is, at least, suggestive.

Historians have always made use of such evidence, but social scientists have probably given the matter more thought and

[13] The figures in current dollars on "Value of Farm Implements and Machinery" are: 1850 = $152 million, 1860 = $246 million, and 1870 = $271 million. The Department of Agriculture which is the source for these figures states: "the data are sufficiently comparable to indicate in a broad way the agricultural progress of the country." United States Department of Commerce, Bureau of the Census, *Historical Statistics of the United States 1789–1945*, Washington, U. S. Government printing Office, 1949, p. 82.

[14] A. H. Cole, *The American Wool Manufacture*, 2 vols., Cambridge, Mass., Harvard University Press, 1926, I, p. 377.

have developed both ingenious indices, and rigorous tests for meaningful correlations between series.

Earl J. Hamilton, an economist by training, has demonstrated the use of price data as an index of many other social phenomena. "Price and wage series," he writes,

disclose changes in the economic positions of different groups such as farmers, fishermen, and industrialists over short periods of time. In combination with data concerning technological development, market relationships, and organizational improvements, price and wage statistics can roughly measure variations in the economic welfare of various groups of producers over periods as long as one or two decades . . . Changes in the ratio of the prices of staple commodities in widely separated producing and consuming centers over long periods of time register alterations in the efficiency of transportation and distributive systems. Variations in the spread between the prices of finished goods at successive steps in the process of distribution likewise measure the efficiency of mercantile agencies . . . Perhaps in very few cases has there been a combination of competition imperfect enough and demand elastic enough over long periods to prevent prices from reflecting, much better than can other attainable historical data, changes in relative technological efficiency. Only through comparative prices could one possibly know, for example, that, as Beveridge pointed out, the increased efficiency in producing steel in Great Britain since the Black Death has been approximately fifty times as great as in producing wheat. It was his encyclopedic knowledge of American price history that enabled Arthur H. Cole to suggest that increasing command of southern staples, especially cotton, over non-southern commodities after the early 1840's may well have had a bearing on the optimism and political ascendancy of the South in the decade of the 1850's.[15]

These are only a few of the uses that Professor Hamilton finds for price indices.

These and other social science methods are not confined to quantitative materials. Instead of inferring a relationship be-

15 E. J. Hamilton, *Use and Misuse of Price History*, in "The Journal of Economic History," Supplement IV (December 1944), pp. 55, 56. For detailed discussion of the use of prices for a limited period of United States history see: A. Bezanson, Assisted by B. Daley, M. C. Denison, and M. Hussey, *Prices and Inflation During the American Revolution: Pennsylvania 1700–1790*, Industrial Research Department, Wharton School, University of Pennsylvania, University of Pennsylvania Press, 1951.

tween a known statistical series and an unknown movement, the mere appearance of a certain factor may be taken as an indication of the existence of a close or invariable correlative. Here again, historians have often used this method, but social science offers suggestions for greater precision. For example, an organized marketing system may usually have been taken as a correlative of the existence of cities, but it required a new development in economic theory to suggest that product differentiation was a correlative of monopolistic or limited competition. Similarly population growth was presumed for centuries to be inversely correlated to urbanism,[16] but only recently have demographers also pointed to correlation between fertility and the business cycle.

In handling all quantitative series, the historian should learn from statisticians certain mathematical tests for the probable truth of the correlation assumed, and retain a healthy skepticism of the reliability of the basic figures.

V

Theoretical constructs or models have value in giving meaning and organization to otherwise diffuse data. The theoretical model does not necessarily have to be true to be useful. In manipulating the empirical findings the model may be modified or destroyed, but almost inevitably the process will have called attention to previously unnoticed characteristics of the evidence.

The following illustration, however, taken from *Railroad Leaders, 1845–1890,* is one in which the model was found to fit the material. Roughly ten thousand extracts bearing on a series of 64 categories were taken from some 100,000 letters written by men who were railroad presidents between 1845 and 1890. Since it is usually not hard to separate statements of attitudes of policy from routine business, "common sense" would have indicated most of the selections chosen. The major problem was what did the selections represent? If the authors gave their real opinions only part of the time, how could true statements be distinguished from deliberate falsification?

At first there appeared to be no organizing principle that would apply. But gradually, it became clear that no matter

[16] See A. O. Aldridge, *Franklin as Demographer,* in "The Journal of Economic History," IX (May 1949), pp. 25–44.

what the reliability as to either fact or attitude in any given statement they all represented the carrying out of a social role.

This concept, rather recently developed by American social scientists "refers to anticipated uniformities in response or behavior when a given type of person, such as a middle aged railroad executive, is confronted with a specific social situation." [17] Expressed another way, a social role is "an understanding shared more or less fully by the members of a group as to what a given position entails for any individuals who occupy it." [18] In general social affairs, the precise group to whose expectations the actor may try to conform is often indefinite and varies with individuals.[19] While in such instances social role is a useful building block for further theory, it is not of much value for handling empirical evidence. But in the modern business corporation these relationships are logical and clearly defined.

For each of these railroads the evidence showed that the board of directors exercised ultimate sanctions on the business activity of the top individuals in the corporate hierarchy. They were the group that prescribed the social role of the chief executives. Individual executives might at times have some other reference groups such as family or church, but this company group had always to be recognized as paramount in business authority.

Since all these executive office letters were available to the board, and might be shown by their recipients to board members, the writers had to be careful to conform. Therefore, the ideas and attitudes shown in the extracts, regardless of their consistency with the writer's personality or knowledge, may be taken as a reasonably reliable representation of the role expected of the railroad executive by his board of directors. Further evidence indicates that the boards, in turn, were dominated by major financiers, so that ultimately we have the projection of the social beliefs of the metropolitan financial communities in railroad management.

17 Th. C. Cochran, *Railroad Leaders*, p. 13.

18 L. H. Jenks, *The Role Structure of Entrepreneurial Personality*, in *Change and the Entrepreneur*, Cambridge, Mass., Harvard University Press, 1949, p. 136.

19 See R. K. Merton and P. F. Lazarsfeld, eds., *Continuities in Social Research: Structures in the Scope and Method of The American Soldier*, Glencoe, Ill. Free Press, 1950.

This social science concept gave meaning and order to the heretofore confusing historical evidence. The reader may think that the device is imprecise in that there are many individual exceptions to the uniform playing of any social role, but the exceptions raise significant problems, bringing aspects of the data that might otherwise be neglected into focus. This is a major function of social theory.

VI

Historians are inclined by their training to think in terms of records, to have an almost irresistible urge to delve into a newly opened collection of important papers without regard to what general social problems they will illuminate. Social scientists, on the other hand, tend like the physical scientist to think first in terms of a challenging problem without immediate regard for the materials that may provide an answer. To put it another way, the logic of the developing system of knowledge in each social science discipline raises certain questions. The scholar wants primarily to answer these questions, and he turns to whatever materials seem likely to be useful. As an economist, Alexander Gerschenkron, has expressed it: "Historical research consists essentially in application to empirical material of various sets of empirically derived hypothetical generalizations and in testing the closeness of the resulting fit, in the hope that in this way certain uniformities, certain typical situations, and certain typical relationships among individual factors in these situations can be ascertained." [20]

The differing approaches of historians and social scientists have been well illustrated at the Research Center in Entrepreneurial History at Harvard, organized by Arthur H. Cole with the aid of the late Joseph A. Schumpeter and others. The initial research group represented economics, history, sociology, and the interdisciplinary group known at Harvard as social relations. The field of study, defined over-simply, was the business man in society as a factor in economic change.[21]

In the beginning the sociologists, particularly Leland H.

[20] A. Gerschenkron, *Economic Backwardness in Historical Perspective,* in B. F. Hoselitz, ed., *The Progress of Underdeveloped Areas,* Chicago, University of Chicago Press, 1952, pp. 3–4.

[21] Efforts at achieving tight definition of purpose or precisely uniform views have been deliberately avoided by the Center.

Jenks, raised the most provocative theoretical questions. But the growth of this theoretical framework proceeded independently of any formal collection of evidence.

Meanwhile the historians, following their usual procedures, were studying business source materials without waiting to formulate exact hypotheses in advance. The Research Center led to easy informal communication between the social scientists and the historians. The latter brought questions arising from studying their materials to the attention of the men from other disciplines, and, in turn, the historians searched their records for data that would support or modify the hypothetical propositions of the sociologists and economists. It was in this context that David Landes and John E. Sawyer applied sociological concepts to qualitative study of the French entrepreneur in the nineteenth century,[22] and role theory was applied to the material on railroad leaders.

In the interplay of trained capacities, or incapacities, the historians were undoubtedly interested by those hypotheses that might be tested by the materials with which they were familiar and somewhat repelled by constructs that seemed difficult to document. But in any case their approach was altered by contact with social scientists in so far as they started with questions and then looked for material that might supply answers.

Hypotheses based on pre-suppositions can be dangerous tools. But so can the implicit or surreptitious pre-suppositions from which no man is free. Of the two dangers, that of implicit bias is by far the greater. Psychologists contend that starting with a well worked out model or series of interrelated questions is perhaps the only reliable aid to objectivity. Since many American historians take the opposite point of view, that a carefully structured theory introduces bias in handling the evidence, and that a relatively blank and "open" mind is best for objective observation, it will be well to illustrate the rather uniformly held views of social psychologists on this matter.

Musafer Sherif has conducted many experiments that show the inability of the individual to avoid surreptitious suggestion or "affect" if he has no system to combat it. One of these

22 D. S. Landes, *French Entrepreneurship and Industrial Growth in the Nineteenth Century*, in "The Journal of Economic History," IX (May 1949), pp. 45–61; J. E. Sawyer, *The Entrepreneur and the Social Order: France and the United States*, in W. Miller ed., *Men in Business*, Cambridge, Mass., Harvard University Press, 1952, pp 7–22.

experiments graphically illustrates this fact. A tiny point of light shines in a dark room. To most observers the light appears to move. "At first, the movements seem chaotic. But they are remarkably responsive to the experimenter's suggestions; his instructions may cause the light to move rapidly to the right, slowly upward, etc. . . . The fact that *external* structure is wanting allows maximum play for *inner* structure-giving factors and for all those which arise in the subject from the verbal and other suggestions of those present." [23] If, however, a thin line of light is placed near the spot, if external structure is supplied, no one can be deluded into seeing motion.

Translating the laboratory experiment into terms of written evidence, the more precise the statement of what is being looked for the less disagreement there will be between scholars as to whether or not that element occurs in a given body of material. Careful advance statement of categories to be examined, questions to be answered, and methods to be used will call attention not only to the anticipated aspects of the evidence but also to those that were not expected. Whereas, if the historian has no external framework for reference these discrepancies might pass unnoticed.

For example, in categories for analysis of the material for *Railroad Leaders* there was a heading "ideas regarding democratic procedure." [24] In this box it was hoped to put opinions on the participation of junior executives or other employees in policy making. The box remained empty. Had it not been there, however, it would have been difficult for either of those who did the research to be sure that some such opinion had not escaped them because they were not looking for it.

Professor Paul F. Lazarsfeld and Allen Barton, sociologists who have studied the use of categories and questions to give order and weight to apparently qualitative material write: "There is a direct line of logical continuity from qualitative classification to the most rigorous forms of measurement, by way of intermediate devices of systematic ratings, ranking scales, multi-dimensional classifications, typologies, and simple quantitative indices. In this wider sense of measurement, social phenomena are being measured every day. . . ." [25] They urge careful

[23] G. Murphy, *Personality: A Biosocial Approach to Origins and Structure*, New York, Harper & Bros., 1947, pp. 347–348.

[24] Th. C. Cochran, *Railroad Leaders*, p. 6.

[25] D. Lerner and H. D. Lasswell, *The Policy Sciences: Recent Developments in Scope and Method*, Stanford, Stanford University Press, 1915, p. 155.

exploration of the logical implications of simple forms of measurement.

One such simple form is "content analysis": noting the frequency of occurrence of certain phrases, concepts, ideas or verbal symbols in a given body of writing. The assumption is that frequency of occurrence will correlate with the interest of the writer or speaker in communicating the idea, and will guard the researcher against being misled by rhetorical emphasis, or his own presuppositions. An application of this technique to historical material can be seen in Ithiel de Sola Pool, *The Prestige Papers*.[26] Editorials in leading newspapers of England, France, Germany, Russia and the United States were studied for the occurrence of some 416 symbols referring to political ideologies from 1890 to the late 1940's. The historian may think that the conclusions do not add greatly to what common sense would lead one to suspect. On this point Bernard Berenson in an introduction that discusses the problems of content analysis, maintains that such studies "develop quantitative measures for concepts previously used on a less formalistic basis. In this monograph the development of an index of stereotyping and instability in political terminology is a case in point. And in the process of verification they qualify the large assumptions that may previously have been made about the nature of political vocabularies over several countries and many years." [27]

VII

So far attention has been focused on aspects of the social sciences and their procedures that have utility for the historian. Lest this presents too optimistic a picture, some of the difficulties in using the social sciences should be mentioned.

The problem of the value for history of non-empirical deductive theory has harassed historians for several generations. Sir John Clapham, one of the fathers of economic history in the English speaking world, wrote: "The central problems of economic theory, although they may be stated in terms of a particular historical phase, are in essence independent of his-

26 Ithiel de Sola Pool et al., *The Prestige Papers*, "Hoover Institute Studies," Series C: Symbols, No. 2., Stanford, Stanford University Press, 1951.
27 *Ibid*, VI.

tory." [28] After listening to sociologist Franklin H Giddings read a paper on social causation in 1903, George L. Burr, editor of the *American Historical Review*, said: "I have listened with much interest to the speculations of Professor Giddings. They are very fine. They may well be true. But the thing of which Professor Giddings is talking is not history. . . ." [29]

Pure theory is a matter of choosing definitions, and its development has to be in the form of corollaries implicit in those definitions. There is no place in it for empirical, or historical, evidence. The applicability of the initial assumptions to a given situation may be questioned, but not their logical consistency.

There is, however, a valid interrelationship between history and pure theory. New elements or lines of investigation that would not occur to the empiricist, whether historian or other social scientist, are often suggested by the results of logical theorizing. Conversely theorists need to know the history of situations in order to make applicable basic assumptions. The two methods should reenforce each other in adding to the scope of awareness.

Another methodological tool of the social sciences that presents difficulties for the historian is the personal interview. As empirical research has gained prestige in anthropology, sociology and social psychology, the personal interview and questionnaire have been increasingly used. Even as applied to current opinion or information, construction or the questionnaire, its administrations, and interpretation of the results have to be considered very carefully. [30] Historical information gained by these techniques varies from moderately accurate to practically worthless.

Experience with an administered questionnaire in the Norristown project illustrated the nature of the variation. On factual historical data intimately associated with the interviewee such as former positions and places of residence, answers appeared to be reasonably accurate as to sequence, but weak on exact dates. On less factual personal history such as how leisure time was

[28] J. Clapham, *Economic History as a Discipline*, in Lane and Riemersma, *Enterprise and Social Change*, p. 419.

[29] "Publications of the American Economic Association," 3rd series, v. V (1904), p. 434.

[30] See H. Hyman, *Interviewing as a Scientific Process*, in *The Policy Sciences*, pp. 203–218.

spent or how the automobile affected their life in former decades the respondents were weak, and in many cases a stereotype
was repeated for each time period, although other evidence in
the interview contradicted the lack of change. Recollections
regarding the character of surrounding society such as changes
in neighborhoods or religious attitudes appeared in the average
questionnaire to be practically worthless. In these latter categories the answers presumably represented present attitudes
projected back in time.

The historical aspects of this part of the Norristown material,
however, suffer from the questionnaire having been given to a
random sample of the population. This meant that most of the
answers came from working class people not used to generalizing regarding their experience. Interviews with citizens selected for their knowledge often yielded richer results, and a
score or more of such interviews on the same topics in the
same location usually gave internal evidence of whether the
statements are true or false. But the results of any single interview, no matter how well informed the person, must be regarded as weak historical evidence.

VIII

This paper has been informal, and illustrative of reading or
research that has left a lasting impression upon the author.
Obviously no effort has been made systematically to survey the
social sciences for those concepts or methods that may be of
most use to the historian. Such eclectic procedure seems justi-
fiable. Experience suggests that a social science approach to
history is largely one of attitude or spirit. It is characterized by
an interest in measurement, norms, precise statement, and systematic conceptual structures.

But an emphasis on system and structure need not prevent
the historian from indulging in the imaginative flights that
have always been associated with his best achievements. No
hypothesis or question need be ruled out as too bizarre or
fanciful as long as it is constantly treated as an unproven assumption. In fact, a major weakness of traditional history, one
that may be strengthened by social science knowledge, is failure
to speculate regarding historically unconventional aspects of
the data or situation.

Furthermore, no one should be enslaved by existing social

science methods. These have, in general, failed to take sufficient account of change over time. The historian with his different orientation may and should be an innovator in method, materials, and hypotheses. He should approach social science in the same spirit that led mathematical physicist P. W. Bridgeman to write: "I am not one of those who hold that there is a scientific method as such. The scientific method, as far as it is method, is nothing more than doing one's damnedest with one's mind, no holds barred." [31]

History as one of the social science disciplines is still history with its intuitive insights and methodological limitations. From inadequate data historians must still piece together qualitative aspects of situations by the process that anthropologist Robert Redfield has called "descriptive integration." Behind the individual exploits of leaders and their rationalization in letters historians have to try to detect underlying environmental trends from fragmentary statistics and to assume patterns of personality from clues that the social psychologist would consider inadequate. To ask that historians regard parts of their discipline as primarily analytic and synthetic rather than merely descriptive is a call to add to the scope of historical research, to cast off the implied limitations of Professor Burr's statement that the study of social causation as such is "not history," to go beyond the admonition that the historian's main object should be describing events as they actually happened, to seek a broader intellectual approach that includes an interest in social theory; and to recognize that since history is a selection of factors from an infinite universe, an explicit basis for selection reduces misinterpretation.

[31] P. W. Bridgeman, *The Prospect for Intelligence*, in "Yale Review," 34 (March 1945), p. 450, quoted in "Bulletin," 64, Social Science, Research Council, p. 30.

22. American History and Social Science*

A. S. EISENSTADT

I

What uses are our historians making of the newer perspectives afforded by the social sciences? The question is more than academic. It touches upon the uses of knowledge in an age of crisis. The constraint of human events turns the kaleidoscope of knowledge to the sight of a particular configuration. A particular type of serviceability dictates to knowledge, defining both what it will be and how it will serve. With respect to what men study and seek to master, an age of crisis is almost necessarily an age of science. Social science models itself upon the forms of science, trying thereby to perform the services of science. It would seem reasonable to expect that historians, who are entrusted with the remembrance of things past, would suit their remembrance to the patterns and formulas of social science. The interesting thing is that, for the larger part, they do not. There are many reasons why they do not, and the reasons reveal not merely the differences between history and social science but also the nature and uses of knowledge in an age such as ours.

That social science has been undergoing a change during the past few decades, and particularly since World War II, there can be little doubt. The change may be analyzed into three separate components: first, the substance with which social

* Reprinted with permission, and with minor revisions, from *The Centennial Review*, VII (Summer, 1963), 255–72.

science is concerned; second, the method it uses to comprehend that substance; and third, the social ideas that serve as a frame for housing both the newer substance and the newer method of social science.

As to its subject matter and substance: social science is becoming more concerned with understanding the regularities in human experience rather than what is unique. It is increasingly concerned with process rather than simply with institutions. It is trying to understand the complexities of the whole social process and to see the various activities of human life in constant interplay with each other. Social science is trying to comprehend the many ways in which an advanced industrial society, caught up in the toils of crisis, articulates its problems and seeks to fulfill its purposes. The social scientist is concerned with dissecting and anatomizing the social process. He is concerned with the structure of society, with various social roles— particularly those of the leader and of the entrepreneur, with the composition and function of groups, with social mobility and stratification, with status and caste, with the emergence of new classes, with the urbanization of life and the rise of the megalopolis, with ethnic and racial minorities, with the growth and forms of mass culture, with the changing sociology of knowledge, with the psychology of leaders and of the led, with economic organization and activity, with the influence of industrialization upon the whole social process, with new cultures in formation and with the reciprocal impact of new cultures and old ones. The social scientist is concerned with the impact of each form and function of human experience upon another and upon a complex of forms and functions, and the permutations and combinations of problems which he contemplates are without number.

No less important than the wide view which social science takes of modern society is the method by which it seeks to insure that the view is accurate and objective. "Indeed," says Robert Bierstedt of New York University ". . . the methods and techniques of empirical research . . . have received perhaps an extra share of attention in recent decades." The newer social science postulates hypotheses about a phase of human activity. It defines rigorous criteria for testing these hypotheses. It uses a variety of devices to insure that its tests are impersonal and valid. These devices include sample surveys, panel studies, projective techniques, interviews, content analysis, and models.

The words which recur as the *leitmotif* of the newer method are measurement and quantification. They summarize the whole current desire to demarcate various aspects of the social process by valid means and to insure the validity of those means by getting tangibly measured data.

In speaking of the newer social science, one would not halt at the line of its newer areas of interest and of its newer methodology. The perspective and method of social science are informed by suggestions deriving from the great social scientists of modern times, from Max Weber, Sigmund Freud, Emile Durkheim, Ferdinand Tönnies, John Dewey, Thorstein Veblen, and a score of others. It would be absurd to suggest that the contributions of these notable individuals are used by modern social science as an integrated whole. Yet it is fair to say that, to the historian's mind surely, the ideas do represent a distinctive approach to the study of human behavior; and however various their arrangement or combination, the ideas form a broad conceptual frame for the newer house of social science.

In trying to understand how far and why historians are using the insights of social science, let me at this point define terms and set limits to my analysis. First, a consideration of the social sciences as a set of disciplines does not imply that they have an organic unity. The social sciences not only differ among themselves but each of them also has serious differences within itself. If the social sciences are considered here as a unit, it is because the path they are taking and the role they are playing differ substantially from those being taken and played by history. Secondly, while I am interested in the question of whether or not history should use the social sciences, my principal interest is in whether or not it does. I am not so much concerned to propose an interdisciplinary alliance as to explain why the proposals for alliance have, in actual practice, not been realized. Third, in talking about history's use of social science I am not talking about social science's use of history. We are all familiar, for example, with the historical orientation of the contribution of David Riesman, Erich Fromm, and C. Wright Mills. My concern here is with the use of social science by professional historians in their regular and continuing researches. Finally, I am confining my analysis to research and writing in the field of American history, which is the field I have myself cultivated and am most familiar with. Much of what I say will no doubt apply to research and writing in other areas of history. This is true, certainly, of my explanation of the relation between American history and social science: since the explanation is itself historical, it deals necessarily with conditions which affected the whole discipline of history (as it arose and developed) rather than with merely one part of it. Yet it is recent work in American history which served me as my vantage ground in arriving at my observations and it is this work which frames the views I am presenting.

The changing conditions of modern American life have altered both the subjects with which social science deals and the purposes which it serves. Inevitably, of course, these changing conditions have raised a question about history's use of social science in dealing with the newer subjects and in serving the newer needs. In its book on *The Social Sciences in Historical Study,* which appeared in 1954, the Committee on Historiography of the Social Science Research Council argued that historians ought to embrace the teachings of the social sciences. In his presidential address to the American Historical Association a few years ago, William L. Langer sustained this argument by designating the application of psychoanalytic knowledge to history as "the next assignment" for historians. Richard Hofstadter has urged his fellow historians to use the new approaches of social science to add "to the speculative richness of history." The liaison between history and social science is the subject of many conferences and is encouraged by many grants. Indeed, some writers assert that history's use of social science has gone beyond the stage of preaching, that it has indeed passed into actual practice. John T. Marcus, in a recent and very stimulating article on "The Changing Consciousness of History," in *The South Atlantic Quarterly* contends that the historical approach has been changing from one that is linear, positivistic, and interested above all in causation, to one that is—as he puts it—configurational, Gestaltist, and multi-directional. Evidences abound that historians are facing up to the problems of history's use of the social sciences.

II

Conspicuous instances may indeed be cited of a new departure in recent American historical writing. Seeking to canvass the whole expanse of the American past, David M. Potter's *People of Plenty* (1954) is almost in a class by itself. Using the tools of behavioral science, Potter shows how economic abundance contributed to the shaping of the American character. Historians have, moreover, been making a goodly use of the insights of social psychology in their studies of groups and of regions, focusing these insights on such questions as status consciousness, social mobility, the relation of minorities to the values of the majority, and the family as a factor in social and political developments. Recent books that are based largely on the substance or method of social science include: Bernard Bailyn's *The New England Merchants in the Seventeenth Century* (1955), Lee Benson's *The Concept of Jacksonian Democracy: New York as a Test Case* (1961), Thomas C. Cochran's *Railroad Leaders, 1845–1890: The Business Mind in Action* (1953), John Hope Franklin's *The Militant South, 1800–1861* (1956), Oscar Handlin's *The Uprooted* (1951), John Higham's *Strangers in the Land: Patterns of American Nativism, 1860–1925* (1955), and Richard Hofstadter's *The Age of Reform* (1955). Mention ought to be made of at least one further area in which history is using the insight of social science: biography. A most conspicuous example here is David Donald's *Charles Sumner and the Coming of the Civil War* (1960) which has availed itself of psychoanalytic knowledge to arrive at a deeper understanding of central episodes in the life of its protagonist.

It would be erroneous to pretend that these examples represent completely the uses of social science by writers of American history. But it would also be erroneous to pretend that there are many more important examples to cite, or that these represent the rule rather than the exception. This is not to deny that the insights of modern social science do filter into current writing on the American past. But one ought not to confuse scattered intelligences gleaned from the social sciences with a social science intelligence. A history which approaches some aspects of American society is far from being a sociological approach to American history. Whatever the preachment of American historians at interdisciplinary colloquia on the social sciences, their practice remains relatively traditional. Indeed, the very fact of the continuing preachment is its own testimony to the continuing absence of the practice. For proof of this, one has but to peruse the last decade's issues of the two principal professional journals in the United States devoted to writings on American history: *The American Historical Review* and *The Mississippi Valley Historical Review*.

No comment is more relevant or pointed here than that of Thomas C. Cochran, of the University of Pennsylvania, who, as much as any other contemporary American historian, has been pleading the case of social science to his fellow guildsmen. "In the field of American history," submits Professor Cochran, ". . . the past fifty years of rapid progress in the development of social science methods and hypotheses have had surprisingly little effect on historical interests, content, or forms of syntheses. This statement applies to American history either as taught in universities and colleges, as presented in textbooks or as reflected in general literature. The main props of a synthetic structure, erected more or less unconsciously by such gifted pioneers as Channing, Hart, McMaster, and Turner, are still securely in place."

If historians are not, for the larger part, using the approaches of social science, what approaches are they using? What are the principal features of contemporary writing on the American past? To begin with, the form in which the writing is cast remains fairly traditional. It is what Cochran calls "narrative synthesis," and by this he means a story centering on great men, generally the major American presidents, and on important events. H. Stuart Hughes of Harvard further suggests that historians still offer simple causal explanations, which they arrive at intuitively. Secondly, the interest in political developments remains the dominant one. Evidence for this could be offered in profusion. A commentary on the vistas of our historiography is afforded by what is clearly the most grandiose and indeed the most important writing venture of our times: Allan Nevins's *Ordeal of the Union,* a ten-volume history of the republic before and during the Civil War. However much he concerns himself with social and intellectual matters, Nevins is principally concerned with politics, and with politics in the traditional sense of the word. Probably the second most important work of our times is Arthur M. Schlesinger, Jr.'s *The Age of Franklin D. Roosevelt.* Here too the primary interest is political and the form of the account narrative.

A third feature of present-day writing is what I would call "the cult of biography." The foremost younger historians of our generation are devoting their talents to this form and are using the form in fairly conventional ways. I am thinking in particular of such luminaries as Frank Freidel of Harvard and his multi-volume work on Franklin D. Roosevelt; John M. Blum of Yale and his work on Tumulty, Theodore Roosevelt, Wilson and the Morgenthau diaries; and Arthur S. Link of Princeton and his distinguished work on Woodrow Wilson. A fourth feature, if not of historical writing then at least of historical effort, is what might be called "the cult of the Founding Fathers." We are passing through an age of spectacular editions of the papers of the founders of the American republic; of Thomas Jefferson, Alexander Hamilton, John Adams, and Benjamin Franklin. From a list of these features it seems fair enough to conclude that the orientation underlying present American historiography is conventional and conservative. For whatever reasons, writers of American history have not walked down the newer paths of social science. For whatever reasons, they seem, as much as ever before, to be abiding by the older canons and interests of their profession.

III

The big question, of course, is why. What are the reasons for which research and writing in the field of American history has tended, for the larger part, to pass by the teachings of social science? I should like to offer some suggestions, which, while they do not apply to all of the social sciences, will surely touch upon some of them. In answering our question about history's use of social science, we shall inevitably have to deal with the nature of history and its relation to the other disciplines. In the process, we may come upon deeper differences between them, differences in their function, their premises, and their methods.

The social sciences grew out of an attempt to find a science of society. Their purposes were practical, their goals utilitarian. They were designed to be an instrument for social understanding and, by means of that understanding, for social improvement. It is only in this light that we understand the great work of Auguste Comte, the French "Utopian" socialists, Herbert Spencer, the classical economists, Marx and Engels, the Fabians, and the whole school of late nineteenth-century American sociology. The continuing interest of social science has been with analyzing the human condition and with taking action based upon that analysis. As Robert K. Merton of Columbia University puts it: sociology seeks ". . . to acquire the knowledge needed to cope with the many social ills man has the inveterate capacity to contract." The social sciences are under the dictate of current events, they have an immediate goal, they serve a social need. If they are not useful, they are nothing.

History also plays a social role, but it is less immediate and practical. In the sociology of knowledge, the role of history might be considered both ideological and utopian. It is ideological in the respect that it conforms to the social myth, to the convention of values by which society lives. It is utopian in the respect that it always second guesses the past, it arraigns the past on a charge of what should have been, it always proceeds in terms of the difference between the imperfections of actual reality and the consummate reality so devoutly to be wish'd. In performing their role, historians often play tricks with the dead. For the larger part, they tell the fables which convention requires for the pursuit of social life.

If the service of social science is to set up a program of action for society, that of history is to serve the national myth. The service of social science is performed by analysis, by studies in arrested motion. That of history is performed by narrative. Historians may aspire to science, but their highest calling is that of troubadours and of bards, of minnesingers and of Homers, recalling to the folk the present meaning of earlier deeds, the heroism and cowardice of earlier men, the nobility or baseness of earlier generations. A folk-singer and myth-maker tells stories; he tells them personally; he commits himself to the narrative. He uses the records of the past—which center, for the larger part, on the unusual and the unique—to serve his cause. Citing the unusual, the historian teaches by example. Drawn from the unique, his portrait is an idealization of social behavior rather than a representation of it.

Differing substantially in their respective uses, it is inevitable that history and social science will differ too in method and theory.

The historian works under the sense that truth is less self-evident and less certain than the social scientist may consider it to be, beset as the latter always is with society's cry for functional truth, the whole functional truth, and nothing but functional truth. Moreover, because the historian cannot possibly know all the social interrelations of a whole scene or of a whole age, and because he cannot presume to deal with less, his account can be little more than (as one historian has put it) an imprecise and impressionistic "explanation sketch." Canvassing the larger frame of experience with which he is perforce concerned, he could not possibly use the narrower and more controlled methods of social science. In their quest for practical truth, social scientists are understandably concerned with how truth is to be found out. They rigorously postulate hypotheses, define areas for inspection, set up charts, classify IBM cards, make the chemistry of human action a matter of quantitative analysis. The historian is both impressed and depressed. If he sees method in their madness, he also suspects madness in their method.

In exploring why history makes only a limited use of social science, we must consider that the social scientist proceeds from the premise that out of a limited sampling of human experience one can arrive at larger generalizations. He proceeds from the instance to the rule. The historian's premises regarding human experience are different. He accepts the uniqueness of experience, the difference of individuals and groups. If the social scientist is looking for rules and laws, the historian has long since come to doubt that they can be found. He is concerned with variables, with the uniqueness of what he is dealing with, with the improbabilities of abstracting a universal out of an instance.

The focal points of history and social science are in many respects different. Social science concentrates on regularities in human experience, on norms, on the recurrent. History concentrates on irregularities, on leaders, on unique events, on the exceptional. The language difference between history and social science both reflects and explains their different approaches and concerns. Writers of books on freshmen English descend zestfully, looking for evidences of what Orwell would probably have called nonspeak, upon the rich, alluvial lands of sociologese. Sociology is considered the worst of the offenders here, but psychology, political science, and economics are often almost as guilty. The sharp difference between history and social science in their uses of language as a means of communication lies deeply in the respective image which each has of its function. The language of social science is impersonal. Talking in ponderous and magisterial tones, using the passive voice instead of the active, it lays claim to the remove of science. By its language shall ye know it. Social science is valid only to the degree that it is above the play and noise of human experience. Any experience is a commentary on all experience, and the language is made bloodless enough to accord with that axiom. But if your premise is, as the historian believes it to be, that any experience is self-sufficient, that it is at best relevant to others, but not as the basis of a model, a norm, a larger hypothesis, or a law, then language must convey the reality of that particular experience, its self-sufficiency, its vitality, dramatic uniqueness. The experience is not an example of life but life itself, and the historian's language seeks to express that very basic difference. My point here is not to enter into an empty argument about the way some social scientists write or speak. It is rather to get beneath the surface of the different uses of language and to see that there is a very fundamental difference in approach to discipline.

IV

The difference between social science and history is the difference between a method which pretends to philosophy and a method which has given philosophy up. Both history and social science are rooted in positivism. Both began in the nineteenth century as quests for certain truth, to be achieved by certain methods. Both appealed to the example of science, and like science, both were to serve society: history by showing the road society had thus far come in its march toward progress and perfection, social science by showing the road it had yet to march. But nineteenth century philosophy has had some very rude shocks. The mythology of the liberal world came clattering down under the assault of two world wars. Western man's sense of his destiny is less of progress than of poverty, less of a certain goal in life than of muddling through. The grand social philosophy of the nineteenth century has found no sequel. Where today is the over-arching ideological structure of Hegel, of Marx, of Darwin, of Spencer? As H. Stuart Hughes of Harvard University puts it: "The chair of speculative social thought stands vacant."

We are living in a world of gods that have failed. We have run the gamut of the grand ideas, of positivistic faith, of belief in science, of conviction about progress, of programs for social reforms, of hopes for human perfectibility and Utopia. But the recent past of man has disabused us of hopes for his present and future. We are not so sure, we do not know, and we do not readily venture into metaphysical systems which, as we now realize, may be more the products of our psyches—whether as projections or as wish fulfillments—than they are of the real world around us. In such a condition of mankind, philosophy cannot flourish. Ideas yield to techniques, metaphysics to methods, ends to means.

All of this has a close relevance to the issue of history's use of social science. If historians still use the methods of positivism, they have long since abandoned a certain belief in its goals. Historians still respect the precepts of Leopold von Ranke about discovering the past *"wie es eigentlich gewesen."* But they are far from being sure about the truth which history will demonstrate or indeed that it will demonstrate truth at all. Which historian would assert, as did J. B. Bury, that history is a science? Which historian would argue, as did E. P. Cheyney, that history is under the governance of laws? Disbelieving in regularities, uniformities, and laws, historians have lost their earlier rapport with social science. The problem of communication between history and social science has arisen, suggests Professor Oscar Handlin of Harvard University, ". . . because historians claimed there was no such thing as a historical 'law' and because many social scientists believed that history conceived in such terms had no utility for them." History has retained its older means of travelling—its positivistic methodology—despite the fact that, paradoxically, it has no place to go. Here indeed may be something of a clue as to why historians, more conscious than ever before of history as an art, are more concerned than ever before with writing, with style, and with form.

What has been the significance for social science of the destruction of nineteenth-century ideology? The truth is that the social sciences cannot give up the goals and the method of science without also giving up their claims as independent disciplines. If they cannot claim to be furnishing society with certain knowledge arrived at by certain methods, they can claim nothing at all. In a world where ideology is under serious doubt, where indeed it seems to be at an end, social science has given up seeking to document truth and has become content with documentating merely a truth. "More and more," says Professor Hughes, "the sociologists, the economists, and the political scientists seem almost exclusively absorbed with the sort of small, neat topics that are alone capable of being dealt with in a methodologically impeccable fashion."

There is, one cannot but feel, a larger significance to the newer tendency toward quantification in social science. It means the abandonment of philosophy, indeed the fear of it. It summarizes the flight from Hegel to the IBM card. The apotheosis of the model and of the number is also the renunciation of ideas. It is perhaps the acceptance of quantity where quality cannot be had. It is the replacement of a thought by a statistic. What is referred to as the recent revolution in social science would seem to reveal that, because their ultimate goals are now so much in doubt, social scientists have, almost defensively, taken refuge in their techniques.

A footnote to this whole tendency may be found in Robert Bierstedt's preface to his recent revision of V. F. Calverton's *The Making of Society*. Abjuring Calverton's Marxist orientation, Bierstedt insists that his own is ". . . both Comtean and orthodox, one that considers sociology 'value-free' in general and politically neutral in particular, and one finally that emphasizes, rather than erases, the distinction between sociology on the one hand and social and political philosophy on the other." Perhaps the comment signifies that in an age of philosophic dismantling, we do not take sides, we only take cover.

Not that the voice of the Jeremiahs is nowhere to be heard in the land. Carle Zimmerman of Harvard has lamented the movement of sociology from an interest in social dynamics to one in social statics. And, in *The Sociological Imagination* (1959), C. Wright Mills attacked the leading schools of American sociology for what he called their abstracted empiricism, their limited practicality, and their bureaucratic ethos. Whatever their points of agreement or disagreement, Zimmerman and Mills both reflect upon the transformation of social science from a system of ideas which prescribes its methods to a system of methods which prescribes its ideas.

In accounting for the difference between history and social science, further illumination may be found in that particular spot where the beams of philosophy, historical relativism, and the sociology of knowledge all converge. It is fair to ask whether the newer theories and methods of social science are not themselves the by-products of a phase of societal or cultural evolution. Every age is an age of self-consciousness and introspection, every age develops the instruments for taking measure of its achievements and shortcomings. The theories and methods of today's social science are peculiarly the product of today's society, they peculiarly fulfill the need of today's world to know itself. The mind and method of social science are accordingly commentaries on the self-cognitive process of a culture beset with problems of mass communication, status revolutions, urbanization, radically altered patterns of social and political behavior. It would be wrong to suggest that none of these problems characterized earlier cultures, but it is fair to ask whether these problems were central to those cultures. If not, then one reason why historians might not have had recourse to social science is that it may not readily have served them, indeed that it may have been inapplicable, in discovering those earlier times and societies with which historians are concerned. Hegel would suggest that social science is an adjunct of social philosophy. The precept for historians is that they cannot accurately measure the philosophy of one age with the yardstick of another.

V

In trying to explain why history does not widely use the social sciences, I have thus far concentrated on what impresses me as the most important reasons: that history and social science differ as to their functions and roles in society, as to their essential premises, and as to their methods. There are, of course, other reasons. For one thing, if history is to borrow the instruction of social science, the latter must be sure of what it has to teach. And it is not. There are not only sharp differences of opinion regarding theory and method among the social sciences but also within them. The language of social science, moreover, is remarkably turgid, murky, and imprecise.

In *The Social Sciences in Historical Study*, one will find a chapter of some fifty long pages, by Thomas C. Cochran, on current concepts in the social sciences. Professor Cochran's conclusion leaves one not unreasonably aghast, though perhaps somewhat comforted: "If the reader is not quite sure that he understands the meaning of the terms and concepts mentioned in this chapter, he is in no worse situation than other social scientists. Even leading scholars in disciplines as closely related as sociology and social psychology find difficulty in precise communication."

The great difference between the data of history and those of social science affords us another reason. How can one seek regularities and norms in typical situations for earlier periods when the sources for discovering them are not to be had? How does one do the equivalent of conducting interviews, taking projective tests, verifying hypotheses, and getting necessary statistics among the dead, particularly the very long dead? The records left for the historian to work with are more likely concerned with irregularities, with deviations from the norm, with men who are not typical, with situations that are unique. Who, after all, bequeaths an archival legacy to the future: John Doe or Woodrow Wilson, a member of yesterday's lonely crowd or their charismatic leader? The way in which the available data might affect the historian's findings has been pointed out by Professor William O. Aydelotte, of the State University of Iowa, who has made a detailed statistical analysis of the House of Commons that was elected in 1841. "The historian's sample . . . ," says Professor Aydelotte, ". . . is apt to be an accidental or biased one, and the very factors which have contributed to the survival of his information may also contribute to skew his results."

One of the reasons why American historians do not too often have recourse to social science is that there is about many of them a regrettable ethnocentrism, a parochialism which seems to put an intellectual iron curtain around the imperial realm of American history. One of the postulates of social science is that societies must be viewed comparatively. This is certainly true of the postulates of cultural anthropology. It is here that American history fails. In his brilliant analysis of *The Liberal Tradition in America,* Louis Hartz has shown us the monolithic features of American politics and political theory. His analysis has relevance to the way we historians construe the American experience. It is, for us, *sui generis.* We are locked up in it. We do not see it as a cultural expression of a particular type. We do not even set up a sufficient contrast between the culture of the whites who came to people the American shores and that of the Indians who were already living there. How far, for example, do we try to understand the differences between the early modern Western culture and that of the Indians of Muskhogean and Iroquoian linguistic stock into whose midst the whites came? Not making even this limited analysis of cultures in apposition, the American historian certainly does not venture farther afield into the realm of comparative sociology or cultural anthropology. His thoughts do not often take the measure of other value systems, he does not often see the American experience as one small adventure in the polymorphous experience of the human animal. His analysis does not often extend to the impact of frontiers in other areas of the planet earth, to other systems of status and caste, to other organized systems of religion, to other arrangements of power and of politics.

A final reason why history does not use the insights of social science is that it takes insight to use insight. For the historian to

avail himself of the perception offered by social science, he has
to have a mind which is able to perceive; to scan the wider
ranges of his subject, he has to be able to scale and to soar.
What is wrong with the sociological imagination is, in its way,
wrong with the historical imagination. Both can get to be pa-
thetically entrapped in tight little sources, in insignificant problems, in narrow perspectives, building frightfully laborious and
horribly dull monuments to the obvious. The imagination of
the historian—to say nothing of his training—is generally in-
capable of meeting the great demands of social science. All too
often he retreats to the narrow perimeter of his sources and to
the very limited confines of his subject. And it is fair enough to
say that the fault lies not in our sources, but in ourselves.

VI

This analysis of history's use of the social sciences would seem
to call for at least two concluding observations. The first deals
with a change of perspective among American historians which
owes little to the social sciences. It is a change which is noted
by C. Vann Woodward's inspired essay, entitled "The Age of
Reinterpretation," in a recent issue of *The American Historical
Review*. In remarking how the momentous issues of our own
times demand a recasting of our historical views, Woodward reminds us that the challenging issues of every age have been the
most important factor in turning the historian's kaleidoscope on
the past. This indeed had been the theme of Geoffrey Bar-
raclough's earlier and very significant essay on "The Historian
and the Changing World." Both essays remind us how fresh
departures in American historical writing were demarcated by
bursts of insight which came at the right time, in the right
place. We are reminded of generations caught up by the imagination of Frederick Jackson Turner's essay on "The Significance of the Frontier in American History," of Charles Austin
Beard's *An Economic Interpretation of the Constitution,* of
Vernon Louis Parrington's *Main Currents in American
Thought.*

The whole matter of imagination, indeed, invites a second
observation. A discussion of the sort we have been having must
perforce face up to the question of whether or not history is a
social science.

My own conviction is that history is *with* the social sciences but not really *of* them. History stands between the social sciences and the humanities. It canvasses both the real world of man and the world of his imagination. In this poise, history inclines toward the sense that our view of reality is also an imaginative one. In getting that view of reality, historians must, even as a condition of their art, seek the insight afforded by the best of social science. But, having done this, they will have qualified only as apprentices and journeymen. For their masterpiece, they must rise ultimately to the challenge of literature and philosophy. The most notable of our historians are men of letters and men who argued, without really proving, a set of values. In these attainments may be found the claim to greatness of George Bancroft, Francis Parkman, Henry Adams, and Charles Beard, to name the irrefutably outstanding among the American historians.

There is of course method to each of these men; each of them adheres to the dictates of historical science. But their histories go beyond method and science. What they say represents their remarkable ability to project themselves into the past and to illumine it with a light which is personal, subjective, imaginative. Distilling the past in a way which is utterly individual, casting the elements of human experience into a private mold, their history is in this way a form of poetry. As such, it has always transcended the rules and formulas of a science of society and, to my own way of thinking, always will.

23. *History as Human Behavior**

Samuel P. Hays

The study of history in both high schools and colleges, it seems to me, suffers from a lack of emphasis on the vital human quality of the past. It is concerned traditionally with the formal and outward aspects of events, and not with human experience, understanding, values, and action. This problem is the central theme of this paper. I hope primarily to suggest a number of ways in which we might approach more closely the human side of the past. By this I mean not simply ways of enhancing the "human interest" factor in history, but ways of systematically studying human experience and behavior so that solid and concrete generalizations emerge. My argument is that if we could develop this approach to history we would not only have a more significant story to tell, but would also arouse greater interest on the part of both high school and college students.

I

Perhaps the best example of formal history is the traditional political history which abounds in our textbooks. Here the major focus of organization centers around presidential administrations: nominating conventions, campaigns, cabinet meetings, the administration's legislative program and its treatment by Congress. This approach has been called "presidential history." Its main justification is not that it conforms to any major movements or changes in American society, but that it follows the rather accidental fact of our four-year presidential

* Reprinted with permission from *Iowa Journal of History*, LVIII (July, 1960), 193–206.

terms. It provides little room for an emphasis on political experience and behavior, nor does it give more than a brief insight into the ebb and flow of activity lying behind the outward events.

Economic history suffers from the same attention to the outward and formal, and the lack of attention to the dynamics of change. In most of our history books we learn about the rise of corporate combinations in the late nineteenth and early twentieth centuries. We describe the legal forms involved—the trust and the holding company—and we relate the number and size of combinations. But rarely do we go into the forces behind this. Rarely do we analyze the economic processes which led to the rise of such large combinations of capital. If we did this, we would spend less time talking about the number and size of combinations, and more about the way in which cheap transportation created, for the first time, a national market; the way in which a national market created, for the first time, intense competition for that market; the way in which producers all over the country tried to protect themselves against competition; and the way in which all economic segments of the nation began to take up collective effort to exercise control over market conditions. These economic processes are far more important than are figures about the number of combinations.

It is precisely this formal approach to history which makes history unsatisfactory to many students. Those who seek an analysis of human society often fail to find it in history and go elsewhere. These views stem from conversations with a great number of students about both their high school and their college history courses. I have come to the conclusion that the more a history course touches the human content of the past the more challenging and satisfying it is to the student. Those courses which are dull and boring seem to consist of memorization of the outward and formal facts of history; those which are more exciting involve a treatment of human experience, human understanding, and human values.

In my own teaching I have observed that the closer one approaches the human situation the more interest rises. I do not mean this in terms of the popular definition of "human interest," such as the last words of Nathan Hale, or the stock market manipulations of Jim Fisk and Jay Gould, or the illegitimate offspring of Grover Cleveland, or Coxey's army. I mean simply the systematic description of human experience, of the universal human situation faced by people in the past and which are faced by students in the present. I find, for example, that students react very positively to such a book as that by Oscar Handlin, *The Uprooted,* an account of the immigrant in America told from the point of view of the immigrant, an analysis of his experience of being uprooted from a traditional and stable European culture and abruptly entering a more mobile and traditionless society. Handlin's major contribution is that he sees history from the inside out. And this I think challenges students and captures their imagination, because all of us inevitably see life from the inside out.

Both of these general concerns point, it seems to me, in one direction—that history must be considered more in terms of human behavior. The reason that much of history is formal and unsatisfying is because the units of history we write and talk and teach about do not consist of types of human experience, thought, and behavior. By changing to this focus we can make history more meaningful from the point of view of the disinterested analyst, and also from the point of view of the student who will inevitably find some contact between his own experience and that of the past.

II

One important way in which we could make this change in focus is to shift attention from top-level affairs to grass-roots happenings. Most of our history is a description of events at the center of national politics, economic affairs, or intellectual life. This is true, for example, of the "presidential history" approach; it focuses on the activities of the office of the President and of Congress. This kind of history is easy to write because materials for it are usually available in a central place. And it is easy to teach because it is a simple way of giving a single focus to history. It is easier to talk about one President than about fifty governors; it is easier to describe the ideas of a few thinkers than of a large number of people. Yet, at the same time, it provides only a partial and limited view, and the limitations of the view can readily be realized once one focuses his attention closer to the grass-roots, to the state, the county, or municipal level. Evidence from this level indicates that top-level history not only leaves out many aspects of the past but often leads to the wrong conclusions.

Consider, for example, the period from 1877 to 1914. According to the traditional approach in history, the major development of the time was the so-called "trust" issue, the growth of business combinations, their influence in politics and government, and the reaction against them on the part of many segments of the community. Most of the chapters in our textbooks for this period are organized around some phase of this question, and evidence from the local or state level is selected to illustrate this national focus. The history of Iowa in the early twentieth century, for example, involves the Progressive revolt within the Republican party, described primarily as a reaction against railroad domination of Iowa politics, and considered to be merely another illustration of a national political trend.

But if one looks at evidence from grass-roots history for its own sake, and not as an illustration of national trends, he frequently comes to an altogether different conclusion. For example, an examination of the precinct voting patterns in Iowa from 1885 to 1918 shows that the matters which most aroused voters, which determined party affiliations, and which filled the local newspapers were not connected with the "trust question" but were largely cultural in nature. They were such questions as the use of foreign language, Sunday observance, and above all prohibition. Defined in terms of how people voted, which is about as close to the grass-roots as one can get, the "trust question" was relatively unimportant, but the prohibition issue was of vast importance. Party differences in voting patterns were cultural, not economic, in nature. If one can argue that a single issue was more important than any other issue in Iowa between 1885 and 1918 it was prohibition.

But prohibition was more than an issue; it was the most specific aspect of a general conflict between patterns of culture in Iowa which dominated the political views of the people of the state for many years. One of these cultural patterns we can call, for want of a better term, Pietism. It stressed strict standards of behavior derived from Puritan sources, especially Sunday observance, and prohibition of gambling, dancing, and, above all, drinking alcoholic beverages. It was evangelistic; it exhorted individuals to undergo a dramatic transformation in their personal lives, to be converted, and it sought to impose these standards of personal character on the entire community by public, legal action. But there were others, whose pattern of culture was altogether different, who resisted these views. They came from a different cultural background, and their religion consisted more of a sequence of rituals and observances through which one passed from birth to death, with the primary focus of religion being the observance of those practices. For many of them Puritan morals meant little; Germans, for example, were accustomed to the continental Sunday of relaxation in beer gardens or to using wine for communion services.

These cultural differences divided groups in Iowa, and the voting patterns follow, to a remarkable degree, the differences in cultural patterns. On the one hand were the native Americans, from English and Scotch extraction, the Norwegians and Swedes, and the German Methodists and Presbyterians. On the other hand were the Irish, Bohemian, and German Catholics and the German Lutherans. In county after county in Iowa the persistently strong Republican precincts from 1885 to 1914 are predominantly from the first group, and the persistently strong Democratic precincts are from the second. Consider, for example, the precincts in Carroll County, Iowa. The eastern tier of townships, Jasper, Glidden, Richland, and Union, all strong native American (77, 84, 83, and 91 per cent, respectively, in 1880), between 1887 and 1914 averaged 33, 26, 34, and 33 per cent, respectively for the Democratic gubernatorial candidate. In the northwestern part of the county, on the other hand, four townships, Kniest, Wheatland, Roselle, and Washington, all heavily German (91, 78, 95, and 80 per cent, respectively, in 1880) and all heavily Catholic, over the same period of time and for the same race averaged 82, 83, 80, and 73 per cent Democratic. In displaying real distinctions in voting patterns, Carroll County is typical of most Iowa counties.

These were persistent distinctions, and led frequently to the importance of such issues as prohibition and woman's suffrage, which was part and parcel of the prohibition movement. In some elections they produced rather violent shifts in voting sentiment. In fact, one can argue that the only violent shifts in voting behavior came when such issues were present. The most striking of these was the gubernatorial election of 1916 when the Republican candidate, William Lloyd Harding, was an avowed "wet" and the Democratic candidate, Edwin T. Meredith, was "bone dry." This reversed the traditional roles of the parties; as a result many traditionally Democratic precincts voted heavily Republican, and some traditionally Republican precincts voted Democratic. There was no gubernatorial election up to the depression of 1929 which stirred voters so deeply.

When one begins to examine grass-roots behavior through election data at the precinct level or through local newspapers, one sees immediately that it was this kind of issue that stirred people deeply, that determined their political attitudes. It was far more important than the trust issue. By using this approach one feels that he is approaching more closely the human content of politics. It is becoming increasingly clear to me that very little of our top-level politics is understandable unless one knows the grass-roots context in which to place the top-level events. And basically what this means is that we have to examine what people feel and think and experience, and see their political action as a product of those inner events.

III

A second important shift in thinking that we must undergo concerns our notion of the significance of the role of government in American life. No phenomenon has more preoccupied historians of recent America than has this one. But it is usually treated in such a way as to obscure rather than to illuminate the meaning of an increasing role of government. We have especially failed to distinguish between government as an end in itself, and government as a means to an end. All instances of increased federal functions, and all movements in that direction are considered by historians to be a part of the same historical trend, while all tendencies opposed to such federal functions are of a different development. "Presidential history" confirms this approach, for the ideology of top-level political battles is usually cast in terms of the desirability of more or less government. But these categories obscure the most important question, namely, what are the purposes to which government is put? History, it seems to me, should be organized around the goals of human action, not the techniques, around the ends rather than the means.

There are many cases in recent American history in which two tendencies, both of which increase the role of government and therefore appear to be of the same historical trend, may involve different and contradictory goals, and therefore be of quite different historical movements. Consider, for example, railroad regulation. The Hepburn Act establishing effective railroad regulation was passed in 1906. During the First World War the United States government operated the railroads under the United States Railroad Administration. After the war there was a debate over whether or not the railroads should be returned to their private owners. The debate culminated in the Transportation Act of 1920, by which the roads were returned. This Act, it has been argued, was a reversal of past trends; the logical extension of the spirit of the Hepburn Act would have been continued government ownership. The Transportation Act of 1920, on the other hand, was merely a part of the dominant private enterprise philosophy of the postwar era, of "the return to normalcy."

This reasoning is logical if one considers the problem purely as one of distinguishing between more or less government action. But the whole question becomes more complex when one asks: who wanted what and why? What groups were involved in the passage of both the Hepburn Act and the Transportation Act of 1920? Evidence concerning this problem discloses that the very groups which wanted more regulation in 1906 and fought for the Hepburn Act opposed continued government operation in 1920 and wanted the railroads returned to their private owners. In terms of the groups involved and their goals, then, the Transportation Act of 1920 with continued private ownership was not a reversal but a continuation of the tendencies behind the Hepburn Act. And if public ownership had become a reality, it would have been a sharp departure from the recent past.

The major force behind railroad regulation consisted of the organized shippers of the country, who wanted lower rates and better services. Although farmers constituted the voting support for the movement, the drive was led by merchants and manufacturers who shipped via railroad and who were organized in the Interstate Commerce Law Convention. After the passage of the Hepburn Act these groups used the machinery of the Interstate Commerce Commission to their advantage. Up until the First World War they were able to prevent attempts by both railroad owners and railroad labor to raise rates. But once the United States government took over the railroads and operated them, these advantages were lost. The powers of the Interstate Commerce Commission were suspended, and as a result the shippers lost a powerful friend at court. The railroads were placed in the hands of leaders in the industry who were brought into the Railroad Administration, and for the first time since the Hepburn Act the roads received substantial rate increases, and labor, in turn, received substantial wage increases. The shippers were unable to protest, for their machinery of appeal no longer existed. It was little wonder, therefore, that following the war shippers asked that railroads be returned to their private owners and that the powers of the Interstate Commerce Commission be restored. These were provided in the Transportation Act of 1920.

These events are easily traceable if one examines as evidence the ideas and actions of the groups themselves which wanted railroad control. In Iowa the two most active of these groups among farmers, for example, were the Farmers Grain Dealers Association of Iowa, a state-wide trade association of farmer-owned grain cooperatives, and the Corn Belt Meat Producers Association, an organization of car-lot shippers of cattle and hogs. Both were concerned with sales problems, and both used railroads heavily for shipping. The proceedings of their conventions and the correspondence of their executive secretaries provide abundant evidence of their shipping problems and of their dissatisfaction with the operations of the United States Railroad Administration. And yet, strangely enough, while historians have written much about such general farm organizations as the National Grange, the Farmers' Union, and the American Society of Equity, they have barely mentioned either the Grain Dealers or the Meat Producers. The reason, it seems to me, is because they cannot be readily used as a local illustration of a nationally-defined top-level political problem. And yet examination of their situation and their views on the state level helps enormously to redefine the character of national politics.

Government can be viewed most effectively by the historian if it is considered not as an end in itself, but as the context within which political struggles take place. All political groups in society contend for the control of the advantages which government has to offer: a shifting of the tax burden, positive financial aid, legal aid to restrict individual action where private groups cannot do so, or restrictions on competing groups. No one group seems to have a monopoly on the desire for positive government or for its elimination. The railroads, for example, were grateful for the stabilization of rates which the Interstate Commerce Commission provided. Consequently, the understanding of any particular government function must rest upon an analysis of the circumstances which give rise to that function, the groups which demand it, and the ends which will be served through it. And the categories in which we organize history must be in terms of those circumstances, groups, and goals, rather than the fact of government itself.

IV

An excellent opportunity for undertaking a grass-roots approach to history is provided by the use of election statistics. But this involves a different approach to the analysis of elections than we have used in the past. Elections are dealt with rather extensively in a "presidential history" approach, but usually only in terms of who won or who lost and by what percentage of the vote. Such an analysis is extremely limited, and yields very little understanding. It would be far more important to know how much change in voting sentiment had occurred since the last election, not just what percentage of the votes a winning candidate received. For the major fact in any election for the historian is change, and the amount of change usually determines the importance of the problem for study.

A "presidential history" approach may completely distort this whole question by emphasizing only the shift from one political party to another, while frequently the most important changes in voting sentiment occur without a change in party dominance. Suppose, for example, that the Democrats won the presidential election of 1948 by 50.1 per cent of the vote, and suppose that the Republicans in 1952 won also by 50.1 per cent. A complete change in party would have involved a change in Republican voting strength of only two-tenths of a percentage point. Suppose, further, that Eisenhower won in 1956 with 60.1 per cent of the vote. This victory involved no change in party, but an increase in 10 percentage points, or 50 times the shift in vote between 1948 and 1952. Which is the more important election? Where is the turning point? A "presidential history" approach would place the break at 1952, but in terms of voting change it would be 1956.

Many important shifts in voting behavior can be obscured not only by a "presidential history" approach, but also by failing to extend the analysis down to the grass-roots level. For example, Herbert Hoover won the presidential election of 1928 by a landslide margin. But one of the most significant facts of the election is that despite Hoover's victory, Al Smith, for the first time in the twenties, and perhaps for the first time since the Civil War, won for the Democratic party a majority of the votes in the nation's twelve largest cities. The Democrats had been gaining in the metropolitan areas in the early 1920's and by 1928 had won a slight majority. These facts have been brought out only in very recent years. They were hidden by the over-all election returns. But they point to the highly significant fact that the Democratic party was gaining strength in crucial areas of the country prior to the depression, and they open up a whole new understanding of the impact of cultural factors in politics in the twenties.

One could give many examples of the possibilities of going behind the results of a single election to see changes in polit-ical behavior, but perhaps a few drawn from Iowa politics would be most appropriate. Consider, for example, political changes since 1950 in the state and specifically in Des Moines. Politics in Des Moines since the early depression has revolved primarily around socio-economic factors, with the lower income groups constituting the center of strength of the Democratic party, and the upper income groups the Republican party. The line of division is very clear geographically; that part of Des Moines west of Harding Road is strongly Republican, and that part to the east is strongly Democratic.

Gubernatorial elections between 1946 and 1956 revealed this split in party majority very clearly, but they also revealed that while the Democratic candidates gained steadily in the county as a whole over that period, they gained most in the lower income areas east of Harding Road. On the other hand, they lost ground in the higher income areas to the west. For example, between 1946 and 1956, five of the precincts west of Harding Road, of the highest socio-economic level, regis-tered a Democratic loss of 19 percentage points, while six to the east of the lowest socio-economic level, registered a Demo-cratic gain of 23 percentage points. The trend, therefore, has been in opposite directions. This is somewhat unusual in elections, for it is more typical for the trend to be toward or away from a party in the same direction in all precincts, with a variation in the degree of the trend from precinct to precinct. A shift in opposite directions at the same time indicates a sharp and unusual cleavage of political interests.

Much of the same kind of problem can be illuminated by examining the voting behavior of precincts in Cedar Rapids since the depression of 1929. Here there are three major groups of voters. In the southwest part of the city are voters of

Bohemian descent who have been traditionally Democratic. To the east and northeast are voters of native American descent, for the most part, of middle and upper socio-economic levels, and traditionally Republican. To the northwest are working class groups largely of native-American extraction; these were strongly Republican up until the depression of 1929, largely because of the cultural issues of nationality, language, and custom which were sharp in Cedar Rapids during that time. But the depression produced a greater concern for economic issues and led to this northwest area of the city voting less and less like the northeast and more and more like the southwest. It has voted Democratic in gubernatorial races since 1944.

In both Des Moines and Cedar Rapids, therefore, one can observe a gradual shifting of political alignments around socio-economic differences. These factors are obscured merely by observing the party strength for the entire county. They can be brought out by examining the returns at the precinct level, which greatly add to our understanding of political behavior.

One type of election which sharply reveals the social and economic structure of a community is the so-called "nonpartisan" municipal contest. Stripped of the restraining influence of party discipline, these elections frequently bring out in full force latent intra-community tensions. Contests over the commission form of government, the so-called Des Moines plan, in Iowa in 1908 are excellent cases in point. In Des Moines, Cedar Rapids and Davenport the plan was pushed forward by the business and professional classes of the community on the one hand, and by native American moral reformers on the other in order to secure political power in municipal affairs and to carry out the various policies that they desired. In each city, however, major elements of the working class and immigrant communities vigorously opposed the plan because they interpreted it as a device to deprive them of political influence and to institute such policies as prohibition which they opposed. In Des Moines workingmen succeeded in defeating the "businessmen's slate" of candidates for the first commission government. In Cedar Rapids, the South-end Bohemian population fought, though unsuccessfully, the commission plan as an attempt by the inhabitants of "piety hill," the northern and eastern sections of the city, to secure control of municipal affairs. And in Davenport the Germans, fearing strict enforcement of anti-liquor laws, succeeded in defeating the proposal to inaugurate a commission government. Precinct and ward voting data in these contests, when related to nativity, religious and income factors, clearly brings out the forces involved in the election and the persistent cultural and socio-economic structure of the entire community.

Much, then, can be gained by using election returns as a device for studying political behavior and changes in that behavior. Perhaps the greatest opportunity this approach can provide in an over-all way is to give us a systematic method of dividing up the units of political history in terms other than presidential administrations. One can construct an index of political change by computing the percentage strength of a particular party in each election, for example, the Republican presidential vote, and plotting it on a graph. Or one can secure an index which reveals change every two years, rather than at four-year intervals, by plotting the party strength in Congress (congressional popular voting statistics are not yet compiled in usable form). Such a graph would provide a rough outline of political change somewhat like a business cycle does for economic change.

This kind of graph reveals several broad trends: (a) from 1874 to 1894 a stalemate between the two parties, with the Democrats winning four of five presidential elections by popular vote, but the Republicans winning three of the five by electoral vote, and with the Democrats winning the House of Representatives eight out of ten times and the Republicans controlling the Senate seven out of ten times; (b) 1894–1910, a period of Republican dominance; (c) a Democratic rise beginning in 1906, reaching a peak in 1914, and declining to a low point in 1920; (d) a Republican rise beginning in 1916, reaching a high plateau from 1920 to 1928, and declining to a low point in 1936; (e) a Democratic rise, beginning in 1924 in the cities, reaching a high point in 1936, and declining to a low point in 1946. These units of political history, it seems to me, are much more appropriate than are presidential administrations. It is curious that many problems which these units pose, such as the reason for the shift from stalemate between 1874 and 1894 to Republican dominance for sixteen years, have never been answered by historians primarily because the questions have never been asked. The value of developing units of voting behavior for study, then, is primarily one of bringing to our attention questions which have heretofore been obscured.

V

Each of these examples—the importance of cultural issues as opposed to the trust question, the analysis of the role of government as a means to an end, and the possibility of using election data to define problems in history—involves a refocusing of attention from the outward formal aspects of history toward the level of human behavior. Each constitutes an attempt to categorize history in terms of types of human experience, types of human understanding of the world, types of human values, and types of resulting human action. This is a group analysis of society in which one sorts out events in history in terms of social organization and behavior. It offers, it seems to me, a much fuller, a more satisfying, and a more provocative approach to the study and writing of history.

There are several factors, however, which make this approach difficult to undertake at the present time. One is the simple fact that few historical studies and many fewer textbooks are written from this point of view. Most texts are organized in a formal, descriptive style, often from the point of view of "presidential history." On the college level most texts have chapters on presidential administrations, with a few on economic or social history sandwiched in between. There is little attempt to integrate all this around patterns of behavior. High school texts, for the most part, follow the same general pattern.

On the other hand, there is considerable reading material which does have a different slant and which can be used. One which I have already mentioned is Oscar Handlin's *The Uprooted*. A book which provides a good picture of the role of cultural groups in political life is Samuel Lubell's *The Future of American Politics*. Two excellent studies of state political life which touch the grass roots closely are V. O. Key, *American State Politics*, and Gordon Baker, *Rural Versus Urban Political Power*. An excellent case study of the goals implicit in public action is Stephen Kemp Bailey, *Congress Makes a Law*, a study of the political forces behind the Full Employment Act of 1946. The movements behind the Interstate Commerce Act of 1887 are examined in Lee Benson, *Merchants, Farmers and Railroads*. These, of course, are only a few of a number of books which provide a slant toward history more in terms of human behavior.

But there is a far more important roadblock which grass-roots history faces, namely, the difficulty in resisting prevailing public assumptions about what ought to be taught in history courses. A behavioral approach immediately raises questions involving group differences in society, differences between ethnic, religious, or socio-economic groups. And in our society it is not considered legitimate to talk about such differences; instead we are expected to paint a picture of a unified, all-community spirit to support a kind of community patriotism and loyalty. Every community resists introspection into its own social, economic, and political structure, and equally resists history which examines the same questions.

For example, would teachers in Carroll, Allamakee, Winnishiek, or Jones counties, in Davenport, Cedar Rapids, or Des Moines feel free to delve into the whole range of cultural and economic differences which have long existed there and which throughout the years have determined the course of politics? How freely does one in Davenport discuss in the classroom the full implications of cultural conflict represented by the different names "Cork Hill" and "Sauerkraut Hill" which used to describe the Irish and German areas, east and west of Brady Street? How freely in Des Moines does one talk about the political differences between Grand Avenue and the downtown area, especially the "bottoms" at the junction of the Des Moines and the Raccoon rivers, and the way in which urban reform for over sixty years has pitted upper-class business and professional people against lower-class laboring groups? How freely can one in Carroll County discuss the religious and cultural differences between the Anglo-Saxon, Protestant eastern tier of townships and the remaining German Catholic townships? Or how freely in almost any small town can one discuss the "pecking order" among the churches, or the community hierarchy of power and control, in the face of the ideology that the community is one big happy family? Two sociologists, Arthur J. Vidich and Joseph Bensman, have done just that in a study called *Small Town in Mass Society*. Their approach would be useful in examining any Iowa small town, past or present, but it brings to light factors in social structure and human behavior which community boosters usually do not appreciate.

And yet the attempt to skip quickly over such fundamental human features of history only does the study of history a disservice, and in my view is one reason why history frequently repels rather than attracts students. Most students know first hand the realities of social and community life, enough to know what is legitimate to talk about and what is not. To obscure these realities in history and social studies courses is to earn a reputation for talking about the unimportant and to court a pose of hypocrisy in the eyes of students. The more we refuse to get down to the human level of history at the grass roots, the more history will be looked upon as dealing only with the formal and the outward and will be shunned. The more we explore the realities of human life, on the other hand, the more students will look upon history as a significant study worth their time and effort.

24. The Next Assignment*†

WILLIAM L. LANGER

Anyone who, like myself, has the honor to serve as president of this association and to address it on the occasion of its annual meeting may be presumed to have devoted many years to the historical profession, to have taught many successive college generations, to have trained numerous young scholars, and to have written at least some books and articles. The chances are great that he has reached those exalted levels of the academic life which involve so many administrative and advisory duties, as well as such expenditure of time and energy in seeing people, in writing recommendations, and in reading the writings of others that he is most unlikely ever again to have much time to pursue his own researches. Nonetheless, his long and varied experience and his ever broadening contacts with others working in many diverse fields have probably sharpened his understanding of the problems of his own profession and enhanced his awareness of the many lacunae in our knowledge of the world and of mankind, both in the past and in the present. It would seem altogether fitting, therefore, that I, for one, should make use of this occasion not so much for reflection on the past achievements of the profession (which is what might be expected of a historian), as for specu-

* Reprinted with permission from *The American Historical Review*, LXIII (January, 1958), 283–304.

† I have benefited greatly from long discussions of this problem with my brother, Dr. Walter C. Langer. I have also to thank Professors Talcott Parsons and Raymond A. Bauer, for stimulating comments on an early draft of the address, and Professors James C. Diggory and A. Pepitone, of the University of Pennsylvania, for allowing me to read their unpublished report on "Behavior and Disaster."

lation about its needs and its future—that is, about the directions which historical study might profitably take in the years to come.

I am sure to sense, at this juncture, a certain uneasiness in my audience, for historians, having dedicated their lives to the exploration and understanding of the past, are apt to be suspicious of novelty and ill-disposed toward crystal-gazing. In the words of my distinguished predecessor, they lack the "speculative audacity" of the natural scientists, those artisans of brave hypotheses. This tendency on the part of historians to become buried in their own conservatism strikes me as truly regrettable. What basically may be a virtue tends to become a vice, locking our intellectual faculties in the molds of the past and preventing us from opening new horizons as our cousins in the natural sciences are constantly doing. If progress is to be made we must certainly have new ideas, new points of view, and new techniques. We must be ready, from time to time, to take flyers into the unknown, even though some of them may prove wide of the mark. Like the scientists, we can learn a lot from our own mistakes, and the chances are that, if we persist, each successive attempt may take us closer to the target. I should therefore like to ask myself this evening what direction is apt to lead to further progress in historical study; what direction, if I were a younger man, would claim my interest and attention; in short, what might be the historian's "next assignment."

We are all keenly aware of the fact that during the past half century the scope of historical study has been vastly extended. The traditional political-military history has become more comprehensive and more analytical and has been reinforced by researches into the social, economic, intellectual, scientific, and other aspects of the past, some of them truly remote from what used to be considered history. So far has this development gone that I find it difficult to envisage much further horizontal expansion of the area of investigation.

There is, however, still ample scope for penetration in depth and I, personally, have no doubt that the "newest history" will be more intensive and probably less extensive. I refer more specifically to the urgently needed deepening of our historical understanding through exploitation of the concepts and findings of modern psychology. And by this, may I add, I do not refer to classical or academic psychology which, so far as I can detect, has little bearing on historical problems, but rather to psychoanalysis and its later developments and variations as included in the terms "dynamic" or "depth psychology."

In the course of my reading over the years I have been much impressed by the prodigious impact of psychoanalytic doctrine on many, not to say most, fields of human study and expression. Of Freud himself it has been said that "he has in large part created the intellectual climate of our time." [1] "Almost alone," remarks a recent writer in the *Times Literary Supplement,* "he revealed the deepest sources of human endeavor and remorselessly pursued their implications for the individual and society." [2] Once the initial resistance to the recognition of unconscious, irrational forces in human nature was overcome, psychoanalysis quickly became a dominant influence in psychiatry, in abnormal psychology, and in personality study. The field of medicine is feeling its impact not only in the area of psychosomatic illness, but in the understanding of the doctor-patient relationship. Our whole educational system and the methods of child-training have been modified in the light of its findings. For anthropology it has opened new and wider vistas by providing for the first time "a theory of raw human nature" and by suggesting an explanation of otherwise incomprehensible cultural traits and practices. It has done much also to revise established notions about religion and has given a great impetus to pastoral care and social work. The problems of mythology and sociology have been illuminated by its insights, and more recently its influence has been strongly felt in penology, in political science, and even in economics, while in the arts almost every major figure of the past generation has been in some measure affected by it.[3]

[1] "Freud and the Arts," London *Times Literary Supplement,* May 4, 1956.
[2] *Ibid.* See also Abram Kardiner, *The Psychological Frontiers of Society* (New York, 1945), p. 11; Goodwin Watson, "Clio and Psyche: Some Interrelations of Psychology and History," in *The Cultural Approach to History,* ed. Caroline Ware (New York, 1940), pp. 34–47; Hans W. Gruhle, *Geschichtsschreibung und Psychologie* (Bonn, 1953), p. 7; *The Social Sciences in Historical Study,* Social Science Research Council Bull. No. 64 (New York, 1954), pp. 61 ff.
[3] See the article by Henry W. Brosin, "A Review of the Influence of Psychoanalysis on Current Thought," in *Dynamic Psychiatry,* ed. Franz Alexander and Helen Ross (Chicago, 1952), pp. 508–53; Ernest Jones, *What Is Psychoanalysis?* (new ed., New York, 1948), pp. 80 ff.; Iago Galdston, ed.,

Despite this general and often profound intellectual and artistic reorientation since Freud published his first epoch-making works sixty years ago, historians have, as a group, maintained an almost completely negative attitude toward the teachings of psychoanalysis. Their lack of response has been due, I should think, less to constitutional obscurantism than to the fact that historians, as disciples of Thucydides, have habitually thought of themselves as psychologists in their own right. They have indulged freely in psychological interpretation, and many no doubt have shared the fear that the humanistic appreciation of personality, as in poetry or drama, might be irretrievably lost through the application of a coldly penetrating calculus.[4] Many considered the whole psychoanalytic doctrine too biological and too deterministic, as well as too conjectural, and they were, furthermore, reluctant to recognize and deal with unconscious motives and irrational forces. Psychoanalysis, on the other hand, was still a young science and therefore lacked the prestige to make historians acquire a guilt-complex about not being more fully initiated into its mysteries.[5] Almost without exception, then, they have stuck to the approach and methods of historicism, restricting them-

---

Freud and Contemporary Culture (New York, 1957). See also J. A. Gengerelli, "Dogma or Discipline?" *Saturday Review,* Mar. 23, 1957; Gardner Murphy, "The Current Impact of Freud upon Psychology," *Amer. Psychologist,* XI (1956), 663–72; A. Irving Hallowell, "Culture, Personality and Society," in *Anthropology Today,* ed. A. L. Kroeber (Chicago, 1953), pp. 597–620; Clyde Kluckhohn, "The Influence of Psychiatry on Anthropology in America during the Past One Hundred Years," in *One Hundred Years of American Psychiatry,* ed. J. K. Hall (New York, 1944), pp. 589–618 and "Politics, History and Psychology," *World Politics,* VIII (1955), 112–23; Harold D. Lasswell, "Impact of Psychoanalytic Thinking on the Social Sciences," in *The State of the Social Sciences,* ed. Leonard D. White (Chicago, 1956), pp. 84–115; R. Money-Kyrle, *Superstition and Society* (London, 1939); Walter A. Weisskopf, *The Psychology of Economics* (Chicago, 1955); Erich Fromm, *Psychoanalysis and Religion* (New Haven, 1950); F. J. Hoffman, *Freudianism and the Literary Mind* (Baton Rouge, 1945); Louis Schneider, *The Psychoanalyst and the Artist* (New York, 1950).

4 Raymond B. Cattell, *An Introduction to Personality Study* (London, 1950), pp. 13–14. H. D. Lasswell, *Psychopathology and Politics* (Chicago, 1930), p. 11, refers to "the obscurantist revulsion against submitting the sacred mystery of personality to the coarse indignity of exact investigation." Keats is said to have feared that spectrum analysis would ruin his enjoyment of the rainbow. See Jones, *What is Psychoanalysis?* pp. 12 ff.

5 Sidney Ratner, "The Historian's Approach to Psychology," *Jour. Hist. Ideas,* II (1941), 95–109.

selves to recorded fact and to strictly rational motivation.[6] So impervious was the profession as a whole to the new teaching that an inquiry into the influence of psychoanalysis on modern thought, written a few years ago, made no mention whatever of history.[7]

This is as remarkable as it is lamentable, for, on the very face of it, psychoanalysis would seem to have much to contribute to the solution of historical problems. Many years of clinical work by hundreds of trained analysts have by now fortified and refined Freud's original theory of human drives, the conflicts to which they give rise, and the methods by which they are repressed or diverted. Psychoanalysis has long since ceased being merely a therapy and has been generally recognized as a theory basic to the study of the human personality. How can it be that the historian, who must be as much or more concerned with human beings and their motivation than with impersonal forces and causation, has failed to make use of these findings? Viewed in the light of modern depth psychology, the homespun, common-sense psychological interpretations of past historians, even some of the greatest, seem woefully inadequate, not to say naïve.[8] Clearly the time has come for us to reckon with a doctrine that strikes so close to the heart of our own discipline.[9]

Since psychoanalysis is concerned primarily with the emtional life of the individual, its most immediate application is

[6] Edward N. Saveth, "The Historian and the Freudian Approach to History," *New York Times Book Review*, Jan. 1, 1956; Gruhle, *Geschichtsschreibung und Psychologie*, pp. 116 ff.; Richard L. Schoenwald, "Historians and the Challenge of Freud," *Western Humanities Rev.*, X (1956), 99–108.

[7] Brosin, "Review of Influence of Psychoanalysis on Current Thought."

[8] Gruhle, *op. cit.*, pp. 127 ff., cites a number of instances from the writings of eminent German historians, and Max Horkheimer, "Geschichte und Psychologie," *Zeitschrift für Sozialforschung*, I (1932), 125–44, argues the complete inadequacy of the psychological concepts of the classical economists. Alfred M. Tozzer, "Biography and Biology," in *Personality in Nature, Society, and Culture*, ed. Clyde Kluckhohn and H. A. Murray (2d ed., New York, 1953), pp. 226–39, plays havoc with the simple-minded biological twist in much biographical writing.

[9] This thought is more or less explicitly expressed by Louis Gottschalk, "The Historian and the Historical Document," in *The Use of Personal Documents in History, Anthropology and Sociology*, Social Science Research Council Bull. No. 53 (New York, 1945), and in *The Social Sciences in Historical Study*. See also Sir Lewis Namier, "Human Nature in Politics," in his *Personalities and Powers* (London, 1955); Schoenwald, "Historians and the Challenge of Freud."

in the field of biography. Freud himself here showed the way, first in his essay on Leonardo da Vinci (1910) and later in his analytical study of Dostoevsky (1928). He was initially impressed by the similarity between some of the material produced by a patient in analysis and the only recorded childhood recollection of the Italian artist. With this fragmentary memory as a starting point, Freud studied the writings and artistic productions of Leonardo and demonstrated how much light could be shed on his creative and scientific life through the methods of analysis. No doubt he erred with respect to certain points of art history. Quite possibly some of his deductions were unnecessarily involved or farfetched. Nonetheless, recent critics have testified that he was able, "thanks to his theory and method, and perhaps even more to his deep sympathy for the tragic and the problematic in Leonardo, to pose altogether new and important questions about his personality, questions which were unsuspected by earlier writers and to which no better answer than Freud's has yet been given." [10]

The striking novelty and the startling conclusions of Freud's essay on Leonardo had much to do with precipitating the flood of psychoanalytic or, better, pseudo-psychoanalytic biographical writing during the 1920's. Almost all of this was of such a low order—ill-informed, sensational, scandalizing—that it brought the entire Freudian approach into disrepute. I have no doubt that this, in turn, discouraged serious scholars —the historians among them—from really examining the possibilities of the new teachings. Only within the last generation has the situation begun to change. The basic concepts of psychoanalysis, such as the processes of repression, identification, projection, reaction formation, substitution, displacement, and sublimation, have become more firmly established through clinical work and have at the same time increasingly become part of our thinking. Meanwhile, concerted efforts have been made to build up systematic personality and character study on a psychoanalytic basis and the so-called neo-Freudians, advancing beyond the narrowly environmental factors, have done much to develop the significance of constitutional and cultural influences.[11]

10 Meyer Shapiro, "Leonardo and Freud: An Art-Historical Study," *Jour. Hist. Ideas*, XVII (1956), 147–78, and other critics there cited.

11 Fromm, "Die psychoanalytische Charakterologie und ihre Bedeutung für die Sozialpsychologie," *Zeits. f. Sozialforschung*, I (1932), 253–77, and *Psy-*

While recognized scholars in related fields, notably in political science, have begun to apply psychoanalytic principles to the study of personality types and their social role, historians have for the most part approved of the iron curtain between their own profession and that of the dynamic psychologists. It is, indeed, still professionally dangerous to admit any addiction to such unorthodox doctrine.[12] Even those who are in general intrigued by the potentialities of psychoanalysis are inclined to argue against its application to historical problems. They point out that evidence on the crucial early years of an individual's life is rarely available and that, unlike the practicing analyst, the historian cannot turn to his subject and help him revive memories of specific events and relationships. To this it may be answered that the historian, on whatever basis he is operating, is always suffering from lack of data. Actually there is often considerable information about the family background of prominent historical personalities and the sum total of evidence about their careers is in some cases enormous. Furthermore, the experiences of earliest childhood are no longer rated as important for later development as was once the case, and the historian, if he cannot deal with his subject as man to man, at least has the advantage of surveying his whole career and being able to observe the functioning of significant forces.[13] In any event we historians must, if we are to retain our self-respect, believe that we can do better with the available evidence than the untrained popular biographer to whom we have so largely abandoned the field.

The historian is, of course, less interested in the individual as such than in the impact of certain individuals upon the

---

chology and Religion, pp. 10 ff.; Karen Horney, *The Neurotic Personality of Our Time* (New York, 1937), chap. 1; Franz Alexander, *Fundamentals of Psychoanalysis* (New York, 1948), chap. VI; Ralph Linton, *The Cultural Development of Personality* (New York, 1945); Kardiner, *Psychological Frontiers of Society*, esp. chap. XIV; Gerald S. Blum, *Psychoanalytic Theories of Personality* (New York, 1953); Gordon W. Allport, *Becoming: Basic Considerations for a Psychology of Personality* (New Haven, 1955); Georges Friedmann, "Psychoanalysis and Sociology," *Diogenes*, No. 14 (1956), 17–35.

[12] Bernard Brodie, in his review of the excellent study of *Woodrow Wilson and Colonel House* (New York, 1957) by Alexander and Juliette George, notes that the authors, while using very effectively the concepts of psychoanalysis, are scrupulous not to mention the fact. "A Psychoanalytic Interpretation of Woodrow Wilson," *World Politics*, IX (1957), 413–22.

[13] Gruhle, *Geschichtsschreibung und Psychologie*, pp. 127 ff.

society of their time and, beyond that, in the behavior of men as members of the group, society, or culture. This leads us into the domain of social or collective psychology, a subject on which much has been written during the past twenty-five years, especially in this country, but in which progress continues to be slight because of the difficulty of distinguishing satisfactorily between large groups and small groups, between organized and unorganized aggregations, between such vague collectivities as the crowd, the mob, and the mass.[14] Much certainly remains to be done in this area, especially in the elaboration of a theory to bridge the gap between individual and collective psychology.

Freud himself became convinced, at an early date, that his theories might have a certain applicability to historical and cultural problems.[15] He accepted the conclusions of Gustave Le Bon's well-known study of the psychology of crowds (1895) and recognized that a group may develop "a sort of collective mind." [16] As the years went by, his clinical work led him to the conclusion that there were close parallels between the development of the individual and of the race. Thus, the individual's unconscious mind was, in a sense, the repository of the past experiences of his society, if not of mankind.[17] In his most daring and provocative works, *Totem and Taboo* (1913) and his last book, *Moses and Monotheism* (1939), Freud tried to determine the effect of group experience on the formation of a collective group mind.

Anthropologists, like historians, will probably continue to reject Freud's historical ventures as too extravagantly speculative, but the fact remains that anthropological and sociological researches suggest ever more definitely that certain basic drives and impulses, as identified by Freud, appear in all cultures and that the differences between cultures derive largely from varying methods of dealing with these drives.[18]

14 Gustave Le Bon, *La psychologie des foules* was published in 1895. The earliest texts, those of William McDougall, *An Introduction to Social Psychology*, and of Edward A. Ross, *Social Psychology*, were first published in 1908. See M. Brewster Smith, "Some Recent Texts in Social Psychology," *Psychological Bull.*, L (1953), 150–59.

15 Freud's letter to C. G. Jung, July 5, 1910, quoted in Ernest Jones, *The Life and Work of Sigmund Freud*, II (New York, 1955), 448–49.

16 Freud, *Group Psychology and the Analysis of the Ego* (New York, 1921).

17 Jones, *What is Psychoanalysis?* pp. 20 ff

18 Geza Roheim, *Psychoanalysis and Anthropology* (New York, 1950).

Furthermore, social psychologists are increasingly aware of the similarity in the operation of irrational forces in the individual and in society.[19] Everett D. Martin, an early but unusually discerning student of the subject, noted in 1920 that the crowd, like our dream life, provides an outlet for repressed emotions: "It is as if all at once an unspoken agreement were entered into whereby each member might let himself go, on condition that he approved the same thing in all the rest." A crowd, according to Martin, "is a device for indulging ourselves in a kind of temporary insanity by all going crazy together." [20] Similarly, Freud's erstwhile disciple, C. G. Jung, has characterized recent political mass movements as "psychic epidemics, i.e., mass psychoses," and others have noted that the fears and rages of mass movements are clearly the residue of childish emotions.[21]

All this, as aforesaid, still requires further exploration. It does seem, however, that we shall have to learn to reckon with the concept of "collective mentality," even on the unconscious level, and that the traits of that mentality—normally submerged and operative only in association with others or in specific settings—can best be studied as a part of, or extension of, individual psychology. That is to say that progress in social psychology probably depends on ever more highly refined analysis of the individual—his basic motivations, his attitudes, beliefs, hopes, fears, and aspirations.[22]

Perhaps I may digress at this point to remind you of Georges Lefebvre's long-standing interest and concern with the character and role of mobs and crowds in the French Revolution, and especially of his impressive study of the mass hysteria of 1789 known as "The Great Fear." Although Lefebvre thought Le Bon superficial and confused, he was convinced by his own researches that there was such a thing as a "collective mentality." Indeed, he considered it the true causal link be-

---

[19] Kluckhohn, "The Impact of Freud on Anthropology," in *Freud and Contemporary Culture*, pp. 66–72.

[20] *The Behavior of Crowds* (New York, 1920), pp. 35–36. Martin was well versed in the psychoanalytical literature of his time.

[21] Jung, quoted by Ira Progoff, *Jung's Psychology and Its Social Meaning* (New York, 1953), p. ix; Erik H. Erikson, "The First Psychoanalyst," *Yale Rev.*, XLVI (1956), 40–62; Melitta Schmideberg, "Zum Verständnis massenpyschologischer Erscheinungen," *Imago*, XXI (1935), 445–57.

[22] See esp. Fromm, "Über Methode und Aufgabe einer analytischen Sozialpsychologie," *Zeits. f. Sozialforschung*, I (1932), 28–54.

tween the origins and the effects of major crises.[23] Without specific reference to psychoanalytic concepts, Lefebvre arrived at conclusions altogether consonant with those of modern psychology. His truly impressive studies in a sense prefaced the more recent analyses of totalitarian movements which, in my estimation, have so clearly demonstrated the vast possibilities that have been opened to social scientists by the findings of dynamic psychology.[24]

As historians we must be particularly concerned with the problem whether major changes in the psychology of a society or culture can be traced, even in part, to some severe trauma suffered in common, that is, with the question whether whole communities, like individuals, can be profoundly affected by some shattering experience. If it is indeed true that every society or culture has a "unique psychological fabric," deriving at least in part from past common experiences and attitudes, it seems reasonable to suppose that any great crisis, such as famine, pestilence, natural disaster, or war, should leave its mark on the group, the intensity and duration of the impact depending, of course, on the nature and magnitude of the crisis. I hasten to say in advance that I do not, of course, imagine the psychological impact of such crises to be uniform for all members of the population, for if modern psychology has demonstrated anything it is the proposition that in any given situation individuals will react in widely diverse ways, depending on their constitution, their family background, their early experiences, and other factors. But these varying responses are apt to be reflected chiefly in the immediate effects of the catastrophe. Over the long term (which is of greater

23 Lefebvre, "Foules révolutionnaires," in his *Études sur la Révolution Française* (Paris, 1954), pp. 271–87, and *La grande peur de 1789* (Paris, 1932). Philip Reiff, "The Origins of Freud's Political Psychology," *Jour. Hist. Ideas*, XVII (1956), 233–49, is equally hard on Le Bon.

24 To mention a few titles: Nathan Leites, *A Study of Bolshevism* (Glencoe, Ill., 1953); Gabriel A. Almond, *et al., The Appeals of Communism* (Princeton, 1954); Hannah Arendt, *The Origins of Totalitarianism* (New York, 1951); the essay by Henry Pachter in *The Third Reich,* ed. M. Baumont, J. H. E. Fried, and E. Vermeil (New York, 1955) and the discussion of it by Carl E. Schorske, "A New Look at the Nazi Movement," *World Politics,* IX (1956), 88–97. See also Hadley Cantril, *The Psychology of Social Movements* (New York, 1941), for a discussion of various modern mass movements, and Raymond A. Bauer, "The Psycho-Cultural Approach to Soviet Studies," *World Politics,* VII (1954), 119–32, for a critical review of several analyses of Soviet society.

interest to the historian) it seems likely that the group would react in a manner most nearly corresponding to the underlying requirements of the majority of its members, in other words, that despite great variations as between individuals there would be a dominant attitudinal pattern.

I admit that all this is hypothetical and that we are here moving into unexplored territory, but allow me to examine a specific problem which, though remote from the area of my special competence, is nevertheless one to which I have devoted much study and thought. Perhaps I may begin by recalling Freud's observation that contemporary man, living in a scientific age in which epidemic disease is understood and to a large extent controlled, is apt to lose appreciation of the enormous, uncomprehended losses of life in past generations, to say nothing of the prolonged and widespread emotional strain occasioned by such disasters.[25] Some exception must be made here for historians of the ancient world who, since the days of Niebuhr, have concerned themselves with the possible effects of widespread disease and high mortality on the fate of the Mediterranean civilizations. Some have made a strong case for the proposition that malaria, which seems to have first appeared in Greece and Italy in the fourth or fifth centuries B.C., soon became endemic and led on the one hand to serious debilitation, sloth, and unwillingness to work, and on the other to excitability, brutality, and general degradation. Recent researches suggest that malaria may have been one of the main causes of the collapse of the Etruscan civilization and may have accounted, at least in part, for the change in Greek character after the fourth century, especially for the growing lack of initiative, the prevalent cowardice, and the increasing trend toward cruelty. With reference to the fate of the Roman Empire, Professor Arthur Boak has recently reexamined the striking loss of population in the third and fourth centuries A.D. and has attributed it largely to the great epidemics of A.D. 165–180 and 250–280, thus reaffirming the view of Niebuhr and others that the Empire never really recovered from these tragic visitations.[26]

[25] Freud, "Thoughts for the Times on War and Death" (1915), in *Collected Papers* (London, 1924–1934), IV, No. 17.

[26] W. H. S. Jones, *Dea Febris: A Study of Malaria in Ancient Italy* (n. p., n. d.) and *Malaria and Greek History* (Manchester, 1909); Jones, Major R. Ross, and G. G. Ellet, *Malaria, a Neglected Factor in the History of Greece*

The literature on these and subsequent epidemics is, however, devoted largely to their medical and sanitational aspects, or at most to their economic and social effects. My primary interest, as I have said, is with the possible long-range psychological repercussions. To study these I think we may well pass over the great plague of Athens in 430 B.C., so vividly reported by Thucydides, and the so-called plague of Justinian of the sixth century A.D., not because they were unimportant but because there is much more voluminous and instructive information about the Black Death of 1348–1349 and the ensuing period of devastating disease.

Western Europe seems to have been relatively free from major epidemics in the period from the sixth to the fourteenth century and it may well be that the revival of trade and the growth of towns, with their congestion and lack of sanitation, had much to do with the spread and establishment of the great mortal diseases like plague, typhus, syphilis, and influenza.[27] At any rate, the Black Death was worse than anything experienced prior to that time and was, in all probability, the greatest single disaster that has ever befallen European mankind. In most localities a third or even a half of the population was lost within the space of a few months, and it is important to remember that the great visitation of 1348–1349 was only the beginning of a period of pandemic disease with a continuing frightful drain of population. It is hardly an exaggeration to say that for three hundred years Europe was ravaged by one disease or another, or more usually by several simultaneously, the serious outbreaks coming generally at intervals of five to ten years.[28] Professor Lynn Thorndike, who thirty years ago

and Rome (Cambridge, 1907); Nello Toscanelli, La malaria nell'antichità e la fine degli Etrutschi (Milan, 1927), esp. pp. 237 ff.; A. E. R. Boak, Manpower Shortage and the Fall of the Roman Empire in the West (Ann Arbor, Mich., 1955).

27 Bernard M. Lersch, Geschichte der Volksseuchen (Berlin, 1896), pp. 52 ff.; L. Fabian Hirst, The Conquest of Plague (Oxford, 1953), p. 10. It is highly likely that the arrival of rats in Europe in the twelfth century had an important bearing on the spread of bubonic plague. See Hans Zinsser, Rats, Lice and History (Boston, 1935), pp. 195 ff.; Major Greenwood, Epidemics and Crowd-Diseases (New York, 1937), pp. 289 ff.

28 August Hirsch, Handbook of Geographical and Historical Pathology, trans. Charles Creighton (London, 1883–1885), I, chap. x; Georg Sticker, Abhandlungen aus der Seuchengeschichte und Seuchenlehre, I, Die Pest (Giessen, 1908), pp. 74 ff.; Hirst, Conquest of Plague, p. 13; Josiah C. Rus-

wrote in the *American Historical Review* of the blight of pestilence on early modern civilization, pointed out that the period of greatest affliction was that of the Renaissance, and especially the years from about 1480 until 1540, during which period frequent severe outbreaks of bubonic plague were reinforced by attacks of typhus fever and by the onset of the great epidemic of syphilis, to say nothing of the English Sweat (probably influenza) which repeatedly devastated England before invading the Continent in 1529. The bubonic plague began to die out in Western Europe only in the late seventeenth century, to disappear almost completely after the violent outbreak at Marseilles in 1720. But the Balkans and Middle East continued to suffer from it until well into the nineteenth century and the pandemic that broke out in India in the 1890's was evidently comparable to the Black Death in terms of mortality and duration.[29]

The extensive records of the Black Death have been long and carefully studied, not only with reference to their medical aspects, but also in connection with the economic and social

---

sell, *British Medieval Population* (Albuquerque, N. Mex., 1948), pp. 2, 14 ff.; Lynn Thorndike, "The Blight of Pestilence on Early Modern Civilization," *Amer. Hist. Rev.*, XXXII (1927), 455–74; C. W. Previté-Orton, *Cambridge Medieval History* (Cambridge, 1932), introd.; David A. Stewart, "Disease and History," *Ann. Medical Hist.*, N. S., VII (1935), 351–71; Herman B. Allyn, "The Black Death, Its Social and Economic Results," *ibid.*, VII (1925), 226–36; the excellent, succinct review by Yves Renouard, "Conséquences et intérêt de démographique de la peste noire de 1348," *Population* [Paris], III (1948), 459–66, and "La peste noire de 1348–1350," *Rev. de Paris* (Mar., 1950), 107–19. According to Charles Mullett, *The Bubonic Plague and England* (Lexington, Ky., 1956), p. 18, there were no less than twenty attacks in England in the course of the fifteenth century.

29 Hirsch, *Handbook . . . Pathology*, I, chaps. III, X, XI; II, chap. II; Justus F. K. Hecker, *The Epidemics of the Middle Ages*, trans. B. G. Babington (London, 1844), pp. 188 ff.; Charles Creighton, *A History of Epidemics in Britain* (Cambridge, 1891), I, chap. VIII; Hermann Meyer, "Zur Geschichte der Pest im 15. und 16. Jahrundert," *Schauinsland*, XXVIII (1901), 13–32; Hirst, *Conquest of Plague*, p. 16. It is highly likely that the replacement of the black rat by the brown rat in Europe in the early eighteenth century had an important bearing on the decline of the plague, since the black rat was much more domesticated than the brown (see Zinsser, *op. cit.*, pp. 195 ff.), and it may well be that the growing severity of the European climate, beginning with the late sixteenth century, may have reduced the reproduction rate of the rat flea which is the carrier of the plague bacillus. See Gustaf Utterström, "Climate Fluctuations and Population Problems in Early Modern History," *Scandinavian Econ. Hist. Rev.*, III (1955), 3–47.

effects of so sudden and substantial a loss of population. The English population is estimated to have fallen from 3,700,000 in 1348 to 2,100,000 in 1400, the mortality rates of the period 1348–1375 far exceeding those of modern India. While the figures for continental countries are less complete, the available data suggests that the losses were comparable.[30] Cities and towns suffered particularly, but in some areas as many as 40 per cent of the villages and hamlets were abandoned, the survivors joining with those of other settlements or moving to the depopulated towns where opportunity beckoned.[31] Although a generation ago there was a tendency, especially among English historians, to minimize the social effects of the Black Death, more recent writers like G. G. Coulton, for example, acknowledge that the great epidemic, if it did not evoke entirely new forces, did vastly accelerate those already operative.[32] The economic progress of Europe, which had been

[30] Julius Beloch, "Bevölkerungsgeschichte Europas im Mittelalter," *Zeits. f. Sozialwissenschaft*, III (1900), 405–23; Russell, *British Medieval Population*, pp. 263 ff., 375, and "Medieval Population," *Social Forces*, XV (1937), 503–11; Renouard, "Conséquences . . . de la peste noire"; Maxim Kowalewsky, *Die ökonomische Entwicklung Europas* (Berlin, 1911), V, 277 ff., 321 ff., 362 ff., 400 ff.

[31] On the desertion of villages and the depopulation of the countryside see Francis A. Gasquet, *The Great Pestilence* (London, 1893), pp. 28 ff., 54, 68, and chaps. IX, X, *passim*; Creighton, *History of Epidemics*, I, 122, 177, 191; Maurice Beresford, *The Lost Villages of England* (London, 1954) who, however, attributes the abandonment of villages to increasing enclosures for grazing, at least in the first instance. By far the best treatments are those of Friedrich Lütge, *Deutsche Sozial-und Wirtschaftsgeschichte* (Berlin, 1952), pp. 144 ff., and Wilhelm Abel, *Die Wüstungen des ausgehenden Mittelalters* (2d ed. Stuttgart, 1955).

[32] So far as Germany is concerned the reaction to exaggerated claims was first expressed by Robert Hoeniger, *Der Schwarz Tod in Deutschland* (Berlin, 1882), pp. 77 ff. In England the reversal of opinion was brought about largely through the researches of A. Elizabeth Levett, "The Black Death on the Estates of the See of Winchester," *Oxford Stud. in Social and Legal Hist.*, V (1916), 1–120, and was strongly reflected in such writings as Helen Robbins, "A Comparison of the Effects of the Black Death on the Economic Organization of France and England," *Jour. Polit. Econ.*, XXXVI (1928), 447–79. For the best-informed recent evaluations, see Coulton, *The Black Death* (London, 1929), chap. v; also the very judicious review by Eileen E. Power, "The Effects of the Black Death on Rural Organization in England," *History*, N. S., III (1918), 109–16; the basic study for Spain by Charles Verlinden, "La grande peste en Espagne: Contribution à l'étude de ses conséquences economiques et sociales," *Rev. belge de philol. et d'hist.*, XVII (1938), 101–46; and the admirable summaries by Renouard, cited above, fn. 28.

phenomenal in the thirteenth century, came to a halt and was soon followed by a prolonged depression lasting until the mid-fifteenth century and in a sense even into the seventeenth.[33]

I make only the most fleeting reference to these questions, because my chief concern, as I have said, is to determine, if possible, what the long-term psychological effects of this age of disease may have been. The immediate horrors of great epidemics have been vividly described by eminent writers from Thucydides to Albert Camus and have been pictured on canvas by famous artists like Raphael and Delacroix.[34] At news of the approach of the disease a haunting terror seizes the population, in the Middle Ages leading on the one hand to great upsurges of repentance in the form of flagellant processions and on the other to a mad search for scapegoats, eventuating in large-scale pogroms of the Jews.[35] The most striking

[33] So eminent an authority as Wilhelm Abel, "Wachstumsschwankungen mitteleuropäischer Völker seit dem Mittelalter," *Jahrb. f. Nationalökonomie u. Statistik*, CXLII (1935), 670–92, holds that pestilence, famine, and war were not enough to account for the enormous decline in population and that psychological forces, as yet unanalyzed, led to a reluctance to marry and raise a family. E. J. Hobsbawm, "The General Crisis of the European Economy in the 17th Century," *Past and Present* (1954), No. 5, 33–53 and No. 6, 44–65, notes that the economic crisis, which had been in process since about 1300, came to an end at just about the time the plague died out. On the general economic depression see especially M. Postan, "Revisions in Economic History: The Fifteenth Century," *Econ. Hist. Rev.*, IX (1939), 160–67; John Saltmarsh, "Plague and Economic Decline in England in the Later Middle Ages," *Cambridge Hist. Jour.*, VII (1941), 23–41; Edouard Perroy, "Les crises du XIV° Siècle." *Annales*, IV (1949), 167–82, who stresses the fact that the Black Death created a demographic crisis, superimposed on a food crisis (1315–1320) and a financial crisis (1335–1345); Robert S. Lopez, "The Trade of Medieval Europe: The South," *Cambridge Economic History of Europe*, II (Cambridge, 1952), pp. 338 ff.; Postan, "The Trade of Medieval Europe: The North," *ibid.*, pp. 191 ff.; and Lopez's review of M. Mollat's *Le Commerce maritime normand à la fin du moyen âge*, in *Speculum*, XXXII (1957), 386.

[34] Cf. the realistic account in Camus, *La Peste* (Paris, 1947), with the contemporary·account of the yellow fever epidemic in Philadelphia in 1793 in Howard W. Haggard, *Devils, Drugs and Doctors* (New York, 1929), p. 213. Recent, as yet unpublished, studies of modern epidemics by Professors James Diggory and A. Pepitone of the University of Pennsylvania, bear out all the main features of earlier descriptions. Some striking plague paintings are reproduced in Raymond Crawfurd, *Plague and Pestilence in Literature and Art* (Oxford, 1914).

[35] Although the appearance of flagellantism and the beginnings of the Jewish pogroms antedated the Black Death, they reached their fullest devel-

feature of such visitations has always been the precipitate flight from the cities, in which not only the wealthier classes but also town officials, professors and teachers, clergy, and even physicians took part.[36] The majority of the population, taking the disaster as an expression of God's wrath, devoted itself to penitential exercises, to merciful occupations, and to such good works as the repair of churches and the founding of religious houses. On the other hand, the horror and confusion in many places brought general demoralization and social breakdown. Criminal elements were quick to take over, looting the deserted houses and even murdering the sick in order to rob them of their jewels. Many, despairing of the goodness and mercy of God, gave themselves over to riotous living, resolved, as Thucydides says, "to get out of life the pleasures which could be had speedily and which would satisfy their lusts, regarding their bodies and their wealth alike as transitory." Drunkenness and sexual immorality were the order of the day. "In one house," reported an observer of the London plague of 1665, "you might hear them roaring under the pangs of death, in the next tippling, whoring and belching out blasphemies against God."[37]

opment in 1348–1349. See the basic accounts by Karl Lechner, "Die grosse Geisselfahrt des Jahres 1349," *Historisches Jahrbuch*, V (1884), 437–62; of Heine Pfannenschmid, "Die Geissler des Jahres 1349 in Deutschland und den Niederlanden," *Die Lieder und Melodien der Geissler des Jahres 1349*, ed. Paul Runge (Leipzig, 1900), pp. 89–218; Joseph McCabe, *The History of Flagellantism* (Girard, Kans., 1946), esp. 33 ff.; Norman Cohn, *The Pursuit of the Millenium* (London, 1957), chap. VI. See further Hecker, *Epidemics of the Middle Ages*, pp. 32 ff.; Hoeniger, *Der Schwarz Tod;* Johannes Nohl, *The Black Death* (London, 1926); A. L. Maycock, "A Note on the Black Death," *Nineteenth Century*, XCVII (1925), 456–64. As late as 1884 in Italy physicians were suspected as agents of the rich to poison the poor, and in 1896 British officials in Bombay were charged with spreading the plague. See Melitta Schmideberg, "The Role of Psychotic Mechanisms in Cultural Development," *Internat. Jour. Psychoanalysis*, XI (1930), 387–418; René Baehrel, "La haine de classe au temps d'épidémie," *Annales*, VII (1952), 351–60, who analyzes the popular reaction to the cholera epidemic of 1831–32; and Ilza Veith, "Plague and Politics," *Bull. Hist. Medicine*, XXVIII (1954), 408–15.

36 The extent of such exodus may be judged from the fact that during the yellow fever epidemic of 1878 about 60 per cent of the population fled the city of Memphis (unpublished MS by James C. Diggory).

37 Quoted in Walter G. Bell, *The Great Plague in London in 1665* (London, 1924), p. 222. In addition to the classic accounts of Thucydides (*Peloponnesian War*, Book II) and Boccaccio (*Decameron*, introd.), see also the

The vivid description of the Black Death in Florence, in the introduction to Boccaccio's *Decameron*, is so familiar that further details about the immediate consequences may be dispensed with. Unfortunately neither the sources nor later historians tell us much of the long-range effects excepting that in the late nineteenth century a school of British writers traced to the Black Death fundamental changes in the agrarian system and indeed in the entire social order; the English prelate-historian, Francis Cardinal Gasquet, maintained that the Black death, with its admittedly high mortality among the clergy, served to disrupt the whole religious establishment and thereby set the scene for the Protestant Reformation. Though this thesis is undoubtedly exaggerated, it does seem likely that the loss of clergy, especially in the higher ranks, the consequent growth of pluralities, the inevitable appointment of some who proved to be "clerical scamps" (Jessopp), and the vast enrichment of the Church through the legacies of the pious, all taken together played a significant role in the religious development of the later Middle Ages.[38]

But again, these are essentially institutional problems which

---

notes of the great physician, Ambroise Paré, *De la peste* in *Oeuvres complètes* (Paris, 1841), III, 350–464; Mullett, *op. cit.*, p. 118, on the London plague of 1603; F. P. Wilson, *The Plague in Shakespeare's London* (Oxford, 1927), chap. v on the London plague of 1625. Much evidence is adduced in B. S. Gowen, "Some Psychological Aspects of Pestilence and Other Epidemics," (Winchester, Tenn., 1907; enlarged reprint from the *Amer. Jour. Psychology*, XVIII [Jan., 1907] 1–60); Karl Lechner, *Das grosse Sterben in Deutschland* (Innsbruck, 1884), pp. 93 ff.; and the books of Creighton, Kowalewsky, Hecker, Nohl, Gasquet, and Coulton, all cited above.

[38] On the high mortality of the clergy in England see especially Russell, *British Medieval Population*, pp. 222 ff., 367. On the general problem see Gasquet, *Great Pestilence*, pp. xvi–xvii, 203 ff.; Augustus Jessopp, *The Coming of the Friars and Other Historical Essays* (New York, 1889), pp. 245 ff.; Coulton, *The Black Death*, p. 48, and particularly his chapter on the Black Death in *Medieval Panorama* (New York, 1938); Hoeniger, *Der Schwarz Tod*, pp. 126 ff.; Anna M. Campbell, *The Black Death and Men of Learning* (New York, 1931), 136 ff.; A. Hamilton Thompson, "The Registers of John Gynewell, Bishop of Lincoln, for the Years 1349–1350" and "The Pestilences of the 14th Century in the Diocese of York," *Archeol. Jour.*, LXVIII (1911), 301–60, LXXI (1914), 97–154. According to Peter G. Mode, *The Influence of the Black Death on the English Monasteries* (Chicago, 1916), chaps. II, VI, the heads of at least 120 monasteries had died and some of those who succeeded proved to be veritable gangsters. Verlinden lays great stress on the enrichment of the Church in Spain through donations and legacies.

may reflect but do not explain the underlying psychological forces. That unusual forces of this kind were operative in the later Middle Ages seems highly probable. Indeed, a number of eminent historians have in recent years expatiated on the special character of this period.[39] I will not attempt even to summarize the various interpretations of the temper of that age which have been advanced on one side or the other. None of the commentators, so far as I can see, have traced or determined the connection between the great and constantly recurring epidemics and the state of mind of much of Europe at that time. Yet this relationship would seem to leap to the eye. The age was marked, as all admit, by a mood of misery, depression, and anxiety, and by a general sense of impending doom.[40] Numerous writers in widely varying fields have commented on the morbid preoccupation with death, the macabre interest in tombs, the gruesome predilection for the human corpse.[41] Among painters the favorite themes were Christ's passion, the terrors of the Last Judgment, and the tortures of

---

[39] Johan Huizinga's *The Waning of the Middle Ages* (London, 1927) was, in a sense, the counterpart to Jakob Burckhardt's *The Civilization of the Renaissance in Italy* (London, 1878). Of the more recent books the following seem to me particularly significant: Rudolf Stadelmann, *Vom Geist des ausgehenden Mittelalters* (Halle, 1929); Will-Erich Peuckert, *Die grosse Wende. Das apokalyptische Saeculum und Luther* (Hamburg, 1948); Hermann Heimpel, "Das Wesen des Spätmittelalters," *Der Mensch in Seiner Gegenwart* (Göttingen, 1954).

[40] Huizinga, *op. cit.*, chap. i; Stadelmann, *op. cit.*, pp. 7, 13; Peuckert, *op. cit.*, pp. 21, 144; Willy Andreas, *Deutschland vor der Reformation* (5th ed., Stuttgart, 1948), p. 202; Otto Benesch, *The Art of the Renaissance in Northern Europe* (Cambridge, 1945), p. 10. In a broad way, Renouard (works noted in fn. 28) and Lucien Febvre ("La peste noire de 1348," *Annales*, IV [1949], 102–103) have suggested the psychological and religious repercussions of the great epidemics. Some authors speak of hysteria, paranoia, and mental disease. See Willy Hellpach, *Die geistigen Epidemien* (Frankfurt, 1905), pp. 84 ff.; Gregory Zilboorg, *A History of Medical Psychology* (New York, 1941), pp. 153 ff.; Norman Cohn, *Pursuit of the Millenium*, p. 73.

[41] See esp. Frederick P. Weber, *Aspects of Death and Correlated Aspects of Life in Art, Epigram and Poetry* (London, 1918), pp. 157 ff.; Erna Döring-Hirsch, *Tod und Jenseits im Spätmittelalter* (Berlin, 1927), *passim*. See also Huizinga, *Waning of the Middle Ages*, chap. xi; Peuckert, *Die grosse Wende*, pp. 95 ff.; and esp. Émile Mâle, *L'Art religieux de la fin du moyen âge en France* (Paris, 1908), pp. 375 ff., 423 ff. Paul Perdrizet, *La Vierge de Miséricorde* (Paris, 1908), chap. ix. Michelangelo on one occasion wrote to Vasari: "No thought is born in me which has not 'Death' engraved upon it" (quoted in Piero Misciatelli, *Savonarola* [English trans., Cambridge, 1929], p. 103).

Hell, all depicted with ruthless realism and with an almost loving devotion to each repulsive detail.[42] Altogether characteristic was the immense popularity of the Dance of Death woodcuts and murals, with appropriate verses, which appeared soon after the Black Death and which, it is agreed, expressed the sense of the immediacy of death and the dread of dying unshriven. Throughout the fifteenth and sixteenth centuries these pitilessly naturalistic pictures ensured man's constant realization of his imminent fate.[43]

The origins of the Dance of Death theme have been generally traced to the Black Death and subsequent epidemics, culminating in the terror brought on by the outbreak of syphilis at the end of the fifteenth century. Is it unreasonable, then, to suppose that many of the other phenomena I have mentioned might be explained, at least in part, in the same way? We all recognize the late Middle Ages as a period of popular religious excitement or overexcitement, of pilgrimages and penitential processions, of mass preaching, of veneration of relics and adoration of saints, of lay piety and popular mysticism.[44] It was apparently also a period of unusual immorality

[42] See Mâle, pp. 477 ff.; Millard Meiss, *Painting in Florence and Siena after the Black Death* (Princeton, 1951), esp. chap. II; Crawfurd, *Plague ... in Literature and Art,* chap. VIII. On the German painters see Joseph Lortz, *Die Reformation in Deutschland* (3rd ed., Freiburg, 1940), I, 102; Benesch, *Art of the Renaissance,* pp. 10 ff.; Arthur Burkhard, *Matthias Grünewald* (Cambridge, 1936), pp. 74 ff.; Gillo Dorfles, *Bosch* (Verona, 1953).

[43] On the artistic side see Crawfurd, chap. VIII; Mâle, pp. 383 ff.; Curt Sachs, *The Commonwealth of Art* (New York, 1946), pp. 88 ff. See also Andreas, *Deutschland vor der Reformation,* pp. 206 ff.; Stadelmann, *Vom Geist des ausgehenden Mittelalters,* pp. 18 ff.; and the specialized studies of Gert Buchheit, *Der Totentanz* (Berlin, 1926); Henri Stegemeier, *The Dance of Death in Folksong* (Chicago, 1939); Wolfgang Stammler, *Der Totentanz* (Munich, 1948); and the particularly significant historical analysis of Hellmut Rosenfeld, *Der mittelalterliche Totentanz* (Münster, 1954), pp. 33 ff., 59 ff.

[44] The subject is too large to permit of even a cursory analysis, but see Stadelmann, chap. III; Lortz, I, 99 ff.; Andreas, chap. III and pp. 191 ff.; and Heimpel, noted above. See also Evelyn Underhill, *Mysticism* (12th ed., London, 1930), esp. 453 ff.; and "Medieval Mysticism," *Cambridge Medieval History* VII (New York, 1932), chap. XXVI; Margaret Smith, *Studies in Early Mysticism in the Near and Middle East* (London, 1931), pp. 256–57. As long ago as 1880 the eminent orientalist Alfred von Kremer suggested the connection of mysticism (Sufism) with the great plague epidemics in the Middle East. See his "Über die grossen Seuchen des Orientes nach arabischen Quellen," *Sitzungsberichte der phil.-hist. Classe der kais. Akad. Wissenschaften, Wien,* XCVI (1880), 69–156.

and shockingly loose living, which we must take as the continuation of the "devil-may-care" attitude of one part of the population. This the psychologists explain as the repression of unbearable feelings by accentuating the value of a diametrically opposed set of feelings and then behaving as though the latter were the real feelings.[45] But the most striking feature of the age was an exceptionally strong sense of guilt and a truly dreadful fear of retribution, seeking expression in a passionate longing for effective intercession and in a craving for direct, personal experience of the Deity, as well as in a corresponding dissatisfaction with the Church and with the mechanization of the means of salvation. as reflected, for example, in the traffic in indulgences.[46]

These attitudes, along with the great interest in astrology, the increased resort to magic, and the startling spread of witchcraft and Satanism in the fifteenth century were, according to the precepts of modern psychology, normal reactions to the sufferings to which mankind in that period was subjected.[47] It

[45] James W. Thompson, "The Aftermath of the Black Death and the Aftermath of the Great War," *Amer. Jour. Sociol.*, XXVI (1920–1921), 565–72, on the continuing degeneration.

[46] Wallace K. Ferguson, "The Church in a Changing World: A Contribution to the Interpretation of the Renaissance," *Amer. Hist. Rev.*, LIX (1953), 1–18; review by Kurt F. Reinhardt of Friedrich W. Oedinger, *Über die Bildung der Geistlichen im späten Mittelalter* (Leiden, 1953), in *Speculum*, XXXII (1957), 391–92; Lortz, I, 99 ff.; Andreas, pp. 152–153, 169 ff.; and the eloquent pages on the Church in the mid-fourteenth century in Henri Daniel-Rops, *Cathedral and Crusade: Studies of the Medieval Church, 1050–1350* (London, 1957), pp. 593 ff. Norman Cohn, *The Pursuit of the Millenium,* is devoted entirely to a study of the "revolutionary chiliastic movements" in Europe from the Crusades onward.

[47] On the triumph of astrology see Lynn Thorndike, *A History of Magic and Experimental Science,* IV (New York, 1934), 611 ff.; H. A. Strauss, *Psychologie und astrologische Symbolik* (Zurich, 1953); Mark Graubard, *Astrology and Alchemy* (New York 1953), chaps. IV, V. On the reemergence of pagan superstitions, the practice of magic, and the belief in witches as a heretical sect devoted to worship of the devil and the perpetration of evil see Thorndike, *op. cit.,* IV, 274 ff.; Peuckert, pp. 119 ff.; Andreas, pp. 28 ff., 217 ff.; Joseph Hansen, *Zauberwesen, Inquisition und Hexenprozess im Mittelalter* (Munich, 1900), pp. 326 ff.; Margaret A. Murray, *The Witch-Cult in Western Europe* (Oxford, 1921), esp. pp. 11 ff.; Harmanns Obendiek, *Satanismus und Dämonie in Geschichte und Gegenwart* (Berlin, 1928); Montague Summers, *The History of Witchcraft and Demonology* (2d ed., New York, 1956), pp. 1 ff.; Gregory Zilboorg, *op. cit.* It may be noted, for what it is worth, that in the fifteenth century witches were accused of inhibiting human fertility: possibly a reflection of popular concern over the

must be remembered that the Middle Ages, ignoring the teachings of the Greek physicians and relying entirely upon Scripture
and the writings of the Church fathers, considered disease the
scourge of God upon a sinful people.[48] All men, as individuals,
carry within themselves a burden of unconscious guilt and a
fear of retribution which apparently go back to the curbing and
repression of sexual and aggressive drives in childhood and the
emergence of death wishes directed against the parents. This
sense of sin, which is fundamental to all religion, is naturally
enhanced by the impact of vast unaccountable and uncontrollable forces threatening the existence of each and every
one.[49] Whether or not there is also a primordial racial sense of
guilt, as Freud argued in his *Totem and Taboo* (1913), it is perfectly clear that disaster and death threatening the entire community will bring on a mass emotional disturbance, based on a
feeling of helpless exposure, disorientation, and common guilt.[50]

---

rapidly diminishing population. It is also interesting to observe that witch
trials died out in Europe concurrently with the disappearance of the plague
in the eighteenth century.

[48] God might, of course, act through natural phenomena such as comets,
floods, droughts, or miasma. For a good discussion of this point see G. G.
Coulton, *Five Centuries of Religion*, II (Cambridge, 1927), p. 394; Hirts,
Conquest of Plague, chap. II; Kenneth Walker, *The Story of Medicine* (New
York, 1955), pp. 71 ff.; and esp. Paul H. Kocher, "The Idea of God in
Elizabethan Medicine," *Jour. Hist. Ideas*, XI (1950), 3–29. This explanation
was generally accepted through the early modern period and undoubtedly
presented a great obstacle to the development of medical and sanitational
measures. See Mullett, *Bubonic Plague and England*, pp. 74, 88. Recent
studies on modern disasters indicate that it is still widely held, despite the
discoveries of Pasteur and his successors. See Martha Wolfenstein, *Disaster:
A Psychological Study* (Glencoe, Ill., 1957), pp. 199 ff.

[49] The crucial problem of guilt feelings has not been much studied except
by Freud and his successors. See Freud, "Thoughts for the Times on War
and Death," (1915) and the succinct discussion in Jones, *What Is Psychoanalysis?* pp. 101 ff., 114. For the continuance of this feeling in modern times
see Wolfenstein, *Disaster*, p. 71. Cantril, *The Invasion from Mars* (Princeton,
1940), pp. 161 ff., quotes one man as saying: "The broadcast had us all
worried, but I knew it would at least scare ten years' life out of my mother-
in-law."

[50] A later explanation of the sense of communal guilt, as it appears among
the Jews, was advanced by Freud in his *Moses and Monotheism* (1939). Still
another, quite different and quite persuasive, argument is presented by
Theodor Reik, *Myth and Guilt: The Crime and Punishment of Mankind*
(New York, 1957), esp. pp. 34 ff., 146 ff. Oskar Pfister, *Das Christentum und
die Angst* (Zurich, 1944) has examined the relation of anxiety to guilt feelings and the magnification of communal anxieties in the face of disaster.
For concrete studies of medieval mass hysteria see Louis F. Calmeil, *De la*

Furthermore, it seems altogether plausible to suppose that children, having experienced the terror of their parents and the panic of the community, will react to succeeding crises in a similar but even more intense manner. In other words, the anxiety and fear are transmitted from one generation to another, constantly aggravated.

Now it has long been recognized by psychologists that man, when crushed by unfathomable powers, tends to regress to infantile concepts and that, like his predecessor in primitive times, he has recourse to magic in his efforts to ward off evil and appease the angry deity.[51] It is generally agreed that magic and religion are closely related, both deriving from fear of unknown forces and especially of death, and both reflecting an effort to ensure the preservation of the individual and the community from disease and other afflictions.[52] Death-dealing epidemics like those of the late Middle Ages were bound to produce a religious revival, the more so as the established Church was proving itself ever less able to satisfy the yearning for more effective intercession and for a more personal relationship to God.[53] Wyclif,

---

folie (Paris, 1845); René Fülöp-Miller, *Leaders, Dreamers and Rebels* (New York, 1935); and esp. the admirable scholarly study of Cohn, *Pursuit of the Millenium,* which stresses the analogies between individual and collective paranoia.

51 Jung, "After the Catastrophe," *Essays on Contemporary Events* (London, 1947). See also Johann Kinkel, "Zur Frage des psychologischen Grundlagen und des Ursprungs der Religion," *Imago,* VIII (1922), 23–45, 197–241; Henry E. Sigerist, *Civilization and Disease* (Ithaca, 1943), chap. VI; Arturo Castiglioni, *Adventures of the Mind* (New York, 1946), pp. ix, 2, 11, 19; Bronislaw Malinowski, *Magic, Science and Religion* (Boston, 1948), pp. 15, 29, 116; Charles Odier, *Anxiety and Magic Thinking* (New York, 1956), pp. 38 ff.; Melitta Schmideberg, "Role of Psychotic Mechanisms in Cultural Development"; Franz Alexander, "On the Psychodynamics of Regressive Phenomena in Panic States," *Psychoanalysis and the Social Sciences,* IV (1955), 104–11. Hirst, *Conquest of Plague,* has noted the reversion to magic during all great plague epidemics and reports that charms and amulets were never more prevalent among even educated Englishmen than during the epidemic of 1665. Jessopp, *Coming of the Friars,* p. 166, remarked that in his day the threat of any epidemic still brought on "wild-eyed panic" and resort to all kinds of superstitious practices.

52 James H. Leuba, *The Psychological Origin and the Nature of Religion* (London, 1921), pp. 4, 81; George F. Moore, *The Birth and Growth of Religion* (New York, 1924), pp. 3, 8, 17; W. B. Selbie, *The Psychology of Religion* (Oxford, 1924), p. 32; Malinowski, *Magic, Science and Religion,* p. 29; Willy Hellpach, *Grundriss der Religionspsychologie* (Stuttgart, 1951), pp. 6 ff.

53 In this connection the great expansion of the cult of the Virgin Mary and even more of her mother, St. Anne, is worth noting; also the fact that

himself a survivor of the Black Death, is supposed to have been deeply affected by his gruelling experience, and there is nothing implausible in the suggestion that Lollardy was a reaction to the shortcomings of the Church in that great crisis.[54] In this connection it is also worth remarking that the first expression of Zwingli's reformed faith was his *Song of Prayer in Time of Plague*.[55]

Most striking, however, is the case of the greatest of the reformers, Martin Luther, who seems to me to reflect clearly the reaction of the individual to the situation I have been sketching. Luther left behind almost a hundred volumes of writings, thousands of letters, and very voluminous table-talk, suggesting an unusually self-analytical and self-critical personality.[56] From all this material it has long been clear that he suffered from an abnormally strong sense of sin and of the immediacy of death and damnation. Tortured by the temptations of the flesh and repeatedly in conflict with a personalized demon, he was chronically oppressed by a pathological feeling of guilt and lived in

---

among the ten or twelve most popular saints of the late fifteenth century, the so-called "plague saints" (St. Anthony, St. Sebastian, St. Roch), were particularly favored. See Huizinga, *Waning of the Middle Ages*, chap. XII; Crawfurd, *Plague . . . in Literature and Art*, chap. VIII; and esp. Mâle, *Art religieux*, pp. 157 ff., 193 ff. and Perdrizet, *La Vierge de Miséricorde, passim*.

[54] *The Last Age of the Church*, written in 1356 and first published in 1840, is a violent denunciation of the depravity revealed in the time of the Black Death. It was long believed to have been the first work of Wyclif but is now attributed to an unnamed Spiritual Franciscan. See James H. Todd, *The Last Age of the Church, by John Wycliffe* (Dublin, 1840); J. Foster Palmer, "Pestilences: Their Influence on the Destiny of Nations," *Trans. Royal Hist. Soc.*, I (1884), 242–59; H. B. Workman, *John Wyclif: A Study of the English Medieval Church* (Oxford, 1926), I, 14; Robert Vaughan, *The Life and Opinions of John de Wycliffe* (London, 1928), I, 238 ff.; and, on the general problem, Coulton, *The Black Death*, p. 111, and Mullett, *Bubonic Plague and England*, p. 34.

[55] This very moving appeal for divine aid (1519) is reprinted in Georg Finsler, *et al., Ulrich Zwingli: Eine Auswahl aus seinen Schriften* (Zurich, 1918), pp. 17–19. See also Pfister, *Das Christentum und die Angst*, 321 ff., according to whom Calvin was terror-stricken by the plague and, unlike Luther, was unwilling to stick at his post during severe epidemics. He firmly believed that a group of thirty-four men and women witches had for three years spread the plague in Geneva and that in their case even the most extreme forms of torture were justified.

[56] Karl Holl, "Luthers Urteile über sich Selbst," *Gesammelte Aufsätze zur Kirchengeschichte*, I, *Luther* (Tübingen, 1921); Heinrich Böhmer, *Road to Reformation; Martin Luther to the Year 1521* (Philadelphia, 1946), foreword; Karl A. Meissinger, *Der katholische Luther* (Munich, 1952), p. 2.

constant terror of God's judgment. So striking were these traits that some of Luther's biographers have questioned his sanity.[57]

Here it is interesting to recall that one of our own colleagues, the late Professor Preserved Smith, as long ago as 1913, attacked the problem in an article entitled "Luther's Early Development in the Light of Psychoanalysis."[58] Smith, who was remarkably conversant with Freudian teaching when psychoanalysis was still in its early stage of development, considered Luther highly neurotic—probably driven to enter the monastery by the hope of finding a refuge from temptation and an escape from damnation, and eventually arriving at the doctrine of salvation by faith alone only after he had convinced himself of the impossibility of conquering temptation by doing penance. It may well be that Smith overdid his thesis, but the fact remains that his article was treated with great respect by Dr. Paul J. Reiter, who later published a huge and greatly detailed study of Luther's personality. Reiter reached the conclusion, already suggested by Adolf Hausrath in 1905, that the great reformer suffered from a manic-depressive psychosis, which, frequently associated with genius, involved a constant struggle with, and victory over, enormous psychological pressures. The point of mentioning all this is to suggest that Luther's trials were typical of his time. In any event, it is inconceivable that he should have evoked so great a popular response unless he had succeeded in expressing the underlying, unconscious sentiments of large numbers of people and in providing them with an acceptable solution to their religious problem.[59]

57 Hartmann Grisar, *Luther* (London, 1913–1917), I, 110 ff.; VI, chap. xxxvi, discusses many of these views but Grisar takes a more moderate stand. The most recent Catholic biography is that of Joseph Lortz, *Die Reformation in Deutschland*, which is a very model of reasonableness.

58 *Amer. Jour. Psychology*, XXIV (1913), 360–77.

59 Hausrath, *Luthers Leben* (Berlin, 1905); Reiter, *Martin Luthers Umwelt, Charakter und Psychose* (Copenhagen, 1937, 1941); Wilhelm Lange-Eichbaum, *Genie, Irrsinn und Ruhm* (4th ed., Munich, 1956), pp. 375–78. See also Walther von Loewenich, "Zehn Jahre Luther-forschung," in *Theologie und Liturgie*, ed. Liemar Hennig (Cassell, 1952), pp. 119–70 and Martin Werner, "Psychologisches zum Klostererlebnis Martin Luthers," *Schweiz. Zeitsch. für Psychologie*, VII (1948), 1–18, who follows Smith's thesis closely. The argument hinges on the harshness of Luther's upbringing and the extent of his father fixation. Smith noted that on at least one occasion Luther asserted that he had entered the monastery to escape harsh treatment at home. His father's unalterable opposition to this step may have played a part in Luther's later decision to leave the monastery. According to Roland

I must apologize for having raised so lugubrious a subject on so festive an occasion, but I could not resist the feeling that the problems presented by the later Middle Ages are exactly of the type that might be illuminated by modern psychology. I do not claim that the psychological aspects of this apocalyptic age have been entirely neglected by other students. Indeed, Millard Meiss, a historian of art, has written a most impressive study of Florentine and Sienese painting in the second half of the fourteenth century in which he has analyzed the many and varied effects of the Black Death, including the bearing of that great catastrophe on the further development of the religious situation.[60] But no one, to my knowledge, has undertaken to fathom the psychological crisis provoked by the chronic, large-scale loss of life and the attendant sense of impending doom.

I would not, of course, argue that psychological doctrine, even if it were more advanced and more generally accepted than it is, would resolve all the perplexities of the historian. Better than most scholars, the historian knows that human motivation, like causation, is a complex and elusive process. In view of the fact that we cannot hope ever to have complete evidence on any historical problem, it seems unlikely that we shall ever have definitive answers. But I am sure you will agree that there are still possibilities of enriching our understanding of the past and that it is our responsibility, as historians, to leave none of these possibilities unexplored. I call your attention to the fact that for many years young scholars in anthropology, sociology, religion, literature, education, and other fields have gone to psychoanalytic institutes for special training, and I suggest

---

H. Bainton, *Here I Stand: A Life of Martin Luther* (New York, 1950), pp. 288 ff., Luther's decision (in 1525) to marry was at least in part due to his wish to gratify his father's desire for progeny. Recent writers tend to explain away the harshness of Luther's youth, which indeed was probably less unusual and less important than Smith supposed. See Otto Scheel, *Martin Luther* (Tübingen, 1916); Böhmer, *Martin Luther;* Meissinger, *Der katholische Luther;* Robert H. Fife, *The Revolt of Martin Luther* (New York, 1957), pp. 5, 9, 99, 117 ff.; Bainton, *Here I Stand*, pp. 23, 25, 28 and chap. XXI *passim*, who insists that Luther's psychological troubles were of a strictly religious character, due to "tensions which medieval religion deliberately induced, playing alternately upon fear and hope."

[60] Meiss, *Painting in Florence and Siena after the Black Death,* while dealing with a restricted subject and a limited period, is in my opinion a masterpiece of synthesis and one of the very few books to recognize the full and varied impact of the Black Death. See also Hans Baron, *The Crisis of the Early Italian Renaissance* (Princeton, 1955), II, 479–80.

that some of our own younger men might seek the same equipment. For of this I have no doubt, that modern psychology is bound to play an ever greater role in historical interpretation. For some time now there has been a marked trend toward recognition of the irrational factors in human development, and it is interesting to observe the increased emphasis being laid on psychological forces. May I recall that perhaps the most stimulating non-Marxist interpretation of imperialism, that of the late Joseph Schumpeter, which goes back to 1918, rests squarely on a psychological base? Or need I point out that recent treatments of such forces as totalitarianism and nationalism lay great stress on psychological factors? [61] Indeed, within the past year two books have appeared which have a direct bearing on my argument. One is T. D. Kendrick's *The Lisbon Earthquake,* which is devoted to a study of the effects of that disaster of 1755 upon the whole attitude and thought of the later eighteenth century. The other is Norman Cohn's *The Pursuit of the Millenium,* which review the chiliastic movements of the Middle Ages and comes to the conclusion that almost every major disaster, be it famine, plague, or war, produced some such movement and that only analysis of their psychic content will help us to explain them.

Aldous Huxley, in one of his essays, discusses the failure of historians to devote sufficient attention to the great ebb and flow of population and its effect on human development. He complains that while Arnold Toynbee concerned himself so largely with pressures and responses, there is in the index of his first six volumes no entry for "population," though there are five references to Popilius Laenas and two to Porphyry of Batamaea.[62] To this I might add that the same index contains no reference to pestilence, plague, epidemics, or Black Death. This, I submit, is mildly shocking and should remind us, as historians, that we cannot rest upon past achievements but must constantly seek wider horizons and deeper insights. We find ourselves in the midst of the International Geophysical Year, and we all know that scientists entertain high hopes of enlarging through cooperation their understanding as well as their knowledge of the universe. It is quite possible that they may throw further

[61] See, for example, Hannah Arendt, *The Origins of Totalitarianism,* and Boyd C. Shafer, *Nationalism: Myth and Reality* (New York, 1955).

[62] Huxley, *Tomorrow and Tomorrow and Tomorrow* (New York, 1956), p. 221.

light on such problems as the influence of sunspots on terrestrial life and the effects of weather on the conduct of human affairs.[63] We may, for all we know, be on the threshold of a new era when the historian will have to think in ever larger, perhaps even in cosmic, terms.

[63] Fully a generation ago a Soviet scientist thought he could establish an eleven-year cycle of maximum sunspot activity and that these periods were also those of maximum mass excitability as revealed by revolutions and other social disturbances. Furthermore, his correlation of periods of maximum sunspot activity with cholera epidemics in the nineteenth century seemed to reveal a remarkable coincidence. See the summary translation of the book by A. L. Tchijevsky, "Physical Factors of the Historical Process," as read before the American Meteorological Society, December 30, 1926, and now reprinted in *Cycles* (Feb., 1957). Of the many studies of climatic, nutritional, and similar influences on human affairs, see Ellsworth Huntington, *Civilization and Climate* (New Haven, 1915); *The Character of Races* (New York, 1924); *Mainsprings of Civilization* (New York, 1946); Willy Hellpach, *Geopsyche* (5th ed., Leipzig, 1939); Louis Berman, *Food and Character* (Boston, 1932); C. C. and S. M. Furnas, *Man, Bread and Destiny* (Baltimore, 1937); E. Parmalee Prentice, *Hunger and History* (New York, 1939); Josué de Castro, *The Geography of Hunger* (Boston, 1952).

25. Can "American Studies" Develop a Method?*

HENRY NASH SMITH

I must ask the reader to accept for the present occasion two definitions. By "American Studies" I shall mean "the study of American culture, past and present, as a whole"; and by "culture" I shall mean "the way in which subjective experience is organized."

The problem of method in American Studies arises because the investigation of American culture as a whole does not coincide with the customary field of operations of any established academic discipline. The phrase "as a whole" does not, of course, imply a global attack directed simultaneously toward all the aspects of our culture. The defining characteristic of American Studies is not the size of its problems but the effort to view any given subject of investigation from new perspectives, to take into account as many aspects of it as possible.

In order to illustrate the need for such a shift of perspective, I should like to draw upon my own experience by considering the example of Mark Twain. He was a writer and his work belongs to the traditional field of American literature. But I can think of no other man whose work so clearly needs to be placed in a social setting before it can be fully understood. No other American writer of comparable importance is so unmistakably of the people. He took his materials and his technique from American culture, and he developed in collaboration with his audience. He served his apprenticeship in newspaper offices; he

* Reprinted with permission from *American Quarterly,* IX (Summer, 1957), 197–208.

perfected his style by practicing the art of oral story-telling. His work is an almost uninterrupted commentary on matters uppermost in the minds of his readers and hearers, and he had a remarkable ability to objectify the memories and dreams of his public. It would be peculiarly artificial to try to deal with his books as if they were self-contained autonomous universes.

But how can one do justice to this central phenomenon of nineteenth-century American culture? It is true that much study of Mark Twain's life and work needs to be undertaken along perfectly conventional lines: his dependence upon literary predecessors, for example, has even yet not been fully investigated. Yet the student of this remarkable career soon finds himself asking questions that lead beyond the usual limits of literary history or criticism. One question, which is probably at bottom anthropological, concerns the matter of taboos governing what may be said, what may be represented, what may be published. Since Van Wyck Brooks's *The Ordeal of Mark Twain* (and that is now thirty-five years) a great deal has been written about the supposed censorship of Mark Twain's work, either imposed by others or self-imposed. The subject is of primary importance in the study of Mark Twain; at the same time it bears very widely on the recent history of American literature, and on the development of attitudes in the culture generally. But no one knows very much about it. We are at a loss if we ask to what extent the taboos evident in Mark Twain's work are individual idiosyncrasies and to what extent they were actually (as he often maintained) imposed by the culture. It is even more difficult to determine whether these canons of propriety were enforced uniformly throughout the society, or whether they varied according to geographical regions (as Bernard De Voto assumes in his chapter on "Cryptorchism") or according to social classes (as is implied in Santayana's celebrated identification of a "genteel tradition" in America).

The literary historian approaches this problem by examining the fiction published in magazines and books during this period; the correspondence between editors and writers; and book reviews, especially those which comment adversely upon supposed violations of taboos. But the information gathered from these sources needs to be interpreted in the light of a thorough knowledge of class structure, of the stratification of taste according to levels of sophistication, and of the different audiences to which different magazines and publishing houses addressed themselves.

I do not believe, for example, that the usual methods of literary history enable us to explain why Harriet Beecher Stowe's "The True Story of Lady Byron's Life," published in the *Atlantic Monthly* in 1869 under the editorship of William Dean Howells after careful revision by Oliver Wendell Holmes, should have cost the magazine fifteen thousand subscribers—more than one-fourth of its list. The incident suggests that the public which read books (and literary magazines, among which the *Atlantic* enjoyed the highest status) had an appreciably stricter sense of decorum than did Howells and Holmes. The New York *Tribune,* mouthpiece for a larger but still relatively literate segment of public opinion, asserted that *Innocents Abroad* showed "an offensive irreverence for things which other men held sacred." Yet Howells published a highly favorable review of *Innocents Abroad* in the *Atlantic.* At the other end of the spectrum of tastes, or of degrees of sophistication, *Innocents Abroad* had an enormous sale among people who seldom read anything except newspapers. Perhaps the exaggerated concern for literary propriety came neither from the extreme highbrows nor from the public at large but from a kind of upper-middlebrow audience defined by the subscription lists of the literary magazines. If there were regional differences among segments of this audience, they have not been clearly defined.

In any event, during the 1870's Mark Twain had a complex problem of adaptation to his various audiences. Howells was introducing him to the world of polite letters through the pages of the *Atlantic.* The canvassers for the American Publishing Company were selling tens of thousands of his books to quite unliterary purchasers. On the lecture platform Mark Twain himself was in direct contact with large miscellaneous audiences —in the Middle West, in the East, and (as early as 1872) in England. He was, in fact, one of the pioneers in the discovery and the formation of the mass audience which is so conspicuous in the twentieth century. In these circumstances, he could obviously not have been the free creative artist in the Romantic mode that seems to have been Brooks's ideal. The autonomy of Mark Twain's works was impaired before they were written, and by forces that were in large part internalized in the author. It does not take us very far to conclude, as Brooks did, that this is a scandal. We must recognize that the inhibitions on literary expression (that is, the demands of various special audiences and of the embryonic mass audience) were a complex trait of the culture in which Mark Twain lived. We need to understand them in order to understand Mark Twain's work. We also need to understand them in order to understand the culture.

Indeed, it may turn out that one of the distinctive fields of American Studies is precisely this ambiguous relation between works of art and the culture in which they occur. Certainly the student of Mark Twain is confronted at every turn with problems arising in this area. Let me cite another example. In his early work, especially in *Innocents Abroad* and *Roughing It,* Mark Twain uses three distinct prose styles. One of these is a vernacular style, based on the everyday speech of men with little formal education—rivermen, stagecoach drivers, prospectors. The second is patterned on the ornate, elevated rhetoric of the pulpit and of political oratory in the manner of Daniel Webster. The third is a direct, unpretentious style representing the impersonal attitude of the skilled reporter. The vernacular style is felt to be appropriate to characters of low social status and reflects various attitudes toward them—sometimes a little patronizing, more often sympathetic and admiring. The elevated style embodies an aspiration toward genteel culture, for which indeed it serves as a matrix; it is often used with perfect seriousness, yet is also often burlesqued. The direct style is apparently felt as being neutral, as being somehow outside the hierarchy of classes. The relation of these styles to one another, and Mark Twain's development (never complete) toward an integrated personal idiom, are delicate indices to his perception of distinctions among social classes, of his own place in the status system, and of the status of the audience he believes himself to be addressing.

An examination of these aspects of Mark Twain's style requires a careful discrimination between attitudes toward social status that he has taken over unconsciously from the culture, and attitudes that spring from his conscious recognition of social stratification and of his place within the status system. It is possible, for example, that his most satisfactory style might turn out to depend on his achievement of a personal autonomy—an achievement that was intermittent rather than accomplished once and for all. Furthermore, we have to recognize drastic changes in Mark Twain's relation to the status system at different periods of his career. Especially in the five or six years immediately preceding his marriage in 1870, and for a year or two after it, he shows the signs of rapid upward social mobility, and this movement along the dimension of social status is inextricably involved with his development as a writer. Thus almost concurrently he moved from California to the East coast; he ceased being a newspaper correspondent to become a platform 'lecturer,' a contributor to literary magazines (including the *Atlantic*), a writer of books, and even a dramatist; after several years of a hand-to-mouth Bohemian existence he began to make a large income from his writing; and despite the perfectly rational misgivings of the Langdon family, he married Livy. He made his celebrated efforts at reform by trying to give up liquor and profanity, and to become a Christian as that term was understood in Elmira. He built his expensive house in Hartford. In place of Steve Gillis, Joe Goodman and the members of the San Francisco Minstrel Troupe, he acquired as friends the Rev. Joseph Twichell, Charles Dudley Warner and William Dean Howells. These biographical facts point in two directions: toward American culture (or the varieties of American regional subcultures) at the end of the Civil War, and toward the literary development recorded in Mark Twain's writings. The problem is at once biographical, historical, sociological and literary.

Mark Twain's attitudes toward American society found expression not only in his style, but in the use of recurrent figures or types of character: in his early work, for example, what has been called the vernacular character (most fully illustrated in Huck Finn); in his later work, a figure that might be called the transcendent character (the best illustration being Young Satan in *The Mysterious Stranger*). These figures occur in many different guises over a long period of time. They are persistent themes in Mark Twain's writing, and they exert a strong influence on the shaping of plots in his works of fiction, on his imagery and especially on his language (what would *Huckleberry Finn* be if the language were altered?). Both figures embody the author's attitudes toward society, or rather his reading of social situations. The vernacular character is, so to speak, outside society because he is beneath it; the transcendent character is outside society because he is above it. There are strong hints here of Mark Twain's own alienation from the society. His principal problem as a novelist was how to conceive of significant action for characters whose relation to society was so special. The problem was evidently forced upon him by the culture of late nineteenth-century America. It lies at the center of his literary development, yet it cannot be adequately dealt with by literary methods alone. What is needed is a method of analysis that is at once literary (for one must begin with an analytical reading of the texts that takes into account structure, imagery, diction, and so on) and sociological (for many of the forces at work in the fiction are clearly of social origin). Such an analysis would not only take us much farther into Mark Twain's fictive universe than criticism has gone in the past; it would also give us a new insight into American society of the late nineteenth century, for the vernacular figure and the transcendent figure are not peculiar to Mark Twain. They were widely current in American literature and thought; they are cultural, not merely private and individual, images.

The final problem I shall mention that is posed by Mark Twain's career is his relation to the established role of the Man of Letters, the Author, as that role had been defined by New England in the place accorded Emerson, Longfellow, Lowell, Holmes, and so on. This role, one of the massive features of nineteenth-century American culture, was undergoing rapid change during Mark Twain's lifetime, and by the time of his death it had, I think, all but disappeared. In our own day the figure of the Alienated Artist has to some extent taken the place of the figure of the Man of Letters. Mark Twain felt the impact of the social forces that created both the older and the newer role of the artist in America, and at the same time his unprecedented popularity gave tantalizing glimpses of yet another role for the artist—that of the darling of the mass audience, a poker-faced bard whose jokes concealed his Whitmanian function of bringing the great democracy to knowledge of itself. This last possibility was never more than a possibility, but the partial extent to which it was realized defines one dimension of the unique achievement of *Life on the Mississippi, Huckleberry Finn* and *A Connecticut Yankee*. After the 1880's the pressures of personal misfortune and even more importantly of cultural change prevented this kind of achievement. *Pudd'nhead Wilson, The Mysterious Stranger* and the lesser works of Mark Twain's last two decades are written from the perspective of alienation (an alienation which, it should be pointed out, was accompanied by increasing fame and popularity). To explain the shift in the direction of his development has long been a capital problem of criticism. It is an equally important problem of cultural history, and neither can be solved without full exploration of the other. To find out what was happening to the man and to the society we have to ask questions which lead simultaneously to literary analysis and to analysis of social change.

Yet I must confess that the inquiries I have described are largely hypothetical. The student who tries to explore American culture even in this limited fashion by drawing upon the techniques of literary criticism and of the social sciences soon encounters difficulties.

The difficulties are due in part to the trend of literary studies in this country during the past two or three decades, which has moved away from rather than toward the social sciences. Just recently there are signs of a major shift of direction in literary criticism which may conceivably lead to more interest in the social setting of works of art. Such a change of direction would be most welcome. The techniques of analysis that have been developed by recent literary criticism should ultimately make it possible to deal with the relation between literature and culture at a much more profound level than has been attainable in the past. But change of this sort does not occur overnight, and the dominant force in literary studies is likely for some time yet to continue to be what we are familiar with as the New Criticism. This means that in general, the guiding principle will be a concern for the autonomy of the work of art.

If the New Criticism is about to give way to an even newer criticism, there is all the more reason to acknowledge its solid accomplishments. Like all literary revolutions, the New Criticism proposed to *écraser l'infâme*: it set about purifying criticism from the contamination of everything that was not literary. Again like other revolutions, this one brought with it a remarkable élan. It improved the morale of literary studies. It gave to scholarship and criticism a new penetration and intensity, and it markedly raised the level of literary instruction in American colleges and universities.

But these results were achieved only at a certain cost. The New Criticism has made it extraordinarily difficult to relate literature to the culture within which it occurs and of which it is indisputably a part. From the beginnings of the movement in the work of Ezra Pound and T. S. Eliot, it has borne the imprint of the image of the alienated artist. The cult of pure literature has implied a strongly negative attitude toward society, which within this tradition is habitually viewed as irredeemably Philistine and depraved: in Eliot's phrase, a "panorama of futility and anarchy." Although the actual techniques were largely invented and applied by other men, the master image of the movement has been Eliot's *The Waste Land,* and the critical undertaking has been strongly influenced by Eliot's idea of literature as a timeless order of eternal objects. This order he calls tradition, but it is very different from the usual conception of tradition because it is outside time and thus unhistorical or even anti-historical.

The pioneer technician of the New Criticism, I. A. Richards, had a somewhat different set of assumptions—he was at the outset, during the 1920's when he exerted his greatest influence on literary studies, an avowed Benthamite. His effort to state the doctrine of pure literature in positivist terms seems at first glance quite remote from the ideas of Pound and Eliot. But the effect of his teaching was essentially the same. Although he has now modified his original distinction between the statements of science, capable of being verified by empirical tests, and the pseudo-statements of poetry, which seem to be verifiable propositions but actually have no referent outside themselves, it has had great influence. And it separates art from society just as drastically as does Eliot's supernaturalism or Pound's denunciations of the "old bitch gone in the teeth," the "botched civilization."

Despite the sincere desire of some of the leaders in the movement to recognize the intimate relation between a work of art and its social setting, the effect of the New Criticism in practice has been to establish an apparently impassable chasm between the facts of our existence in contemporary society and the values of art. In this respect, the philosophical position of the New Criticism seems to me to bear a striking resemblance to Edgar Allan Poe's conception that art belongs to a non-empirical realm of 'ideality' totally divorced from the sordid or commonplace facts of everyday life. The root of the matter is the belief in an extreme dualism of nature and spirit. If society is taken to be a part of the natural order, and art is assigned to the realm of spirit, it becomes impossible to relate art (except negatively) to the actual culture within which it occurs.

We are no better off if we turn to the social sciences for help in seeing the culture as a whole. We merely find society without art instead of art without society. The literary critic would cut esthetic value loose from social fact; the social scientist, despite his theoretical recognition that art is an important aspect of culture, uses techniques of research which make it difficult or impossible for him to deal with the states of consciousness embodied in serious art.

To a student of literature, the social scientists seem to proceed ordinarily as if certain tangible values inherent in society were the only values that need to be taken into account. They find their reality in observed fact, and like all other scholars they have defined facts as the data which their methods of inquiry enable them to discover and record. The extreme form of this tendency is the emphasis on quantification, on the use of data susceptible of statistical treatment. The sociological studies of literature which I have encountered characteristically involve a 'content analysis' of large numbers of works of popular fiction or drama. The assumption on which they are based is, in the words of one such study, that popular literature "can be regarded as a case of 'social fantasy'—that the psychological constellations" in such material "indicate sensitive areas in the personalities of those for whom the work has appeal; their needs, assumptions and values are expressed ('projected')" in the play or novel or short story. Popular literature is used as if it were a body of material resulting from a series of projective psychological tests. This seems to me entirely justified, although I am not sure one can accept Lyman Bryson's contention that "today's popular art did not come out of yesterday's fine art . . . [but] is something developed out of natural social habits and needs by the machine." Popular art is certainly notable for its lack of originality; it is meant to be a homogeneous product identified by brand labels that the customer can count on. Its characters and situations are indeed, as another sociological study maintains, "ubiquitous mass symbols," extremely limited in range at any given moment. The relative homogeneity of popular art lends itself to the quantitative methods of content analysis.

But is nothing of consequence about a culture to be learned from its serious art? I suppose that when we speak of a serious novel, for example, we have in mind a work whose meaning is not exhausted by the identification of stereotyped ideas and attitudes in it. It is serious precisely because it differs in some respects from the mass of popular literature with which it is contemporary and with which, to be sure, it probably has something in common. The serious work has its period flavor but it also has other qualities, and some of these other qualities may be quite unique. Yet what the serious work uniquely expresses is not on that account unreal, or on that account alone unrepresentative. A description of the culture within which this book of permanent interest was created would be incomplete if we left it out of account. Subtract the work of a few dramatists from what we know of Periclean Athens, or of Elizabethan England, and our image of the culture undergoes a drastic change, quite apart from merely esthetic considerations.

The procedures of content analysis do not seem to be adapted to the analysis of works of art differing appreciably from popular art. The content that is analyzed is too rudimentary; it is, again by definition, a factor common to large numbers of works, which means a factor that is very far from exhausting the particularity of even a simple work of art. We need a method that can give us access to meanings beyond the range of such a systematic simplification—meanings that are not, so to speak, homogenized. Lacking such a method, the sociological study of the arts will inevitably yield an image of the culture which is truncated. Contemporary American culture is no doubt frightening enough, but it is made unnecessarily appalling by studies of popular art which by implication define the culture without reference to any subtleties beyond the horizon of the mass media. There is more to us than that!

In fact, there is more than that in the sociological findings. Reading the articles in the journals, one may easily forget that after all, the same culture which produced the soap opera has also produced the sociological journals. Yet if the mass culture is there, so also are the observers and interviewers, the statisticians and the appraisers. Only, they have hidden themselves. The man who conducts the content analysis and identifies the obsessive fantasies in the movies describes a world from which freedom is entirely absent and in which consciousness itself is rudimentary. He silently assumes that he and the colleagues to whom he reports his findings monopolize freedom and consciousness. The mores of his craft (borrowed from the natural sciences) oblige him to conceal his own consciousness behind statistical tables, and he seeks to deny his own individuality by a ceremonial avoidance of the first person. A kind of automation is suggested by these devices of rhetoric: the third person and the passive voice seem to establish as the model of the society a self-contained mechanism from which consciousness has been banished. The scientific observer is outside the field of his observations. He simply makes dial-readings.

I have suggested that the rhetoric of the social sciences seems to reflect an effort to minimize the role of consciousness. This observation can be justly extended to other aspects of the attitude toward language that an outsider encounters in reading current scholarship in these fields. Content analysis of works of literature, for example, requires the investigator to leave entirely out of account the actual words of the individual texts. The content which is extracted for counting and comparison with the content of other texts is detached from its original form of expression and thereafter exists (if it exists at all) in the neutral linguistic matrix of paraphrase. Here again, a procedure which may be suitable in dealing with texts lacking distinction of style is inappropriate in dealing with a serious work of literature. For what can be paraphrased is a small part of the whole meaning of such a work. The range of possible human experiences beyond the limits of paraphrasable meaning is the province of imaginative or poetic language. The complex modes of statement which characterize the truly imaginative use of language (and I would be understood here as referring to the different vocabularies of the several arts) are the only instruments we have for embodying and communicating the full content of consciousness.

These more complex meanings are just as real as are the stereotyped fantasies of popular art; in fact, they are more real, because they are more precisely and durably embodied in the medium. And they are part of the culture. A hundred years ago it might have been said that they make up the whole of culture. We believe differently now, and I trust I have made it clear that I have no intention of trying to reinstate a conception of the arts as existing in a separate esthetic realm which contains all values. But I believe the social sciences have reacted too strongly against Matthew Arnold's view of culture. A fully adequate science of society will recognize the existence and the importance of the experiences and attitudes with which Arnold was concerned. And this recognition is possible only for one who is aware of the almost infinite subtlety and complexity of imaginative modes of statement. To recognize no serious and accurate function of language except its use as an instrument of precise denotation is to reduce the scope of consciousness and to deny the significance of whole universes of human experience. The result is a mutilated image of man and of culture.

I have described a situation in which, as it seems to me, the characteristic methods of literary criticism and the social sciences exhibit, each in its own way, serious shortcomings from the standpoint of the enterprise of understanding American culture as a whole. The social sciences seem to me to assume too hastily that all value is implicit in social experience, in group behavior, in institutions, in man as an average member of society. Current literary criticism assumes, also too hastily, that value lies outside society, in works of art which exist on a plane remote from the Waste Land of our actual experience. I have sincere respect for the accomplishments of American scholarship in all these areas, and I recognize that these accomplishments have been made possible only by the rigorous narrowing of fields of inquiry, by the specialization of interests that has been so marked a feature of scholarship in this country during the past half-century. On the other hand, I also believe that the desire to study American culture as a whole, which underlies the nascent movement toward American Studies, has valid motives behind it, and that without disturbing sociologists or literary critics in their important undertakings we can properly ask whether a method can not be found for investigating the whole of the culture.

The concept 'culture' seems, in the abstract at least, to embrace the concepts 'society' and 'art.' Why may we not say quite simply that the problem of method in American Studies can be solved by presupposing a value implicit in culture which includes and reconciles the apparently disparate values assumed in the disciplines of, say, literature and sociology? From this point of view, the problem of method in American Studies might seem to find its answer in the already existing field of cultural anthropology. But is this formula more than a verbal solution to the dilemma? The central question is whether cultural anthropology can take account of the full range of meanings available to us in the arts of complex modern societies like our own. From a sketchy acquaintance with some of the scholarship in this field, I gain the impression that when it undertakes the study of complex societies, it tends to resemble sociology, with perhaps a stronger inclination to invoke comparisons between advanced and preliterate cultures. Moreover, cultural anthropology does not seem to differ appreciably from sociology in its assumptions about the relation of fact and value.

I conclude, in short, that no ready-made method for American Studies is in sight. We shall have to develop one for ourselves, and I am afraid that at present we shall have to be content with a very modest program. The best thing we can do, in my opinion, is to conceive of American Studies as a collaboration among men working from within existing academic disciplines but attempting to widen the boundaries imposed by conventional methods of inquiry. This implies a sustained effort of the student of literature to take account of sociological, historical and anthropological data and methods, and of the sociologist or the historian to take account of the data and methods of scholarship in the fields of the arts. I am optimistic enough to believe that inquiries which have their starting-points in various academic departments can converge as they are brought to bear upon a single topic, namely, American culture past and present.

Method in scholarship grows out of practice, or rather out of repeated criticism of practice intended to remedy observed shortcomings. In the inadequacies of answers we have found to our questions we discover clues to the reformulation of the questions, and the reformulated questions in turn suggest new ways of finding answers. If I insist that the development of a method for American Studies is bound up with an effort to resolve the dilemma posed by the dualism which separates social facts from esthetic values, I do not imagine that a new method can be deduced from philosophical premises. A new method will have to come piecemeal, through a kind of principled opportunism, in the course of daily struggles with our various tasks. No one man will be able to redesign the whole enterprise. What will count is the image in our minds of the structure we believe we are helping to build. Such an image will influence a long series of particular decisions, will determine a tendency over a period of time rather than give us a new apparatus all at once.

From the standpoint of the social sciences the lines of investigation I have mentioned probably seem of limited value because they point to the analysis of specific, individual cases. This is an inevitable consequence of the nature of literary and historical inquiry. But I venture to suggest that individual instances embody whatever uniformities may exist in a culture, and that a really exhaustive knowledge of the concrete case—a work of art, a specific situation, a career—might well lead to the recognition of aspects of the culture which have previously escaped attention. At the very least one might hope for suggestions capable of being formulated as hypotheses and then tested against more extensive evidence. Why is it not conceivable that the masterpiece of literature, or the exceptionally productive career, might turn out to be an expression of the culture in ways beyond the scope of stereotyped examples of popular art or merely average life-patterns?

26. The Historical Dimension*

C. Vann Woodward

It would seem to be high time for some Southern historian to abandon temporarily the standoffishness of his guild and make his bow to Southern men of letters. Not that it is necessary at this late date to acknowledge that the literary men have earned the greater acclaim and distinction. That goes without saying. What is really needed is some acknowledgment of the genuine debt the historians owe to the poets, playwrights, and novelists—particularly the novelists—as well as an acknowledgment of vital relations between the crafts.

The generation of Southerners who went to college in the 1920's usually took a defensive attitude toward the history of their region, or affected indifference. It was an attitude compounded of several components: the college boy's revolt against the ideas and values of his parents, the striving to cover up a consciousness of provincialism, and an eagerness to appear abreast of the times, if not a little in advance. Even so staunch a traditionalist as Donald Davidson admitted the force of these impulses when he wrote in 1926: "The gallantries of the Lost Cause, the legends of Southern history—these he may admire, but they came to him mouthed over and cheapened . . . the treacly lamentations of the old school."

Being "old school" in the 1920's was the worst possible offense against the canons of the collegian, and he strove with all his might to avoid the charge. He readily gathered from the literary monitors of fashion and taste whom he admired that there was nothing issuing from his native region in the

* Reprinted with permission from *The Virginia Quarterly Review*, XXXII (Spring, 1956), 258–267.

way of arts and letters that was worth his notice. When "The Sound and the Fury" appeared in 1929 he was assured by the New Republic that it "signified nothing." He also absorbed the impression from numerous quarters that the history of the South was generally discreditable if not faintly ridiculous. All things considered, it was not the most auspicious background for one who aspired to become a Southern historian.

The Southerner who was graduated about 1930 was soon aware of new voices in the land and new forces astir. He doubtless derived some encouragement from the contemporary awakening of historical scholarship, particularly if he hoped to be a historian. But it was soon apparent that the stir among historians was only a minor aspect of a wider intellectual awakening in the South. The most brilliant manifestation was in the field of letters and literary criticism. To mention only a few books of one author, within the three years beginning in 1929 there appeared William Faulkner's "Sartoris," "The Sound and the Fury," "As I Lay Dying," "Sanctuary," and "Light in August"—a one-man renaissance by 1932. Katherine Anne Porter's first book, "Flowering Judas," appeared in 1930. Shortly before that there arose the bright star of Thomas Wolfe with the appearance of "Look Homeward, Angel." Of all American novels, that is the book of the young man, especially the young Southerner, and no one who read it in his youth will forget the strange excitement of the experience. The early thirties were stirring years to be discovering the South and its history and spending the years of one's youth.

The spice of controversy and polemic was added by the Nashville manifesto, "I'll Take My Stand," in 1930. Counterblast provoked counterblast, and the controversy raged on in the pages of Davidson's "Attack on Leviathan" and in successive numbers of the American Review and later in the Southern Review. With the establishment of the latter in 1935 the center of the avant garde of American literary criticism shifted temporarily to the banks of the Mississippi at Baton Rouge. Gradually the pundits and critical moguls on the Hudson began to alter their tone about the "Sahara of the Bozart." An occasional note of praise, then of cautious respect, were succeeded by fulsome acclaim and eventually by a sort of awed puzzlement at this sudden flowering of the cultural desert. The young Southerner took a vicarious pride in all this achievement, a pride that did wonders for his provincial inferiority complex. He hailed the

new names as they appeared—Robert Penn Warren, Eudora
Welty, Tennessee Williams—and new ones kept on arriving
upon the scene.

Allen Tate spoke of this outpouring as "quite temporary" in
1935 and thought that year marked "the height of the Southern
literary renaissance." But in 1935 some of the brighter luminaries had not yet appeared on the horizon. Again, in 1945
Tate wrote that "that Renascence is over. . . ." But in 1955
Andrew Nelson Lytle could declare: "The Renascence has been
going on for thirty years with little sign of diminishment." The
fact is that we have grown up with this movement, and it will
remain for a later generation to fix its limits and assess its
achievements.

Our concern here is with its significance for the historian
rather than with its place in history. It was early apparent that
the new Southern writers had something special to say to the
historian, something that no other living American writers—
and few dead ones—-seemed to say. If he had read any American
literature in college it was not likely to have been of Southern
origin. The literary awakening of the Middle West was still in
the public eye in the twenties, and the collegian of that era
plowed through his Theodore Dreiser, Edgar Lee Masters, Sherwood Anderson, and Sinclair Lewis. There was little in their
pages to increase his respect or deepen his appreciation for the
uses of history. The characters in the novels of Dreiser, Anderson, and Lewis appear on the scene from nowhere, trailing no
clouds of history, dissociated from the past. They seem to have
left it behind them in New England, or Norway, or Bavaria,
and along with their past they checked their forebears, their
historical roots and associations. One has the feeling that they
considered that heritage a good riddance. They rarely discuss
it, and one gathers there was no room for it in such baggage as
they brought along to Gopher Prairie, Winesburg, or Chicago.

In the work of some later writers the historical perspective is
even more flat. Hemingway's characters appear to live completely in the present. To emphasize their historical rootless-
ness, they are invariably pictured as expatriates, as wanderers,
as soldiers or adventurers. They are temporarily in Italy or
Spain, in France or Africa, in Cuba or the Florida Keys. A
Hemingway hero with a grandfather is inconceivable, and he
is apparently quite as bereft of uncles, aunts, cousins, and in-
laws, not to mention neighbors and poor relations. With Dos

Passos the story is somewhat different. But for all his marvelous gift for evoking a given place or a period of the recent past (a gift historians can but envy), his characters are exclusively preoccupied with personal problems or with social problems of their own time. They are haunted by no ghosts of the past, and the past does not seem to be part of the present. If our collegian was coached through a reading of the literary flowering of New England that took place a century or more ago, he will have discovered little more of the historical dimension than he found in the more recent schools. The New Englanders, with the exception of Hawthorne, regularly pictured the individual starkly alone with his problems, his wilderness, or his God. Cooper and Henry James offer a certain amount of historical depth, but the characters of Melville appear to live entirely in the present or the future and to concern themselves seldom with the past.

To discover the new school of Southern fiction after 1930 was to enter suddenly upon a new world of the imagination, a world in which the historical imagination played a supreme part. In his essay on "The Profession of Letters in the South," Allen Tate has fixed upon "The peculiarly historical consciousness of the Southern writers" as the secret spring of creative energies that has fed the whole literary movement in the South during the last three decades. Tate has also suggested an historical explanation for the intellectual awakening of the South and the heightening of historical consciousness so characteristic of it. He suggests that after the First World War the South arrived at a crossroads of history where an old traditional order was being rapidly obliterated and a new modern order was being simultaneously brought to birth. Caught at these crossroads, the Southerner was made more keenly conscious at once of the present and of the past. His sensitivity to present change heightened his awareness of past differences, and his intensified remembrance of things past added corresponding poignancy to his awareness of things present. As Tate put it, "that backward glance gave us the Southern renascence, a literature conscious of the past in the present."

A claim to what Tate called "the peculiarly historical consciousness of the Southern writer" was made by Ellen Glasgow in her posthumously published autobiography. "I had been born," she wrote, "with an intimate feeling for the spirit of the past, and the lingering poetry of time and place." In the last of his ten volumes Arnold Toynbee advances the theory that "the vividness of historical impressions is apt to be proportionate to their violence and painfulness," and speculates that "a child who had lived through the American Civil War in the territory of the Southern Confederacy would be likely to grow up more historical-minded than one who had lived through the same experience at the North." In this connection a statement of Katherine Anne Porter has some relevance. "I am a grandchild of a lost War," she writes in "The Days Before," "and I have blood-knowledge of what life can be in a defeated country on the bare bones of privation."

In emphasizing the place that historical consciousness plays in contemporary Southern writing, I have no reference to the vogue of the conventional historical novel. The South has produced its share of the historical romance output, and during the early years of the present century when the market reached one of its peaks, Southern romancers produced considerably more than their share of best-sellers. But production figures reveal no particular regional concentration. The Northern and Western writers have proved themselves as handy at this craft as the Southern. Their product has little to do with Tate's "literature conscious of the past in the present." And it might be observed parenthetically that modern craftsmen of that school sometimes reverse Tate's description and tend at times to interject a dubious awareness of the present in the past. At any rate, we are not concerned here with the historical romance—whether its purpose is to score some point about the present or to settle some score about the past.

It is interesting but quite tangential to the argument that the first books of two leading figures of the Southern Renaissance were not in the field of fiction but of history. These were Allen Tate's biography of Stonewall Jackson, published in 1928, and Robert Penn Warren's biography of John Brown, published in 1929. It is also a source of great fascination to the historian—though still neither essential nor quite relevant to the thesis—that some of our most gifted novelists have chosen historical periods or figures or movements as subjects. Ellen Glasgow set out early in her career to write what she described as "a social history of Virginia" from 1850 to 1912. It must be admitted, however, that none of her "Novels of the Commonwealth," as she called them, are among her best works. Faulkner has been engaged for the better part of three decades in rounding out his Yoknapatawpha world of McCaslins, Sartorises, and Compsons; its MacCallums, Bundrens, and Snopeses; its Joe Christmases, Lucas Beauchamps, and Charles Bons. While this saga so far represents the supreme creation of the Southern Renaissance, it is not history in any usual sense. And it is not unlikely that the Faulkner critics have gone astray in thinking of the Yoknapatawpha novels as Southern history in microcosm, or as representing any very consistent ideas or theories about Southern history. In the universality of their meaning they are more, and in their immediate application, less than that.

The Southern novelist who comes nearest approaching an historical subject after the manner of an historian is Warren. Yet Warren is careful and perfectly correct to warn the reader of "Night Rider" that "Although this book was suggested by certain events which took place in Kentucky in the early years of the century, it is not, in any strict sense, a historical novel." What Warren has pronounced "the bone-headedness or gospel-bit hysteria" or those who insist upon making either history or a political tract out of "All the King's Men" drives the author to despair. He quotes Louis Armstrong as remarking, "There is some folks that if they don't know, you can't tell 'em." While Warren selects the same sort of subject matter as the historian—the Black Patch War in Kentucky during the first decade of the century, a financial tycoon of Tennessee in the twenties, or a demagogue of Louisiana in the thirties—he could rightly say of them all, as he said of the first, that they are not historical novels in any strict sense. At the same time it could be as accurately said that they quicken and vivify our consciousness of history in a way that conventional historical novels, as well as many bona fide histories, do not.

The relevance of the theme of "historical consciousness" in Southern letters would have been the same had the novelists never tackled a historical subject or treated any period prior to Appomattox. It is not the period or the subject that is the point but, in Tate's words, the consciousness of the past in the present. Here, among many possible illustrations, one thinks of Katherine Anne Porter's Miranda, in "Old Mortality," seeking through the years of her youth to find and come to terms with her family's past and her own past and to relate them to the present. Or of Thomas Wolfe's Eugene Gant, "the haunter of himself, trying for a moment to recover what he had been part of . . . a stone, a leaf, an unfound door," and lyrically imploring, "Ghost, come back again." Or of Faulkner's Quentin Compson in "Absalom, Absalom!" groping through the convolutions of Colonel Sutpen's incredible legend for an answer to Shreve McCannon's questions in 1910. Or of Warren's Jack Burden in "All the King's Men" brooding endlessly over the faded letters and diaries of Cass Mastern for a lost meaning to the past and a key to the present in the 1930's.

This preoccupation, this almost obsessive concern of Southern writers with the past in the present has been expressed often explicitly as well as implicitly in their stories. Thus John Peale Bishop wrote in his essay, "The South and Tradition," that "without a past we are living not in the present, but in a vague and rather unsatisfactory future." Katherine Anne Porter remarks of Miranda's family that "their hearts and imaginations were captivated by their past," but while the author never treats that past as such, it is constantly obtruding itself into the present she does treat. On the other hand, Ellen Glasgow did repeatedly treat historical episodes and epochs, but her most successful use of the past was probably in such unhistorical novels as "Barren Ground" and "The Sheltered Life." For all his reference to the Old South, Faulkner has never attempted a full-bodied treatment of the Civil War, as much as it impinges on his major themes. His themes have been preponderantly those of the post-bellum South. Still, he has Gavin Stevens say in "Intruder in the Dust," "The past is never dead. It's not even past." In the course of a bear hunt we are taken all the way back to tribal life among the aborigines of Mississippi through Sam Fathers, their descendant. For the Southern school the present is a fleeting segment of the cumulative past, and might be described by the concluding words of "All the King's Men": ". . . out of history, into history and the awful responsibility of Time."

Another deeply embedded trait of the Southern novelists that has strong appeal to the historian is their way of treating man not as an individual alone with his conscience or his God, as the New Englanders were inclined to do, or alone at sea with a whale or a marlin, or alone in a ring with a bull, but as an inextricable part of a living history and community, attached and determined in a thousand ways by other wills and destinies of people he has only heard about. Herbert Marshall McLuhan has remarked that "The sense of belonging to a great chain of persons and events, passive yet responsible, is everywhere in Faulkner." And he quotes T. S. Stribling on "the chain of wrongs and violences out of which his life had been molded." In his most recent novel Warren has its narrator say, "You live through time, that little piece of time that is yours, but that piece of time is not only your own life, it is the summing-up of all the other lives that are simultaneous with yours." This, in sum, is also the way the historian tries to see the individual and the forces that mold him.

Francis B. Simkins has urged that "The historian of the South should join the social novelist who accepts the values of the age and section about which he writes." The trouble lies in the ambiguities of the verb "to accept." And there is also the question of which values and what age. Faulkner certainly never accepted the values of the Snopeses, nor of the Compsons either. For it is just the tragedy of the Compsons in "The Sound and the Fury" that in the person of Jason Compson they *did* accept the values of the age—the age of the Snopeses. The historian like the novelist should not change his values with his ages, whether it is the age of Colonel Sutpen or of Jason Compson. This was precisely the mistake of the John B. Gordons and Basil Dukes and their generation. They did.

The best of the Southern novelists have never set out to defend the values or the prejudices or the errors of any particular age or section. It is true that their books are often filled with tales of horror and lust and betrayal and degradation. But they have not paused to reckon their popularity in attacking the values of their own age or any other. They have not set up as defenders of a cause, either one lost or one still sought. They have proved themselves able to confront the chaos and irony of history with the admission that they can fit them into no neat pattern and explain them by no pat theory.

The historian is fortunate, I think, in sharing a period with literary men of great talent who share so many of his own values, so much of his own outlook and point of view, and so much of his own subject matter. He can afford to take pride in their achievements and comfort in their example. This is no plea for the relaxation of the severe limitations of the historian's discipline, nor for his borrowing the novelist's license. But once the historian abandons an old and false analogy with the natural sciences and sees that his craft employs no special concepts nor categories nor special terminology, he will admit that he attempts to "explain" history in the same way he explains events in ordinary life—his own as well as that of his fellow men—and with much the same language. moral and psychological. He should then be willing to acknowledge that Southern men of letters have advanced many of the aims he shares. They have helped us penetrate the romantic haze of an older generation as well as the cynical stereotypes of our own. They have endowed the denigrated and emotionally impoverished New South with a sense of tragedy and dignity that history had hitherto reserved for the Old Régime, and they have enriched our consciousness of the past in the present. They have helped to bring the Negro into intelligible focus without the glasses of sentimentality. And they have given history meaning and value and significance as events never do merely because they happen. These are things the historian also strives to do, and he should seek to do them with the same fortitude and honesty.

PART SEVEN

Research and Writing

Introductory Notes

In the preceding sections of this book, our subjects have been the premises and substance of historical writing, the way these have changed, and why. In this section, our subject is the actual process of historical writing, the several operations by which an idea is pursued through research and expressed in words.

In his paper on "The Problems of the Working Historian," Bernard Bailyn suggests that the two subjects have no practical, tangible connection, that the writing of history is unaffected by considerations about the nature and premises of historical inquiry. Two things ought to be said about Professor Bailyn's comment. First, there was a close connection between both subjects in the writings of our foremost historians, men such as Bancroft, Henry Adams, Turner, Becker, and Beard, each of whom was remarkably self-conscious and explicit about the relevance of premises to practice, and of thinking about the nature of history to the actual writing of history. Second, the fact that an individual has not explicitly considered how historical "philosophy" shapes historical writing does not mean that the writing is without philosophy—that what may not have been admitted formally through the front door did not enter informally through the back. There are more things in historical writing than are dreamt of as "philosophy."

Yet Professor Bailyn's comment has its own significance. It reminds one of Tocqueville's observation that Americans are more given to practical science than to theoretical: "They mistrust systems; they adhere closely to facts and study facts with their own senses." Indeed, in the usual course of historical study in the United States, systems and an awareness of systems are passed by; the pursuit and presentation of facts, generally gleaned from a hitherto untapped body of source materials of whatever significance, are the principal work of seminars. The slogan of the seminarian is the slogan of any other pugilist in the American entrepreneurial arena: go out there and write.

Professor Bailyn's paper lists three major problems that face the working historian: selecting a topic, conducting research, and presenting the material. This list will serve us well as a thematic guide to the essays contained in this section. Walter Prescott Webb's essay on the historical seminar argues that the topic of research is the essence of a meaningful seminar, that research has an inner spirit only when it is conducted in pursuit of an important idea. The problem of conducting research is considered in the four essays that follow Webb's. Douglas E. Leach explains how certain types of sources—the town records of early New England—may be used to reconstruct the everyday life of a community. Richard B. Morris details the several important bodies of materials that are available for the study of labor history prior to the Civil War. The papers of the Adams family constitute one of the richest sources for the study of American history; concentrating on the respective eras of their interest, Merrill Jensen, Samuel Flagg Bemis, and David Donald discuss these papers in terms of both their substance and significance. In "History This Side the Horizon," Allan Nevins reminds us that the sources of tomorrow's history lie close at hand in today's experience. The final problem facing the working historian is the written presentation of his material. This problem is discussed by George F. Kennan, not so much from the standpoint of the technicalities of writing, but rather from that of the writer's involvement in the history he is writing.

The writers of the following essays bring very substantial qualifications to the subjects they are discussing. Nothing more need be added about the two whom we have already met: Allan Nevins and Bernard Bailyn. Walter Prescott Webb, who died in March 1963, taught for four and a half decades at the University of Texas; best known for *The Great Plains* (1931), he also wrote *The Texas Rangers* (1935), *Divided We Stand* (1937), and *The Great Frontier* (1952). He was president of both the Mississippi Valley Historical Association and the American Historical Association. Douglas E. Leach teaches at Vanderbilt University and is the author of *Flintlock and Tomahawk: New England in King Philip's War* (1958). Richard B. Morris is Gouverneur Morris Professor of American History at Columbia University and one of America's leading colonial historians. He is co-editor of the New American Nation Series, of which some twenty volumes have thus far appeared. His many writings include *Government and Labor in Early America* (1946) and *The Peacemakers* (1965).

Merrill Jensen teaches at the University of Wisconsin; his two volumes, *The Articles of Confederation* (1940) and *The New Nation* (1950) are indispensable to an understanding of the revolutionary era. Samuel Flagg Bemis, who taught at Yale University until his retirement in 1961, is one of our outstanding diplomatic historians. His writings, which center mainly on the early national period, have twice earned him the Pulitzer Prize, and include two volumes of the diplomatic career and achievement of John Quincy Adams. David Donald, who is Harry C. Black Professor of American History at the Johns Hopkins University, has rapidly established himself as a first-rate scholar in the field of Civil War and Lincoln studies. His works include *Lincoln's Herndon* (1948), *Lincoln Reconsidered* (1956), and *Charles Sumner and the Coming of the Civil War* (1960), for which he won the Pulitzer Prize. Together with his wife, Aïda Di Pace Donald, he has edited the early years of the diary of Charles Francis Adams, two volumes of which have recently appeared.

George F. Kennan is Professor of the School of Historical Studies (of the Institute of Advanced Study) at Princeton. He served for many years in various diplomatic missions in Europe and was our ambassador to Yugoslavia from 1961 to 1963. His concern with modern international relations in general and with Russo-American relations in particular, underlies all his writings: *American Diplomacy, 1900–1950* (1950); *Realities of American Foreign Policy* (1954); *Russia, the Atom, and the West* (1958); *Russia and the West under Lenin and Stalin* (1961), and a multi-volume history of *Soviet-American Rela-*

tions, 1917–1920, of which two volumes have thus far appeared.

The essays that follow will afford the student rich suggestions about the kinds of problems he will meet in historical
research and writing, and also about possible solutions of them.
But he will understand from several of the essays that a command of the historian's craft rests on more than a command
of sources and of style. The trouble with much historical training in the United States is, as Walter Prescott Webb suggests,
that it is training in techniques rather than in ideas. Indeed,
techniques often substitute for ideas. "But history," as the
great French medievalist, Marc Bloch, has said, "is neither
watchmaking nor cabinet construction. It is an endeavor toward better understanding. . . ."

To achieve that better understanding, the student must ex-
ceed mere technical proficiency. Far more significant than the
sources a historian has canvassed is the perception with which he
has canvassed them. To write meaningful history one must ask
meaningful questions. Posing important questions makes the
meanest subject important; posing no questions, or petty ones,
reduces the grandest subject to insignificance. Doing research
on the past without searching it profoundly is a mindless indul-
gence. Too often the student supposes that by staking out his
claim to a body of sources he has insured the value of his contribution. Using manuscript materials in master's and doctoral
theses tends frequently to become an empty, unthinking ritual;
all too often, though purporting to signify the student's mature
entry into the mysteries of his profession, it signifies merely that
precedence has been taken by ceremony over cerebration, by
footnote over theme, by matter over art. Canvassing the sources
is only one part, and not the most important, of writing history:
far more important is exercising a creative and informed intelligence in order to command the whole process of thinking and
writing about the past.

The student must do more than seek answers to questions
about the particular subject he is studying. He must also seek
answers to basic questions about historical inquiry, such questions indeed as we have been considering all through this book:
about the nature and uses of historical inquiry; about the possibility of achieving truth and objectivity in history; about the
degree to which history is science and the degree to which it is
art; about the role of the historian—whether he is a reporter, an
impartial judge, a critic, or all three. No full answer to these

questions is possible, but no valid historical writing is possible which does not at least seek to answer them. The working day of the historian may not require a regular review of the basic premises of historical inquiry, but if it does not rest on these premises and proceed from them, then it is a day and work misspent.

Writing history demands too a sense of the past, a retrospective imagination which brings the writer back to the pressing realities of an earlier period, to a point at which the men he is writing about are alive with prospects and the problems before them are as yet unsolved. In this respect, as George F. Kennan so well tells us, the historian stands alone, writing about an earlier world in which only he is alive, but living in the world of his own day, to which he must be partly dead. That he must possess a retrospective imagination means ultimately that the historian's function is, in the words of C. V. Wedgwood, "neither more nor less than that of any other creative writer. All literature arises from human experience and therefore all literature arises in the ultimate resort from historical material. The discipline and technique to which the historian submits his material is different from that of the imaginative writer. But the nature of his material is the same and the historian, in so far as he stands or wishes to stand within the bounds of literature at all, has the same task as the creative artist." This is indeed the very point that Arthur M. Schlesinger, Jr. has made in a superb essay in a recent article in the *Atlantic* magazine, entitled "The Historian as Artist."

A sense of the past requires something beyond retrospective imagination. It requires a view of the past as the outworking of human will and social tendencies. It requires a deep insight into both individuals and society, insight that is informed and chastened by intelligences from all areas of knowledge, particularly from social science. And it requires no less significantly commitment to values, moral decision, judgment about right and wrong. These are the qualities, certainly, that distinguish the foremost historians of our own age, men such as Allan Nevins and C. Vann Woodward, and they have distinguished no less the principal historians of other ages and other countries: Gibbon, Ranke, Macaulay, Burckhardt, Kliuchevskii, Maitland, Croce. One would add only this, that a sense of the past requires a sense of human purpose and of the tendency of human life. Let the student seek and find where he will, whether it be with Toynbee's credo of the Church Militant, with Reinhold Niebuhr's view that history is paradox, or with Herbert Muller's conclusion that man's inspiration must begin with a tragic view of his history.

The study and writing of American history ought to include a survey of those who have contributed signally to the treasury of our historical literature: Bradford, Bancroft, Parkman, Prescott, Motley, Henry Adams, Nevins, to cite the indisputable masters. The student ought to know the several qualities which have put these historians at the top of their calling, and how the combination of qualities has differed from one historian to the next. He should know too the values which served each writer as the canvas on which to draw his particular portrait of an age, and how these values have varied from one historian to another and from one age to the next. The shifting premises of historical inquiry must be a component of the student's knowledge. It is fair to say that historical inquiry, while it should not end merely with the concept of relativism, can not validly begin without it.

But if a master historian is a guide to the historical writing of his age, he is at best a guide to only a part of it. However much they subscribe to many of the major values of their age, not all contemporary historians see the past in the same way. The cult of Clio is variously practiced. One has but to consider a few of its most distinguished present-day practitioners —Edmund Sears Morgan, Oscar Handlin, David Donald, Richard Hofstadter, Arthur S. Link, and Arthur M. Schlesinger, Jr.—to realize that a larger faith may be consummated by a rich diversity of works.

In his pursuit of the past, the student will surely wish to consider Sir Lewis Namier's suggestion that "the historical approach is intellectually humble" and Carl Becker's list of the qualities of a good historian: ". . . intelligence, experience of men and things, insight into human conduct, literary ability, and last but not least knowledge. . . ." At every turn, he will come upon the sentiment of our foremost historians that the discipline of history requires vision no less than effort, imagination no less than research, and that a historian's sense of the past is more than the sum of his sources.

The study and writing of American history offer the novice

both a challenge and a reward. The challenge is that of serving a devoted apprenticeship and of striving for a distinguished mastery. It is not merely one of commanding a wide body of materials and skills, but of making of them something individual and personal. To the achievement of science, the student must ultimately add the insight of art. But this will be his reward. Pursuing the craft of history will bring him more than the entertainment of reading a great literature; it will bring him more than the instruction that a knowledge of the past affords those studying the directions of the present. The student will have achieved, through both his study and writing, something that is uniquely his own. He will have defined his relation to his calling: his purview, his premises, his commitment, his abilities, himself.

The study and writing of history are in this sense a work of self-consciousness, of self-identification. Like every work of scholarship and thought, they require that the scholar and thinker come to grips with his society and his age. Speaking one's mind about the past is no mean act. The student and writer of American history is ultimately Emerson's American scholar, sharing with him the trials and triumphs of Man Thinking.

Suggestions for Further Reading

Baker, Sheridan, "Scholarly Style, or the Lack Thereof," *AAUP Bulletin,* XLII (Autumn 1956), 464–470.

Benison, Saul, "Oral History and Manuscript Collecting," *Isis,* LIII (March 1962), 113–117.

—————, "Reflections on Oral History," *American Archivist,* XXVIII (January 1965), 71–77.

Binkley, William C., "A Historian Looks at the National Union Catalog of Manuscript Collections," *American Archivist,* XXVIII (July 1965), 399–407.

Boyd, Julian P., "God's Altar Needs Not Our Pollishings," *New York History,* LVI (January 1958), 3–21.

Butterfield, Lyman H., "Bostonians and Their Neighbors as Pack Rats," *American Archivist,* XXIV (April 1961), 141–159.

—————, "Whatever You Write, Preserve," *American Heritage,* X (April 1959), 27–33, 88–93.

Caswell, John E. "Archives for Tomorrow's Historians," *American Archivist,* XXI (October 1958), 409–417.

Fishbein, Meyer H., "Business History Resources in the National Archives," *Business History Review*, XXXVIII (Summer 1964), 232–257.

Hays, Samuel P., "Archival Sources for American Political History," *American Archivist*, XXVIII (January 1965), 17–30.

Jennings, Francis P., "A Vanishing Indian: Francis Parkman Versus His Sources," *Pennsylvania Magazine of History and Biography*, LXXXVII (July 1963), 306–323.

Koch, Adrienne, "The Historian as Scholar," *Nation*, CXCV (November 24, 1962), 357–361.

Leland, Waldo G., "The Prehistory and Origins of the National Historical Publications Commission," *American Archivist*, XXVII (April 1964), 187–194.

Lurie, Edward, "Some Observations on Research in Nineteenth Century Science," *Isis*, LIII (March 1962), 21–30.

Morison, Elting E., "Some Thoughts on the Roosevelt Papers," *Library of Congress Quarterly Journal of Current Acquisitions*, XV (May 1958), 101–105.

Morrissey, Charles T., "The Case for Oral History," *Vermont History* XXXI (July 1963), 145–155.

Morton, Louis, "Sources for the History of World War II," *World Politics*, XIII (April 1961), 435–453.

Olson, James C., "The Scholar and Documentary Publication," *American Archivist*, XXVIII (April 1965), 187–194.

Stewart, William J., "The Sources of Labor History: Problem and Promise," *American Archivist*, XXVII (January 1964), 95–102.

Wright, Louis B., "Huntington and Folger: Book Collectors with a Purpose," *Atlantic*, CCIX (April 1962), 70–74.

27. The Problems of the Working Historian: A Comment*

BERNARD BAILYN

Professor Gershoy, in his paper on the problems of the working historian, has reached conclusions with which I both agree and disagree.

He has asked, first, "what constitutes the raw material of historical inquiry?" His answer is: facts, which are pieces of information, themselves inert and meaningless, charged with significance by the inquiring mind of the historian noting their relevance to the matter at hand. In this sense the "effective existence" of facts is a creation of the historian's consciousness. He has considered, second, the double question of the extent to which history is a science and the degree of objectivity that historians can achieve. His conclusion is that historians can "come closer to the objective procedures of the modern scientist than the relativist critics of Ranke had imagined possible," for though the historian's hypotheses are subjective in that they "exist in [his] mind" and though "the knowledge that the historian derives from historical facts is of a different nature than the knowledge that the scientist obtains from his instruments," nevertheless historical investigation is not so very different from scientific investigation: the scientist too makes hypotheses with his mind and he too does not obtain 100 percent certainty in his conclusions. As for the related question of how far one can generalize from the historical particular to the general and hence use history as the basis for predicting

* Reprinted with permission from *Philosophy and History: A Symposium,* ed. Sidney Hook (New York: New York University Press, 1961), 92–101.

the future, Professor Gershoy answers that while generalizations from history have no "universal validity or absolute
predictive certainty, they do . . . suggest the range of the
possible" and furnish "a working measure of probability." In
conclusion, Professor Gershoy describes himself as an optimist
concerning the present tendencies within the discipline of
history. He believes that younger historians, despite the gloomy
things that have been said about them, are in fact agreeing
more and more on "answers to the questions about the kind
of knowledge that the historian seeks and the nature of the
data that he uses," as well as on "the hypotheses they posit
and the empirical facts they assemble and examine." There is,
he feels, a growing sophistication among historians concerning
causation and determinism, free will and inevitability, the
unique and the general.

I find myself on the whole in agreement with these conclusions. I too believe that historians are capable of achieving a
large measure of objectivity and impartiality; I too believe
that raw data become effective facts when they are seen to be
relevant by the historian's inquiring mind; and I agree that
the discipline of history is flourishing, and that gloomy pre-
dictions about its future are unjustified.

What I disagree with is something more basic than these
points. I wonder whether, if what one is concerned with is the
actual problems of the working historian, he should be talking
about such matters as these at all. I believe Professor Gershoy
to have been too generous to a certain tradition in defining
what the problems of historical study are. For there is a
variety of problems involved in historical investigation, and
while they are all in some way related to each other, there are
yet significant distinctions among them. These distinctions are
especially important when it is "the working historian" one is
talking about. Problems of objectivity and subjectivity, the involvement or detachment of the inquiring mind, the nature of
facts, and the predictive value of historical knowledge are obviously exciting and fruitful subjects for anyone, philosopher
or historian, to consider. But they fall more naturally and immediately into the provinces of thought of the working philosopher, of a certain type of interest, than of the working
historian. Let me put it more bluntly and personally. Like
many historians, I have had a good deal of interest in these
questions; and I have pursued them as far as time and ability

have allowed me to. But insofar as my concern has been with understanding, teaching, and writing about what has happened in the past, I have never once felt it necessary to work out precise answers to such questions—questions of objectivity and subjectivity, the nature of fact, etc.—in order to advance my work in history. It may well be that that is too bad for me, that I am just a bad example, that I am intellectually insensitive, and that I would write better history if I spent more time on such matters. The last of these points, at least, I am quite sure is not true. What is more important is that though I have often discussed with other historians such matters as Professor Gershoy has presented, I have never yet heard from them, either, a statement to the effect that their work in history has been affected one way or the other by such considerations.

Let me be clear about this. I am not questioning the value of these problems as such. They are of course part of an important philosophical inquiry, and they are involved in the premises and in the ultimate conclusions to be drawn from historical knowledge; but the study of history is different from the study of the premises of historical thought no matter how intimately the two are related, and history is not, at least as most of us think of it, concerned with ultimate truth.

But why insist? The questions Professor Gershoy has discussed are of obvious importance in certain areas of thought even if they are not the problems of the working historian, and they undoubtedly involve the cosmic periphery and the elemental assumptions of the historian's work even if not its ordinary substance. The distinction is worth insisting upon, I believe, because if we accept the convention that these are *the* systematic problems that relate to historical study, we exclude from the consideration they deserve those other problems—humbler, perhaps, less ultimate, but more immediate problems—which historians must, in some way or other, solve in order to proceed with their work, and which they do in fact solve by extemporizations of varying degrees of crudeness. I realize that not all aspects of historical study need to be, or sensibly can be, dignified by "philosophical" analysis. But since I do not know what the boundaries of philosophy are and believe that philosophers, if not philosophy, can help the historian think more clearly and systematically about the questions with which he is daily confronted, I think it might be profitable if I attempted to sketch here, in a very tentative way, what I consider the problems of the working historian to be.

The work of the historian seems to me to group itself into three phases; and I would place the everyday problems he faces within these categories.

I. The first and, I would say, the least understood if not the most important, phase of historical study is the selection of topic.

The choices of topic modern working historians make appear to be based on observations of three distinct though partly overlapping kinds.

a) Historians decide to study and write about something because they observe that in the present state of the historical literature there is a *need* for such work, a need in the sense that a proper utilization of known resources has not been made. It might be observed, for example, that many valuable monographs and articles have been written on the French Revolution since George Lefebvre's survey was written; this new knowledge available to the specialists, one decides, should now be resynthesized with the old and a new master survey produced. Or, again, there might be a *need* for a textbook in economic history because none exists and one is needed for classroom use. Or one observes that there is a *need* for a good short narrative of the War in the Pacific, or of the Great Crash, or of Jefferson's public career—a need in the sense that the existing knowledge has not been made conveniently or properly available, and that there would be profit (in various senses) in making it available.

b) A second group of topics seems to be defined not by these considerations—considerations that we may call matters of strategy, academic, literary, even social or political—but by observations concerning the state of historical knowledge itself. These are topics that are suggested by what appear to be *gaps* in our knowledge: the consideration, for example, not that a book should be written because our knowledge has not been properly assembled or presented to best advantage, but because we do not have the knowledge of the subject that we wish to have. The motivation here is to learn something new and to present this new information; but the precise issues are not defined. There are no specific questions and no hypothetical answers. Thus the motivation for writing a narrative of a battle may be simply to discover what happened in it; to find out how it was that the victors won it. Or, again, one decides to do research and writing about Wilson's Administration because we are ignorant of it, and any thorough, clear narrative of it will be valuable because it fills an important gap, an evident vacuum.

c) A third group of topics is defined by what I would like to call true historical problems. I mean by true historical problems questions raised by the observation of (1) anomalies in the existing data, or (2) discrepancies between data and existing explanations. An example of the first would be the observation that in 1700, tobacco marketing in the Chesapeake area was handled by consignment to merchants located mainly in London; in 1760, much of it was handled by factors who lived in the colonies and were agents of firms largely located in Scotland. Why the change? The observation of the difference creates a problem of explanation, to solve which one undertakes research and writing. An example of the second type—a discrepancy between existing explanation and the data at hand—would be the following. For many generations, the American Revolution was explained as the spontaneous, unanimous uprising of a liberty-loving people against the heedless, not to say tyrannical, action of a power-hungry administration. But then it is discovered that many leaders in the colonies did not rise up as they were said to have done; indeed, a large number was openly sympathetic with the English actions, and they had the support, tacit or overt, of an estimated one-third of the population. Obviously, there is a problem here: either the Americans were not all liberty-loving, or the ministry's actions were not so heedless or tyrannical as they were thought to be, or perhaps the whole formulation is wrong; perhaps other considerations than tyranny or liberty were primarily involved. Let the subject be studied anew, then, and a more reasonable explanation given.

Needs, gaps, and *problems:* these three categories of topics obviously overlap. But they are perhaps distinctive enough in essence to serve as a starting point for more systematic thought than I believe has yet been given to the nature of historical topic-selection and problem-posing. For not every project we can conceive of that involves historical data is worth pursuing; not every question is a good one. What is the difference between a good historical problem and a poor one? Is there such a thing as a *false* historical problem? What are the criteria for deciding? Most practicing historians know a good problem when they see one; but they have acquired this knowledge from experience alone, and much of that experience is repetitious and wasteful. An efficient conceptualization would help, not in a cookbook sense by dictating the selection of problems to the historian, but by sharpening his awareness of the logic of the work he engages in and by informing him, in shorthand, of the experience that has so far been accumulated in pursuing it. One of the greatest values of the doctoral dissertation, it seems to me, is the almost universal experience gained in the process of writing it of discovering that one has given the right answers to the wrong questions. But such education, essential at one stage, becomes paralyzing if continued indefinitely.

Precise, orderly thought applied to this question would be more valuable to the working historian than volumes of speculation on whether it is conceivable to know the past, or what is the nature of a fact.

II. The second phase of the working historian's activity is the gathering of information: that is, *research*. Here again some systematic thought would be useful. Historical research is an analytical process. It is not, like most research in sociology or social psychology, a matter of creating the data one wishes to have after having defined a problem, expecting that analysis will follow; and it is not, hence, mechanical. It is the opposite of mechanical. It is a matter of creatively thinking one's way through a body of information. *Creatively* in the sense that the historian's great problem is deciding what to reject and what to accept as relevant to the subject he studies; and the determination of relevance can be a subtle process indeed. It has often seemed to me that the historian's research is analogous to the operation of a radar machine: he sends out hundreds of probes into the material and flashes the results back, searching for recognizable patterns. Like the radar operator he shifts his focus to take account of the location and configuration of the patterns he sees forming. This is so not only for the social historian; it is only more complicated for him since the events he depicts have structures that are more deeply submerged than those of the events that biographers or political historians usually describe. Much in historical work can be mechanized, and should be, but research must remain essentially this kind of creative process, a process in which the student, his radar wide open, probes the data with his mind, searching for patterns, for relevance, for significance. Often in the process the investigation becomes transformed. What starts as a gap becomes a true historical problem. Indeed, what starts out as a *need,* projected as a large-scale survey, can easily turn into a *gap* and end up as a *problem,* the solution to which may be properly presented in a pinpoint monograph.

But what are the broad problems worth the philosopher's attention in this connection? One seems to me to be preeminent.

In all their research, in their gathering of data, historians face the problem of the sufficiency or insufficiency of proof. What do historians in fact mean when they say their research has proved something? Often I think they mean only that most qualified historians, given the same information they have examined, would arrive at the same conclusions they have arrived at. But this is more a psychological reflex than a logical explanation. The logic of proof, even in the humble sense in which the historian actually deals with it in his everyday work, would seem to be complicated. Do not the forms of proof differ, for example, according to the types of events we are talking about? Is not a different kind of proof required to demonstrate that Roosevelt died on April 12, 1945, than to prove or disprove Halévy's argument that the rise of Methodism accounts for the failure of a social revolution to take place in eighteenth century England? Are not the forms of proof different in the case of a specific, deliberate act whose evidences are strictly limited, from one which involves the attitudes of masses of people over a long period of time where the evidence is so voluminous that no historian can possibly exhaust it? What proof is there for the accounts historians give of the spirit of an age, the style of a society or a group— accounts like David Cecil's first chapter in his biography of Melbourne, that brilliant piece of impressionism called "The World"? Are the citations in Huizinga's *Waning of the Middle Ages* anything but illustrations of a series of conclusions beyond proof? Yet is not his book historical writing of the highest quality?

III. The final phase of the historian's work is the presentation of his material. The problems here are the most obvious and the least unusual of all those he deals with. But though they are unlikely to appear at first glance to be "philosophical" in character, they are no less susceptible than the others, I believe, to careful analysis at a high level of generality. I would like simply to mention, very briefly, two illustrations of the kind of difficulties the working historian faces in this connection.

The *choice of words* is crucial if only because it affects the way in which the historian handles the problem of *distance*. Where does he stand in relation to the reader on the one hand and to the personalities and events he is describing on the other? Modern sociologists and psychologists, curiously enough, talk a great deal about themselves; that is, they report to the reader what they did in their study and what they discovered. Their writing does not consist solely and strictly of statements about the people or situations they have examined. The statements of this nature that they make most often include passages about themselves, about their methods, experiments, and reasoning. But the historian, like the novelist, writes sentence after sentence, descriptive or analytical, of those other people or situations. His effort is to keep the reader's mind constantly and evenly focused on the historical situation, not on his own; and his success in this can depend to a considerable extent on the kinds of words he chooses. An excessively subjective or connotative word can suddenly dislocate the author in relation to his reader and his subject by injecting the author's personality and forcing the reader to jump from one world to another. This, for example, explains the jarring effect of the single word A. L. Rowse uses to modify the final noun in this characteristic sentence about the English Puritans: "Leicester was on their side, and kept in with them, and spoke their somewhat nauseating language."

Much could be said about this question of word-choices as they relate to the historian's stance: the distance he assumes from the reader and from his subject. It is a problem that students of linguistic exposition are no doubt familiar with. But historians are not commonly aware of it; they do not sense the implications it has for their whole undertaking.

The use of figurative language in historical exposition also presents problems the working historian faces constantly. In what ways are metaphors and similes useful in historical prose? At times, when they are extended and used with great skill, as in Tawney's *Religion and the Rise of Capitalism,* one has the feeling that historical conclusions are being expressed in figurative language that could be expressed in no other way. But can this be justified? Are not metaphorical statements beyond validation?

One could speak similarly of problems of the tone and the economy of language, and of a number of other questions that relate to *presentation.* But the point I hope is clear. The way in which a historian presents his information, the way in which he relates expository flow to the discrete pieces of knowledge he has available—all of this constitutes an important area of problems he faces in his everyday work. It too is worthy of systematic consideration.

28. The Historical Seminar: Its Outer Shell and Its Inner Spirit*

WALTER PRESCOTT WEBB

"It is easy . . . to outline a few external characteristics of the seminary," wrote Herbert Baxter Adams in 1884, "but difficult to picture its inner life." [1] Since Adams wrote this, more than seventy years ago, a great deal of attention has been paid to the external characteristics, the outer shell, and not so much to the inner life and spirit of the historical seminar. I chose the subject for this occasion because the seminar has played an important role in my own work. In discussing it with others, I gained the impression that there was something peculiar in my use of this instrument of graduate instruction; and had the results of my experiment been less satisfying, I might have concluded that what I had was no seminar at all.

Further investigation revealed that I was not quite as original, peculiar, or off-side as I first thought. What had seemed the outer shell soon came to appear as the protective cover for the inner spirit where the vitality exists. My conclusion—which may be stated at the outset—is that the great seminars have been animated and made great not by any method but by the inner purpose, the great program, and the dominating idea of him who conducted it.

The seminar may be defined as a group of mature students or scholars studying and practicing the art of investigation

* Reprinted with permission from *The Mississippi Valley Historical Review*, XLII (June, 1955), 3–23.

[1] Herbert Baxter Adams, "New Methods of Study in History," *Johns Hopkins University Studies in Historical and Political Science* (Baltimore), II (1884), 107.

and research under the direction of an experienced supervisor who sets the goal and sees to it that the best-known procedures are utilized by the group journeying toward it. The question arises as to what is the goal, the aim, of the director. What is he trying to do for these young people who have come for help? What, also, is he trying to do for himself? The answer to the first question is simple: the director is trying to help these young people become historians. He, the master craftsman, is trying to make master craftsmen out of apprentices and journeymen. Years ago I read a story of a German *meister* of the craft of making beer kegs. The master often reminded his apprentices that in his own apprenticeship he made a perfect beer keg. He doubted that any of them would ever make a beer keg as perfect as his had been. He harried them, drove them; he cajoled and bullied them; and in the end the poor apprentices were quite full of beer kegs, and a little tired of the subject. And in time they probably learned that the master's beer keg was not as flawless as he had represented it. But this parallel between making beer kegs and making seminar papers will not be further developed here.

The director of the seminar puts the apprentices through the motions that the historian must make in the production of a finished work. He has them read, collect, analyze, organize; he has them write a paper with preface, outline, notes, and bibliography, and finally present the results of their labor— their own little beer kegs—for the judgment of the master and of their fellows. If there is no aim other than this, then the seminar is a thinly disguised course in pedagogy, the director is conducting a trade school in historical mechanics, and the seminar is overrated, with more space in the graduate curriculum than its importance justifies.

Those who have glorified this sort of seminar have put great stress on the use of documents and original sources. Traditionally here is a place where the last shade of meaning is squeezed out of an official document. There is nothing wrong in putting a document under the microscope or through the critical wringer, analyzing it, looking into the bias and prejudice of him who made it. Nor is there anything wrong in seeking the motives of those who have committed great crimes or performed great services. The ability to do these things is possessed by many people, notably constitutional lawyers, probate judges, and police officers. These skills and critical attitudes can be taught in high school, and have been; they are taught again in college; they should be perfected by any student who has an M. A. degree. In the graduate seminar no student should receive any credit for having them, but should be penalized if he lacks them. These things—mechanics, procedures, and methods—constitute the outer shell, the indispensable minimum equipment needed by the student to qualify for admission to the sort of seminar that I am trying to delineate.

This brings me to the second question: What is the director of the seminar trying to do for himself? The answer is that he is trying to push out the bounds of knowledge. He has got far enough to ask questions, to know what kind to ask, but he has not found the answers. Therefore he calls in a group of graduate students, already equipped with method, takes them as junior partners, and sets them off on the quest for the answers to his questions. He is seeking aid while giving it. It is his hope that one out of ten will strike a trail, pursue it until he makes a field of inquiry his own, and become transformed into a creative historian. The director knows that he is a gambler, gambling in human possibilities, gambling that out of ten technicians there may emerge one who glimpses an idea and in pursuit of it becomes a master. The other nine will be no worse technicians than they were, and some of them may be a little better for having had pointed out to them a far country which they will never enter. That far country, reserved for the few, is the goal of the director. It has been the goal of all directors of all great seminars. Such seminars have been conducted by curious, restless investigators, bold enough to build a program of inquiry and writing around a compelling idea. With such men, and such men only, is found the inner spirit of the seminar.

In this paper I shall review briefly the origin of the seminar in Europe and its importation to this country and some results —good and bad—of its application in both places. Second, I shall show by example that the great seminars have been given by men with great ideas, men who used the seminar as an instrument of investigation. In the third place, I shall relate my own experience with the seminar.

It is generally stated that Leopold von Ranke of Germany was the father of the historical seminar, and it is assumed that he invented or adopted a new method of pursuing historical investigation. The method was already old, and had long been used in philology and in Biblical study. Ranke borrowed it from philology and carried it over into history, applying it to modern official documents rather than to ancient writs.[2] He was contemporary with Lyell, Wallace, Darwin, and Renan, who were applying the analytical and critical method with startling results in their respective fields. He turned the lecture room into a laboratory, using documents instead of a "bushel of clams." He was trying to make history a science, which has turned out to be as simple as making science history, something the scientists have had too much gumption to attempt.

Ranke's emphasis on documents came at a fortunate time in just the right place and was applied to a favorable period, the sixteenth and seventeenth centuries. Situated in Central Europe, he was surrounded by new national states and others in the process of formation, and in each capital were the accumulated official records as yet untouched by historians. Ranke led the way in cracking these treasure houses to set numerous students off on careers of writing national history based on official documents in an era when the volume of official documents was manageable.[3] The documents were mainly political, and the histories based on them became almost entirely so. Ranke and his followers accepted Edward A. Freeman's dictum that "history is past politics and politics is present history" before Freeman phrased it. By such procedure, Ranke believed, history could be written *wie es eigentlich gewesen ist,* but we know better now.

Ranke's method was accepted as a sort of historical Geiger counter, and students flocked to Berlin to acquire this new gadget. The results in two countries, Germany and the United States, are worth notice.

In Germany, Ranke built up a school—known as the German School—which numbered not less than thirty historians who attained in their day a considerable reputation, and many of them were distinguished. Most famous among them were Wilhelm von Giesebrecht, Georg Waitz, and Heinrich von Sybel. Their concern with official documents gave them the official

[2] Edward G. Bourne, "Leopold von Ranke," *American Historical Association, Annual Report,* 1896 (2 vols., Washington, 1897), I, 71.

[3] Historians of contemporary times are appalled by the volume of documents. In a lecture in Austin, Texas, April 8, 1953, Arnold Toynbee stated that the British documents pertaining to World War II would fill a shelf eighteen miles long. Ancient historians are handicapped by a paucity of documents, contemporary historians by a plethora. Ranke hit on a period when they were abundant but still manageable.

view, and they began to tend more and more toward a glorification of the state. Sybel broke away from Ranke, and with the aid of Friedrich Dahlmann founded the Prussian school, which numbered among its members Johann Gustav Droysen and the notorious Heinrich von Treitschke. What they taught by Ranke's method we learned in 1914 and rehearsed in 1941. The study of state documents had led to the worship of the state. Ranke cannot be blamed for this perversion, although it grew naturally out of his basic principle, his belief that by depending on official documents one would arrive at truth as it really is. The Prussian school took the documents and proved to the satisfaction of themselves and many others that the German Empire was the noblest work of political evolution, that Prussia was the crown piece of the Empire, and that the Nordic race, of which Germans were the purest example, was superior to all others.[4] Nothing could better illustrate the danger inherent in any method considered infallible.

The results in the United States were not so fatal. While Ranke was at the height of his power, just before and after the Civil War, Americans began to go to Berlin and other centers, and return to the United States to preach the documentary gospel. They brought back the shell, the idea that they must be scientific, prove every statement with a footnote, that a felicitous style was no longer desirable—nay, it was reprehensible —that imagination was dangerous, too thrilling for the pick and shovel brigade of historians. They brought the method but forgot the substance; they brought what was valuable and needed, but some of them—not all—left behind what was indispensable, something Ranke himself had. They did what disciples often do; they warped and distorted the best work of the master.

These returning natives arrived on the American scene at a fortunate time, in the midst of an educational boom when new states were setting up new universities, when history as a university study was new. In 1880 there were only eleven professors of history in the whole country.[5] Any man who had the prestige

4 For a treatment of the evolution of the German schools of "scientific" history from Ranke on, see James Westfall Thompson, *A History of Historical Writing* (2 vols., New York, 1942), II, chaps. XLII and XLIII. Thompson denies that Ranke himself was objective.

5 Michael Kraus, *The Writing of American History* (Norman, Okla., 1953), 5.

of a European degree, and especially a German degree, could get a job. In 1884, these men took the lead in organizing the American Historical Association, and elected Leopold von Ranke the sole honorary life member. Eleven years later, Edward G. Bourne read a paper before the Association commemorating the hundredth anniversary of his birth.[6]

The cult spread and the newly trained Ph.D's took their Geiger counters into the state and national archives to repeat two generations later what Ranke and his men had done in Europe. They extracted the documents, mainly political, and began to turn out source books of all kinds. The movement culminated when Albert Bushnell Hart launched the *American Nation Series* in 1904, and to use his own words, drove a team of twenty-four historians through the field of American history. These volumes were fairly uniform in style, uniformly dull, heavily documented, primarily political, highly factual, wholly uninspired, and completely divorced from the reading public. In them was none of the savage beauty of Parkman, the insight of Macaulay, the vision of Gibbon, or the restrained yet luminous imagination of Jules Michelet, of whom James Westfall Thompson said: "He not only took history for life, he lived himself into the past to an extent unexcelled before or since." [7] Here was American history with all the blood and guts squeezed out of it. Something that had lived and moved was chopped up into twenty-seven parts so that some 280 years of history could be treated in ten-year blocks. These books had neither the charm of literature nor the exactness of science, and the series is being discarded in favor of a new one equally ephemeral. The conclusion seems to be that in this field of history the method of "science" confers no more immortality than other methods. There is no such thing as immortal history, a way of saying that there is in history no permanent truth; the facts may be permanent, but their meanings are in flux, and the historians only guess at them.

We have witnessed here the results of the seminar in Germany and the United States. The Germans perverted its use with such skill that they led their country down the road to destruction. When the Americans followed the method without imbibing the spirit, they bored the public to extinction. In the land of

[6] Bourne, "Leopold von Ranke," American Historical Association, *Annual Report*, 1896, I, 67–80.

[7] Thompson, *History of Historical Writing*, II, 238.

its origin, the method led to the devil; in the land of its adoption, to dullness. A mighty venture is now on to recapture the lost readers. Almost 100,000 people have indicated their willingness to try *American Heritage*. The editors have received some three-quarter million dollars as evidence that the people can read. Their present anxiety is whether the historians can write.

My second point is this: The great seminars that have most influenced historical writing have been given by men with great ideas. These men have shared their ideas and their programs with their students and used the seminar as an instrument for expanding the idea and executing a program. They have used any and all methods, but the exclusive use of any one method, even a "scientific" one, has proved fatal.

The best analogue to the seminar I am talking about is an exploring party bound for an unknown country. At the head of the expedition is the leader, the one on whom success is likely to depend and on whom blame for failure will inevitably fall. This leader has that which makes him the leader—that is, an idea of destination. He does not know that he can reach it, or the nature of the obstacles in the way, or what it will be like when he does reach it, but the idea dominates him and makes him hazard the risk.

He selects carefully from those who volunteer for the adventure, hoping that each has intelligence, skill, and endurance. He calls the crew around him and speaks to them in this wise:

> You have engaged voluntarily to go with me into a strange and unknown country. You understand that I am not leading you through a park or meadow to show you trails which will, if you follow them, bring you home. I am leading you where there are no trails; we go to blaze a trail that others may follow. I know the direction but I do not know the way; I know the destination I hope we may reach, have an idea of what we will find there, but I am not sure of anything. I know that we shall pass over high mountains and penetrate dark valleys, that we shall see many new vistas, and even though we do not find what we seek, we will find something—an experience to remember all the days of our lives. One more thing I have to say: We are in this expedition together. The idea is mine, and as I share it with you, I want you to share what you find and what you make out of it with us. The campfire will be the clearing house for all.

The director is the leader with the idea of destination, the seminar members are the crew of axe-men, observers, hunters and scouts, front, flank, and rear. The library is the high mountain and the forested valley where inspiring views and depressing confusion alternate. The seminar table is the campfire where the party gathers and each member reports what he has seen and what he thinks about it.

The essential elements of the sort of seminar I am talking about are two: the man and the idea. The important moment in the life of the man is that moment when this idea arrives to possess him and guide his work for a lifetime. In this moment he sees some pattern of truth, real meaning in the miscellaneous facts he has been gathering, and he knows that he has found something neither borrowed nor stolen, something his very own. It is the idea that transforms the mechanic, imitator, or pedant into a creative scholar with a destination and a purpose. The insatiable curiosity as to where the idea leads drives him to prodigious industry and endows him with an energy he never before knew. When the man, the prepared scholar, has received this idea he is ready to become the director of the sort of seminar where students enlist to go on a journey full of adventure and misadventure into an unkown country.

I have used the words "creative historian" and "creative seminar," words which I trust make nobody flinch. Those who do might turn to the etymology of *seminar*. In suggesting this I lay myself open to the charge of redundancy in placing the adjective *creative* before the noun *seminar,* which basically means creativeness. The seminar in this country was first called a seminary, but that term has been released to those less concerned with so profane a subject as history. Seminary and seminar stem from the French, *seminarius,* from Latin *seminarium,* pertaining to seed. Seminal comes from French and Latin *seminalis,* French *semen,* again pertaining to or consisting of seed, source, first principle, germinal, originative. There is nothing in the etymology signifying method or manner. Arthur P. Newton, the British historian of the Empire, thus defined it: "A Seminar (i.e., a bed in which to *sow* the seeds of intellectual effort), is . . . a group of disciples [I don't like the word *disciple* at all] gathered around a Master and inspired by him in a common field of enquiry." [8] If anybody wants to use the seminar in

---

[8] Margaret M. Spector, "A. P. Newton," in Herman Ausubel, J. Bartlet Brebner, and Erling M. Hunt (eds.), *Some Modern Historians of Britain: Essays in Honor of R. L. Schuyler* (New York, 1951), 293.

a creative manner, he will be on clear ground semantically.

Since the idea is so important in the seminar, I want to discuss that exciting moment when the idea arrives; when the idea and the man unite to transform an undifferentiated learner into a dynamic scholar.

Leopold von Ranke's name is synonymous with the "scientific" historical method, but I have never heard anyone speak of his basic idea, his main purpose, or the amazing program of investigation that he carried on for sixty years, resulting in fifty published volumes. He was not an imaginative man; he seemed to evolve slowly from his first task based on a compact body of documents through the history of the popes and of the national states of Europe, culminating his work with a World History, which he completed shortly before his death. One might think he never had that fine moment of insight to set him off on his course and give direction to all he did. I find evidence that he did have that moment, and that it came to him at the age of thirty. In February, 1825, he wrote to his brother: "I am now studying later modern history. Would I might be a Moses in this desert to strike and bring forth the water which is certainly there." [9] Surely here was a man making ready to set off into a desert—a desert of documents—to see if he could emulate Moses in the act of creation. Since he was working with documents, a documentary method was the natural one, incidental to his purpose and materials. "Der Stoff brachte die Form mit sich," he said in commenting on the Venetian papers.[10] The stuff not only determines the form, but it often determines the method.

That Ranke used his seminar to further his program is clear from the following passage:

I am still astonished at the talent and application of the young men who gathered around me. . . . In this circle the work throve. We came upon the *Chronicon Corbiense,* whose spuriousness I first recognized without being able to prove it. The members of the seminar made the investigation which proved its falseness.[11]

As we leave Ranke, I would like to pose this question: What made him in his day the leading historian of the world? Was it

[9] Quoted in Bourne, "Leopold von Ranke," American Historical Association, *Annual Report,* 1896, I, 72.
[10] *Ibid.,* 73.
[11] Quoted in Thompson, *History of Historical Writing,* II, 188.

primarily because of the method he taught or was it because of the vast program he carried out?

Other men have been clearer than Ranke in nailing down the moment of synthesis spoken of by Fustel de Coulanges,[12] the moment of insight which transforms the student with a head full of inert knowledge into a dynamic scholar with a destination. Augustin Thierry spoke of this moment which led to his *History of the Conquest of the English by the Normans*.

> One day [he said] when reading attentively some chapters in Hume, I was struck with a thought which appeared to me a ray of light, and closing the book, I cried, "All this dates from a conquest; there is a conquest at the bottom." Instantly I conceived the project of remaking the history of the English Revolutions by considering them from this new point of view.[13]

Thierry describes the ecstasy with which one who has had this moment of synthesis works. He said that he devoured many pages to extract a single phrase of a word, and in the process, he said,

> my eyes acquired a faculty which astonishes me, and for which I can not account; that of reading, as it were, by intuition, and of falling almost immediately on the passage that ought to have interest for me. . . . In the species of ecstasy which absorbed all my internal faculties . . . I had no consciousness of what passed around me. . . . The officials of the library and curious visitors came and went through the hall; I heard nothing, I saw nothing;—I saw only the apparitions called up in my soul by what I read.

But of all the accounts of how an idea, an obsession if you prefer, transforms a man, that of Heinrich Schliemann, who excavated Troy and the tombs of Mycenae, is to me the most remarkable. Schliemann was not exactly a historian, never had a seminar nor taught one, but had he done so it would have been a good one. His inspiration did not come in a flash, but had its beginnings, as is often the case, in early childhood, when he conceived the idea of finding the lost city of Troy and excavating it.

> If I begin this book with my autobiography [he wrote], it is not from any feeling of vanity, but from a desire to show how the

[12] Fustel de Coulanges is reported to have said: "It requires years of analysis for a day of synthesis."

[13] Thompson, *History of Historical Writing*, II, 230.

work of my later life has been the natural consequence of the impressions I received in my earliest childhood, and that, so to say, the pick axe and spade for the excavation of Troy and the royal tombs of Mycenae were both forged and sharpened in the little German village in which I passed eight years of my earliest childhood.

The chain of events which made him one of the most original scholars of the modern world had its origin, not in a document, but in pure legend of his home village, a legend of buried treasure. In a pond near his home, legend said, each midnight a maiden rose from the water bearing a silver bowl; in a nearby burial ground a robber knight had buried his child in a golden cradle; and in the garden of the village proprietor other treasures were hidden underground. "My faith in the existence of these treasures was so great," said Schliemann, "that, whenever I heard my father complain of his poverty, I always expressed my astonishment that he did not dig up the silver bowl or the golden cradle, and so become rich." This was the first step.

The second step came on Christmas Day, 1829, when the eight-year-old received his father's present, Georg Ludwig Jerrer's *Universal History,* published the year before. In the book was a picture of the massive walls of Troy, but Schliemann's father told him that the picture was an imagination, that no trace of Troy existed, that none knew its location. This the boy could not believe.

"Father," I retorted, "if such walls once existed, they can not possibly have been completely destroyed; vast ruins of them must still remain, but they are hidden away by the dust of ages." He maintained the contrary, whilst I remained firm in my opinion, and at last we both agreed that I would one day excavate Troy.

The third step came at the age of sixteen when Schliemann was clerking in Theodore Huckstadt's grocery store, where one day a drunken sailor entered reciting the Homer he had learned before being expelled from the gymnasium for bad conduct. Schliemann says:

He recited about a hundred lines of the poet, observing the rhythmic cadence of the verses. Although I did not understand a syllable, the melodious sound of the words made a deep impression on me, and I wept bitter tears at my unhappy fate. Three times over did I get him to repeat those divine verses, rewarding his trouble with three glasses of whisky, which I bought with the few pence that made up my whole fortune. From that moment I never ceased to pray God that by His grace I might yet have the happiness of learning Greek.

By the time he was ready to excavate Troy he had mastered English, French, Dutch, Spanish, Italian, Portuguese, Russian, Polish, Modern Greek, Ancient Greek, Latin, and Arabic—thirteen languages in all.

The fourth step came five years later when, at the age of twenty-one, the youth landed as a shipwrecked cabin boy to become a clerk in Amsterdam at £32 a year, half of which he spent on his studies. He knew it would take money to excavate Troy. There were no great foundations like those around which we timid scholars now flutter like candle flies; and had there been such, he would have stood no chance for a grant. Therefore, he made the money with which to excavate Troy. In another twenty-one years, at the age of forty-two, he retired as indigo merchant to Russia and gold merchant to the mines of California with a fortune. He wrote:

Heaven continued to bless all my mercantile undertakings in a wonderful manner, so that at the end of 1863 I found myself in possession of a fortune such as my ambition had never ventured to aspire to. But in the bustle of business I never forgot Troy or the agreement I had made with my father . . . to excavate it. I loved money indeed, but solely as means of realising this great idea of my life.

Five more years passed before Schliemann got to Troy, and then, between 1868 and his death in 1890, he not only found and excavated the lost city of Troy, but also Ithaca, Mycenae, Orchomenus, and Tyrus.[14]

This story illustrates the power of an idea followed by resolution to overcome and burn down all obstructions between the owner and his goal.

Let us now look at some American historians who conducted seminars, and try to determine whether they became notable because they followed a method or an idea. It is often stated

[14] This account is based on Arnold J. Toynbee, *A Study of History* (10 vols., London, 1934–1954), X, 12 ff. Any historian who is hesitating to take a chance on an original idea should read Toynbee's last volume, which bears the title, "The Inspirations of Historians."

that the first seminar was given by Henry Adams at Harvard, but this is an error. The first seminar was given by Charles Kendall Adams at the University of Michigan in 1869 when Henry P. Tappan was president.[15] I have found little record of what went on in this seminar or of its results.

The case is different with Henry Adams at Harvard, where he was an assistant professor from 1870 to 1877. It is quite easy to attribute all his merit to the fact that Adams spent some time in school in Germany, and to the fiction that he there learned how to conduct a seminar and become a great historian because he had mastered the latest wrinkle in German method.

An Adams is never a favorable witness for any Adams, but if we can trust Henry's own testimony, he never attended a seminar, knew little about history, and had no use for method. Here he tells of his activities after reaching Berlin in 1858:

> Within a day or two he [Henry Adams] was running about with the rest to beer-cellars and music-halls and dance-rooms, smoking bad tobacco, drinking poor beer, and eating sauerkraut and sausages as though he knew no better. This was easy. . . . The trouble came when he asked for the education he was promised. His friends took him to be registered as a student of the university; . . . and they led him to his first lecture.

> His first lecture was his last. The young man was not very quick . . .; but he needed no more than one hour to satisfy him that he had made another failure in education, this time a fatal one. . . . He had thought Harvard College a torpid school, but it was instinct with life compared with all that he could see of the University of Berlin. The German students were strange animals, but their professors were beyond pay. The mental attitude of the university was not of the American world.[16]

Instead of continuing in the university, Adams entered the gymnasium, which he spoke of as a public school attended by boys of thirteen. He described this experience as a horror, and the school as "something very near an indictable nuisance." In the spring he left for good, and here is his description of his farewell: "He realized what a nightmare he had suffered, and he made up his mind that, wherever else he might . . . seek for

15 Kraus, *Writing of American History*, 165.
16 Henry Adams, *The Education of Henry Adams: An Autobiography* (Boston, 1918), 75.

The Historical Seminar   221

education, it should not be again in Berlin." [17] He further stated that "He had revolted at the American school and university; he had instantly rejected the German university; and as his last experience in education he tried the German high school. The experiment was hazardous." [18] Of the university he said: "Neither the method nor the matter nor the manner could profit an American education." [19]

On his return to the United States after the Civil War, Adams found a gap of a thousand years—the medieval period—open at Harvard. President Charles W. Eliot gave him the job against his wishes and at four dollars a day. He said that "when he took his chair and looked the scholars in the face, he had given, as far as he could remember, an hour, more or less, to the Middle Ages." [20]

It is interesting to know what procedure Adams, the most nearly perfect American historian, followed. He has told us in these words:

> He frankly acted on the principle that a teacher, who knew nothing of his subject, should not pretend to teach his scholars what he did not know, but should join them in trying to find the best way of learning it. The rather pretentious name of historical method was sometimes given to this process of instruction, but the name smacked of German pedagogy, and a young professor who respected neither history nor method, whose sole object of interest was his students' minds, fell into trouble enough without adding to it a German parentage. . . . Nothing is easier to teach than historical method, but, when learned, it has little use.[21]

Adams said he selected as his victims a half-dozen intelligent boys and started them reading whatever they pleased as a background for law. There must have been something about Adams that touched them off, for, he says:

> The boys worked like rabbits, and dug holes all over the field of archaic society; no difficulty stopped them; unknown languages yielded before their attack, and customary law became familiar as the police court; undoubtedly they learned, after a fashion, to chase

17 *Ibid.*, 81.
18 *Ibid.*, 77.
19 *Ibid.*, 76.
20 *Ibid.*, 300.
21 *Ibid.*, 302.

an idea, like a hare, through as dense a thicket of obscure facts as they are likely to meet at the bar; but their teacher knew that his wonderful method led nowhere.[22]

In view of this evidence, and it is a primary source however unreliable, no one can attribute Adams' greatness, as a conductor of a seminar or as historian, to methodology or to German training. I have not found that the self-depreciatory Adams ever admitted that he had that moment of illumination which determined the way he would go. The only obsession he admitted was the futile pursuit of an education.

Though something called a seminar had been given at Michigan and at Harvard, the institutionalization of this device in this country occurred at Johns Hopkins. Here, in 1876, was established a real university as distinguished from such colleges as Yale, Princeton, and Harvard, fortunate in that it was not cluttered up with undergraduates. Johns Hopkins was a graduate school from the beginning, the only one then worthy of the name. Its reception amazed its founders; its instantaneous success astonished all. Of it Sidney Lanier, in his "Ode to Johns Hopkins," said:

> So quick she bloomed, she seemed to bloom at birth,
> Fore-seen, wise-plann'd pure child of thought and pain,
> Leapt our Minerva from a mortal brain.

A more prosaic writer has said: "To look through the list of first students at the Johns Hopkins University is to obtain a preview of the men who were to become the distinguished members of the faculties of American universities in the thirty or forty years that followed." [23] Within ten years, sixty-nine men had received the Ph.D. degree, and all but thirteen had positions in thirty-two universities. Among the early fellows are such names as Walter Hines Page, Charles Lane Poor, John H. Latané, Herbert Baxter Adams, John Spencer Bassett, W. W. Willoughby, Josiah Royce, John Dewey, and Woodrow Wilson.

The mortal brain that launched this educational meteor was Daniel Coit Gilman, the first president. That he thought men of ideas should outrank men of methods is made pretty clear in his statement of purpose:

[22] *Ibid.*, 303.
[23] W. Carson Ryan, *Studies in Early Graduate Education* (New York, 1939), 32.

It misses its aim if it produces learned pedants, or simple artisans, or cunning sophists, or pretentious practitioners. Its purport is not so much to impart knowledge to the pupils as to whet the appetite, exhibit methods, develop powers, strengthen judgment, and invigorate the intellectual and moral forces.

Again he said:

In forming all these plans we must beware lest we are led away from our foundations; lest we make our schools technical instead of liberal and impart a knowledge of methods rather than of principles. If we make this mistake we may have an excellent *polytechnicum,* but not a *university.*[24]

The first historical seminar was set up at Johns Hopkins by Austin Scott at the time George Bancroft was writing his *History of the Formation of the Constitution of the United States,* published in 1881. Scott was acting as Bancroft's assistant, and the seminar was put to work on the problem. I quote Herbert Baxter Adams:

The seminary had the feeling that they had been admitted to Mr. Bancroft's workshop, and that, by the examination of his materials and his methods, they were being taught the art of constructing history. The very manuscripts which Dr. Scott had prepared while collecting and sifting facts for Mr. Bancroft, were shown to the seminary. Questions still unsolved were submitted to Johns Hopkins students for their consideration, in company with their instructor. . . . The feeling was thus engendered that, in some slight ways, the seminary was contributing to the great volume of United States history.[25]

Here again we see the students assisting the director on a real program of scholarship.

In 1876, Herbert Baxter Adams returned to America with a Heidelberg Ph.D., and became one of the first fellows at Johns Hopkins. I suspect that the seminar he later established would rank at the top in terms of what came out of it. His first idea was to continue to study the Roman and German origins of community life, but this soon proved to be impracticable, and

24 *Ibid.,* 29.

25 Herbert Baxter Adams, "New Methods of Study in History," *Journal of Social Science* (New York), XVIII (May, 1884), 251 ff.

he turned to American Institutional History. His students ranged far and wide over the United States, writing about American institutions.

Need I follow the careers of Edward Channing and John Bach McMaster and answer the question as to why students flocked to their seminars and considered it something to remember that they had studied with such men? Was it their methods or their prodigious program of work that made these men worth while? Need I answer the same question for the man from Portage, Wisconsin? Did he come back from Johns Hopkins to send his name and influence around the world because he had learned mechanics or because he, by looking at his own rude environment, had hit upon a seminal idea which fascinated those who worked with him and set many off on quests to the frontier to create a school of thought?

In 1901, Herbert E. Bolton, a recent graduate from the University of Wisconsin, was exiled to the province of Texas to teach elementary history to the reluctant sons of cowboys. He brought no idea with him, but picked one up on the borderland he had entered, where Anglo-American met Latin-American, English met Spanish, Protestant met Catholic. The archives were at hand, but he could not use them because he knew no Spanish. Deciding to devote himself to the Spanish borderlands, he studied Spanish under Miss Lilia Casis and set to work. He later went to California where he inspired, and sometimes made a little dizzy, his many disciples who have filled the chairs of Latin-American history all over the continent and beyond. In addition, he turned out a volume of work, which if not prodigious, is quite respectable.[26]

Another Californian had a somewhat similar idea long before Bolton. Hubert Howe Bancroft, like Schliemann, Walter Leaf, George Grote, and James Ford Rhodes, took time out to make money before turning historian.[27] The regular gild liked to depreciate Bancroft because of his method, that of hiring better-trained historians than he was and paying them with the money he knew how to make. Thus he got the title of Clio Incorporated. He never had a seminar, never studied method, but he evolved a compelling and expanding idea which would give him no rest. Though historians are reluctant to admit him to

26 Kraus, *Writing of American History*, 286–87.
27 For an account of the business activities of Schliemann, Leaf, Grote, and Rhodes, see Toynbee, *Study of History*, X, 145 ff.

the gild, they must concede that he put the scholarly world into his debt, and that his books, with all their faults, will outlive the *American Nation Series*, old and new.[28]

In all these examples from Leopold von Ranke and Henry Adams to Herbert Bolton and H. H. Bancroft, we find one common denominator. It is not a method, but the presence of an idea or an obsession which creates a driving energy and an insatiable curiosity. In each case where the seminar was used by these men, it was used as a creative instrument to assist the director in extending the area of knowledge.

I speak now of my own experience with the seminar. In my entire life I have had only two ideas which I consider to have any originality. I am here tonight because I followed those ideas, without much regard for method, using that which would facilitate the pursuit. Each idea has resulted in a book. A new seminar was organized around each idea shortly after its arrival, maintained until the book was published, and then abandoned. No idea, no seminar.

The first idea, embalmed in *The Great Plains*, came on a stormy night in February while I was reading in preparation of an article about the Texas Rangers for a magazine sponsored by a crooked oil company intent on fleecing the public. I was writing the article for three reasons: I knew something about the Texas Rangers; I was on an instructor's salary; and the crooked oil company paid well until it was rudely interfered with by a United States marshal. Months of research preceded the exciting incident of that night, the moment of insight and synthesis when the miscellaneous facts I had gathered formed a pattern, fell into place, and took on meaning, that moment when something triggers the mind loaded with what Toynbee calls inert knowledge, and brings understanding.

The Colt revolver, which had often been used as a precipitant, always the favorite weapon of the Texas Rangers, was the grain around which the idea formed. I suddenly saw the six-shooter as the natural weapon of the man on horseback, of men moving in an open treeless country where there was grass for horses and

---

[28] John W. Caughey, *Hubert Howe Bancroft: Historian of the West* (Berkeley, 1946), vii, says: "In the historiography of the West, no name is written larger than Hubert Howe Bancroft's." For Bancroft's account of his method see *The Works of Hubert Howe Bancroft* (39 vols., San Francisco, 1882–1890), XXXIX. This volume was also published separately as *Literary Industries: A Memoir* (New York, 1891).

cattle and room in which to ride. I saw that in weapons a revolutionary change took place where men left the wooded country and entered the treeless land, where men mounted horses to do their traveling, their fighting, and their work. I had as yet practically no proof of what I knew, but I found it shortly and in abundance, and wrote the story of the historical significance of the six-shooter—I called it the American revolver—which was accepted by *Scribner's Magazine* before I had ever taken a seminar.

But more important than that, I now had a bigger question to ask: What other changes took place where men left the forest to dwell on the plains? Nobody could answer that question which had not been asked before, but the question would not go away, and I had to go to work and answer it myself. The big question broke up into smaller ones. Where timber and grass meet, what change took place in geology? What in botany? In zoology? In anthropology? What in the laws of land and water? What in literature? Having specialized in history, I lacked education, knew neither geology, nor botany, nor zoology, little anthropology, nothing of law, and not much more of literature. Hitherto I would have been appalled had anyone suggested that I explore these formidable subjects. Yet my curiosity about these suspected changes was such that it acted like a fire to burn away the obstacle of complete ignorance. I studied all these subjects in so far as they threw light on the questions. Geology and law came hardest, but were quite rewarding.

Because of that quest I understand what Thierry meant when he spoke of the ecstasy of search, of being insensitive to what went on around him, and of reading as by intuition. I could read for my purpose a dozen books a day, and it came to the point where anything pertaining to the Great Plains would jump out of the page at a glance, just as Thierry described.

I was authorized to offer a course on the Great Plains. I did not rate a seminar, and I did not know enough to lecture. I said to the class: I think something important happened to ideas and institutions when men left the woodland to live on the plains in middle America. Will you help me find out what happened to this and that and the other? I surreptitiously converted this class, and succeeding ones, into a seminar—into hunting answers to my questions. My students were good hunters. As Henry Adams said, they scurried about like rabbits; they dug holes all over the Great Plains.

It is difficult to remember how much I stole from them, but I can not forget that I stole something. One student described the Great Plains as a strange land where the wind draws the water and the cows cut the wood. Another explained the collapse of the early farming settlements by saying that in the East civilization stood on three legs—land, water, and timber. In the West, two of these legs were withdrawn, and civilization was left to stand, or topple, on one leg. I took that.

There is evidence that the students got from me and from their fellows something in exchange for what they brought, an understanding of the significance of things hitherto without meaning. This evidence comes in letters containing newspaper clippings on subjects we explored. Students sent specimens of barbed wire, pictures of windmills, and occasionally an old six-shooter. Though nearly twenty-five years have passed since the seminar ceased, the letters and specimens still come.

About ten years elapsed between the stormy February night when the apparition appeared and the hot July day when the book was published. Practically nothing but the *Scribner* article was published in that long interval. Fortunately, I was in Texas, where the ideals of high-pressure scholarship had not then obtruded. Nobody told me I ought to produce, write articles, get in print whether I had anything to say or not.[29] I had time to mature what I was about, to do what I had been preparing for since I was carried to the sun-blistered plains of West Texas at the age of four, and where I saw at an impressionable age

[29] Here I wish to say a word on behalf of young men, especially in the large universities, who are driven to write when they have nothing to say and are fired if they do not say it with documentation. The system is vicious and is providing an oversupply of beer-keg makers. I have devised a substitute system for universities to consider. That would be for the university to pay a flat sum to the young teacher for his services as a teacher and put him on a piece-basis for his so-called production. This would require a scale, a bonus system which would automatically register the worth of the harried young man and relieve his superior from making decisions.

Let us say that the base pay for teaching is $4,500. In addition, here is what the young man gets for production: Full length book, $500; monograph, $100; book review, $15; paper before learned society, $25. For evidence of recognition by his peers, apply this scale: Favorable review of his book, $10.00; unfavorable review, 50 cents; quotation by another author, $5.00 each; reference in footnote, $2.00 each; listing in bibliography, $1.00. All rates would be doubled for foreign publications. This would be a reversal of a system already started of taking from the scholar all he earns outside his salary, a system which I trust will not spread to other institutions.

everything that is in the book except Indians and irrigation. The Indians had just departed, and the water was never there.

The second idea, of greater magnitude but less originality than the first, came to me one spring morning in 1936, and like the first it came when I was working on something not closely related to it—another case of serendipity. Two years later I organized a seminar around the idea, and fourteen years still later the seminar ended with the publication of a book. The central question this time was: What effect did the uncovering of three new continents around 1500 have on the civilization that discovered and for a time owned the continents? Again the central question broke up into specific ones. How did the sudden acquisition and subsequent development of all this new land affect the individual? How did it affect such institutions as absolutism, democracy, slavery, and religious polity? Did it do anything to economic practice and theory? Thirteen years elapsed between the time the idea came and the time I began to write, years of alternating exaltation and misery. Avenues of inquiry radiated in all directions, to new stars in a new hemisphere of astronomy, to the botanical gardens in Europe, to seekers after windfalls of New World gold and silver or hides and fur, to the ensuing booms and bubbles, and to the economic theories and political philosophies that men made to rationalize an unseen revolution.

The young people who joined me on this expedition contributed much to the final result. Their minds were fresh, often they were eager, and they explored far and near. One question I asked was how piracy of the sixteenth to the nineteenth century was related to the frontier. Why did it arise shortly after the frontier opened? Why did it end early in the nineteenth century? Why was it centered in the Caribbean? Three successive students were assigned the subject. The first two returned with nothing—just a passable paper on pirates; but the third found something. Piracy, he said, had headquarters in the Caribbean because the precious metals from the mines of the Great Frontier had to pass that way en route to Europe. Spain owned the mines and would allow no other power in the Caribbean, a closed sea. No nation could break the monopoly. The alternative was to wink at and support all pirates who preyed on Spanish commerce. This England, France, and Holland did, sharing with the buccaneers their good fortune but never their bad. Finally, Spain's monopoly was broken. Pirates were no longer an asset to anybody; all nations turned on them, and their day was over. In the seminar I had spoken of the entrance to the New World symbolically as a golden door. This student suggested, rather shyly, but with some insight, that the subtitle of his essay on pirates might well be "The Thief at the Golden Door." Thus did he wrap his thesis up in a phrase. I have never asked the experts whether we had a proper seminar. I know we traveled together to far places, we worked at exciting tasks, and I think we came to know what Francis M. Cornford meant when he spoke of a "silent, reasonable world, where the only action is thought, and thought is free from fear," and we traveled in "the company of clean, humorous intellect." [30]

[30] Francis M. Cornford, *Microcosmographia Academica, Being a Guide for the Young Academic Politician* (3rd ed., Cambridge, England, 1933), 47.

29. Early Town Records of New England as Historical Sources*

DOUGLAS EDWARD LEACH

The early settlers of New England—Bradford, Winthrop, Williams, and the rest—brought with them from England a firmly established concept and tradition of local community government, in particular town and parish government.[1] Plymouth Plantation reluctantly, and Massachusetts Bay eagerly and with almost unseemly haste, reached out from the original points of settlement to found new towns as offshoots and satellites of Plymouth and Boston. Likewise in Connecticut a number of distinct communities were in existence soon after the original migration from the Bay Colony. In Rhode Island separate towns were established by different groups of contentious reformers and refugees, while along the ocean-scoured coast of Maine still other towns came into being. Thus by the second half of the seventeenth century New England was already dotted with a galaxy of distinct townships, some quite close together and others fairly remote and isolated. One thinks not only of Boston, Hartford, Plymouth, and Providence, but also of such pulsing communities as Medford, Weymouth, Bridgewater, Newport, Saybrook, and Northampton.

By the character of the country and by the deliberate planning of the settlers themselves the township in New England became the unit of government closest to the people and most

* Reprinted with permission from *The American Archivist*, XXV (April, 1962), 173–181.

1 Wallace Notestein, *The English People on the Eve of Colonization 1603–1630*, pp. 240–243 (*New American Nation Series*, ed. by Henry Steele Commager and Richard B. Morris; New York, 1954).

immediately answerable to their needs. Almost without exception—certainly in the early days—these towns were inhabited by people who had come together to live as neighbors for some compelling reason, often religious. At the outset, then, the typical New England town had a strong sense of common interest and common purpose. It has been well observed that in the early New England town the political community, the economic community, and the religious community were virtually identical. These people, for the most part wielders of the hoe and followers of the plow, saw life in relatively simple terms. They wanted to serve God and to prosper—and to be let alone by outsiders. Each family bore the basic responsibility for its own well-being, subject of course to the general good of the community; and the general good of the community was what made town government and the town meeting essential.

From the very day on which a new township was founded the townsmen kept written records of their official transactions. The legal and other reasons for doing so were compelling, and English precedent was deeply ingrained. Just as in our day every newly founded club with some pretensions to lasting importance begins to keep a series of minutes, so the newly formed town would purchase one or more skin-bound volumes of blank pages and begin to keep its own official records. These would include records of grants and sales of land; records of births, marriages, and deaths; and records of questions raised and decisions reached at town meetings. As time passed, the first one or two volumes would become filled, additional ones would be obtained, and sometimes the earliest volume would be identified by marking it "Vol. A" or "Vol. I," with the subsequent volumes following in order.

How important are these town records as historical sources? The answer depends upon what kind of information is being sought. Naturally I can speak with greatest assurance when describing my own experience in exploring the records of some 75 New England towns as part of my study of King Philip's War. The opportunity of learning from someone else's hard experience will, I trust, make you indulgent with my focusing the spotlight on my own work.

Although some of the volumes of town records have been gathered into central repositories of one kind or another, most are still held in the offices of town and city clerks. This means that the researcher must travel extensively, perhaps even adventurously, if he wants to see them all. As an "impecunious party," being then a graduate student, I made the rounds in a battered old wooden-bodied station wagon that required frequent dosing with water on hot days and thick cheap oil in all weathers. In this dubious vehicle I had put a mattress so that I might avoid the expense of staying at hotels, although I did treat myself occasionally to the luxury of a room in the local Y.M.C.A.

Custodians of the town records often appeared slightly astonished and a little bewildered when I appeared before them with my briefcase and cardboard file boxes and demanded to see "Vol. A, Town Votes, 1659–1713." Occasionally this was their first glimmering that such a thing existed anywhere in the world, let alone in their own cluttered precincts. The clerk, or I, or both of us, would then plunge into the interior of the safe and, if lucky, would emerge dirty but triumphant. All too often, however, the desired volume could not be found, although a useful nineteenth-century transcript laboriously made by some devoted local antiquarian might be available. I hasten to add, incidentally, that many town clerks were genuinely interested in the early history of their communities and displayed an intelligent awareness of the precious volumes in their custody.

A passing line or two in a musty volume of town records may help to enlarge our understanding of major events in history, or may simply uncover some homely fact of everyday life in colonial times such as Wallingford's method of plugging up a leak in the mill dam with cartloads of manure.[2] The Warwick town meeting of April 20, 1674, ordered "That pomham [an Indian] be paid out of ye tresury of this towne what is justly dew by order of this towne for killing A woolfe if ther be money in ye tresurry," thereby revealing to posterity something about predatory wildlife, Indian relations, and even the financial embarrassment of a frontier town.[3] The Taunton Proprietors' records depict the sometimes difficult process of buying land from the Indians, in one case a tract owned by King Philip himself. After considerable maneuvering and expenditure of time on the part of Taunton men, the land was "through difficulty obteyned of Philip Sachim" in 1672.

During the dangerous period of the Indian uprising in 1675

2 Wallingford Town Records (transcript), vol. 1, pp. 70–71.
3 Warwick Records (transcript by Marshall Morgan), Town Book A–2, p. 123.

and 1676 many frontier towns had to make drastic alterations in the normal pattern of economic life. A typical trend was toward communal agriculture, even communistic agriculture. In Billerica, for example, the constables were authorized to draft workers for the care of crops belonging to absent soldiers.[4] The men of Westfield ("considering the hand of God upon us in sturing or Leting Lus the heathen upon us So that now wee cannot cary on our ocasons for a lively hood as formerly" and in order to "be in a way of geting food for our familyes") agreed to a plan of communal agriculture under the direction of an appointed committee.[5] Men were to be assigned their tasks in the field, and the harvest would be shared according to need.

Then, when the war was over, the towns began the job of reconverting to normalcy. The town records illuminate this process of transition also, as when Middletown voted to convert its watchhouse into a schoolhouse. Later the town laid plans to build a new schoolhouse near the watchhouse.[6] Even the very layout of a town might be affected by the war and its aftermath. Both for comeliness and for security a Suffield committee decided that the town should be settled "by dwelling pretty neere together." [7] Persons who before the Indian war had constructed homes in the outskirts were now encouraged to build in or near the village.

In some towns the records for the war years were missing altogether, due to war damage or other causes. Even when the sequence of entries was unbroken the war was mentioned, for the most part, only indirectly. Of course much valuable information could be gleaned from tax records and other more or less routine entries. Occasionally one found the town debating such matters as the erection of palisades or the equipping of soldiers, but of lengthy comment upon the great crisis of the times there was none. And naturally so, because the job of the town clerk was to record routine business. Besides, he assumed that everybody knew all about the Indian uprising anyway. So the researcher working in local records must be prepared to probe below the surface of bald and apparently routine entries.

Occasionally—and how bright and shining are those rare

---

[4] Billerica Records (transcript), 1653-85, p. 187.
[5] Westfield Miscellaneous Records, 1675-94.
[6] Middletown Town Votes and Proprietors' Records, vol. 1 (1652-1735), pp. 121, 131.
[7] Suffield Town Records, vol. 1, Sept. 25, 1677.

occasions—one does find a sharply drawn, brief depiction of some episode that except for this record would have been lost forever. Take this entry from the Providence town records by way of example:

> Memorand that on the 25 of August 1676 (so called there came into this Towne One Chuff an Indian so calld in time of peace, because of his Surlines against the English He could Scarce come in being wounded Some few dayes before by Providence Men His wounds were corrupted & stanck & because he had bene a Ring leader all the War to most of the Mischiefs to our Howses & Cattell, & what English he could: The Inhabitants of the Towne cried out for Justice against him threatening themselves to kill him if the Authoritie did not: For which Reason the Cap: Roger Williams Caused the Drum to be beat, the Toun Councell & Councell of War called, all cried for Justice & Execution, the Councell of War gave sentence & he was shot to Death, to the great satisfaction of the Towne.[8]

How much those few sentences tell us about the pitiful condition of the Indians in the closing days of the war and about the bitter vindictiveness of the settlers, against which even Roger Williams apparently did not care to struggle!

Great events such as wars, political upheavals, and religious revivals, colony-wide in scope, may not be systematically chronicled in the records of particular townships, and the researcher may have to scratch very hard to uncover significant material on such topics. But if the purpose of going into town records is rather to feel the pulse of a community year after year, in good times and bad, and to see what were the problems faced by that particular group and how they were dealt with, then town records may prove a rich source indeed. I am inclined to believe that the promising sources have sometimes been neglected by historians, perhaps because of the difficulties of access and use. Town clerks' offices are not the most comfortable places to perch for long hours, but the discomforts and inconveniences may well be compensated a hundredfold.

Where else but in town records can we watch so closely the day-to-day functioning of local government as it deals with all the routine matters of community life? Here we find the titles of the various town officers, from selectmen down to hog reeves,

---

8 *The Early Records of the Town of Providence*, 8:13 (Providence, 1895).

and read the instructions given them by their fellow citizens in town meeting assembled.

> It is ordered that thre men shall be apoynted to warne towne meetings each one in ther severall Circuits, he which warns from John Persons to Mr Nelsons shall have 4 pence a tyme he which warnes the midle of the towne shall have 2 pence a tyme and he which warns Bradford strete shall have 2 pence a tyme, and in Case any pson or famyly that is att home be vnwarned he that warnes in that quarter shall pay for every defecte herein six pence [9]

We find a variety of town regulations designed to protect the well-being of the community.

> Whereas there have bene great danger of great damage by foule Chiminies it is therefore ordered that the second day after the publication hereoft all thached Chiminies in the towne shall be swept and all thached houses shall be swept that day fornight and ol clapboard houses that day month and brick chimnies on the same day alsoe and this to continue till the first of may. . . .[10]

Town finances are often laid before us in these yellowed pages. We can learn how taxes were decided upon, apportioned, and collected, and for what purposes the money was disbursed. In short, the whole functioning machinery of New England town government—simple, direct, relatively democratic, eminently practical—is seen at work.

Anyone who has done research in town records will agree that the town clerks probably used more ink in recording the distribution and sale of land than on any other subject. After all, land was the one great distributable asset of every new township. This land usually was vested in the proprietors or original grantees by the General Court, and often the proprietors kept records of their own, distinct from the records of the town itself. Every piece of land surveyed and distributed to private persons had to be accounted for and subsequently the title had to be maintained.[11] Consequently the local records bulge with entries

---

[9] *The Early Records of the Town of Rowley, Massachusetts, 1639–1672*, p. 57 (Rowley, 1894).

[10] *Ibid.*, p. 91.

[11] George Lee Haskins, *Law and Authority in Early Massachusetts*, p. 172 (New York, 1960).

concerning original divisions of common land, further divisions and subdivisions, and the buying and selling of lots.

A historian interested in watching the growth and development of some particular colonial town can by careful study of the local land records show exactly how the available land was originally divided into home lots and outlying fields and how the remaining undivided land was later distributed. The history of a piece of land through the pages of town records may not be so exciting as the progress of scalping parties in an Indian war or the relations between a pious colonial governor and certain notorious pirates, but it does contribute greatly to our knowledge of how New Englanders settled on a tract of land and, once there, how they met the challenge of growth. This, of course, is an integral part of the story of westward expansion.

Certainly the social historian will find much to interest him in town records. The everyday life of the village, matters of rank and prestige, methods of agriculture, local customs and prejudices, problems of education and religion, and the constant battle against wrongdoing, all are reflected in these pages. Often such matters are clearly depicted with specific information, giving the social historian case after case for his files. But even when the facts are half hidden behind brief routine entries, much may be inferred by the alert and well-informed student. Like an orange, these old records have to be squeezed a bit.

Consider how much we may learn about village life in seventeenth-century New England from just a few sample entries, chosen almost at random from the records of one New England town.[12]

> It is ordered and agreed that all common Gates and perticuler mens fences joyning upon any Corne feild shall be manteined against Great Catle at all times and if they be not sufently made to turne Great Catle at any time when Catle may doe hurte upon Corne. . . .

> Whereas their is hurt done yearly by Cattell eating and treading on mens Rye in the northeast field in winter time upon sudden thaughes and at breaking up of frosts at spring it is therrfore ordered that if any Cattle be found within the said fild after the Publishing hereof that it shall be lawfull for the Pinder to put them in the Pen and to be paid for poundage as for Cattle in other

12 *Early Records of the Town of Rowley*, pp. 55, 74, 88, 95, 109, 148.

places as also the owners are hearby lyable to all damages done by any such Cattle on mens Corne

. . . it is ordered that all maner of swine which shall be found in any Corne or meadow wheresoever they shall be liable to pay double damage notwithstandinge any order or Custome to the Contrary except they be sufficiently yoaked and ringged: which yoake shall be one foot and halfe upward and one foot and eight inches the Cross barre for every hogg of a yeare old and for others ether yunger or elder proportionably acording to the descretion of the overseers

att a leagall towne meeting held the 3 day of the 12 moth 1656 it was agreed by the towne that all male childrin shall pay to the scole men when they are 4 years ould till they Come to be 8 years ould also it was agreed at the same meeting that wiliam bointon shud have five pound lent him out of the churches stock towards the building of an end to his hous upon this condion that if he keep the scolle seven years this five pound is to bee void but in case he leave the scol before seven years be out the said hous end is to be prised by two indiferant men and the one half of the pris of the said hous end soe prised shall the said wiliam bointon is to returne to the church againe

Leutenant Brockellbanke Henry Rily Thomas Wood and John Grant, Jachin Ranor and John Mighill, haveinge ingaged for to make a pen for to catch wolves, had that priviledge granted that no boddy else should make any pen, any where upon the cow commons, duringe the space of three years, and were to have for every wolfe taken by there pen fifty shillings, payed by the towne. It is ordered that noe Inhabitant or owner of any house or land in the Towne shall bring in any Tenant to Dwell thering without the consent of the towne under The penaltie of 19 shillings the moneth every month they continue in the towne or bounds of the towne without consent

It is like wise ordered That noe man shall sell any house or land more or less unto any stranger before he ofer the same to the select Men at an Indeferant vallue upon paine of ninteene shillings the moneth for every percill of land soe disposed of contrary to this order

Lo, the poor farmer in those days! Roving hogs, if not yoked, squeezed between his fence rails to eat his corn; intruding cattle threatened his winter rye; and wolves destroyed his cows. Education for his sons was compulsory but not free. And he lived in what today we should call a "restricted community." No one could dwell there, either as tenant or owner, without permission of the authorities. Communities in those days screened out the indigent, the irresponsible, and the unorthodox.

From these brief entries in a town record book we get quite a bit of information about one town's daily life and everyday problems. If we were willing to spend the time necessary to read carefully the full record for the entire first century of the town's existence, our view would be wonderfully broadened and deepened. Were we to do the same thing for a goodly number of other communities scattered from Maine to Connecticut, we would be in a position to speak with some confidence about New England towns in colonial times.

Town records after the eighteenth century are another matter. Obviously they became more voluminous and complex as communities grew and were confronted with more diverse problems. Improvement in legibility is overbalanced by increasing quantity, and this is true of all governmental records. But fortunately that is a problem for others. I am thankful to be working in the colonial period of our history.

May I conclude with a brief postscript on the condition and custody of New England town records. First of all I must say frankly that my contact with the records themselves in their own habitat occurred some years ago. It may be that conditions have changed greatly since then, but I doubt it. I feel quite confident that my observations of a previous day are still, in the main, valid.

The condition of the original records varies greatly. Some volumes are still firmly bound and easily readable; others are tattered, faded, and crumbling. Many communities, I was happy to notice, have gone to the expense of having their precious early records safeguarded by lamination, but other towns still rely solely upon the custodian's warning to each researcher, "Treat 'em gently!" Time is taking its toll.

I was always glad whenever I found a good transcript available for use with the original records. Many of these transcripts were made in the nineteenth century, and they vary widely in quality. Some omit whole entries, besides committing the lesser sins of altering spelling and punctuation. The only really good transcript, at least for the purposes of the serious scholar, is an exact copy of the original in clear handwriting or typescript. In any case, the careful researcher must frequently compare the transcript with the original, whenever possible, to make sure he is not being led astray by the inaccuracies of a zealous but untrained antiquarian. When used with due caution, however, transcripts can save many hours of close work with the difficult and faded handwriting of an earlier day. Transcribing the early records would be an excellent local project for many communities, the main problem being to find transcribers with the necessary ability and devotion. As is well known, the Works Progress Administration did some good work in this field in the 1930's.

Many towns are even so fortunate as to own published versions of their early records. As in the case of transcripts, when they are good they are very, very good, but when they are bad they are horrid. Everything depends upon the skill and determination of the editor. From the point of view of research, it would be wonderful if all early town records could be brought out in print, with adequate indexes, but the costs are often prohibitive.

Finally, I should like to say a few words about the custody of the original records without, I hope, treading on too many toes. Usually, as I have indicated, the venerable volumes are still held in the office of the town clerk. Many such offices are now reasonably well equipped with fireproof vaults, and there the records are reasonably safe, although all kinds of persons do gain admission to the vaults for all kinds of purposes. Too often, however, town records are still stored rather haphazardly in places difficult of access and not absolutely proof against fire. I even found one set of colonial records in a farmhouse kitchen. Would it not be possible to persuade the towns to transfer custody of their colonial records to some central authority, which would house them properly and make them readily available to all legitimate researchers? As an alternative, State governments might undertake an extensive program of microfilming. This would not only increase the usefulness of town records by making it unnecessary for the eager but financially embarrassed graduate student to travel and sleep in a nondescript vehicle but would also assure their preservation for future generations. These towns records of colonial New England are truly valuable historical sources, and should be so treated.

30. American Labor History Prior to the Civil War: Sources and Opportunities for Research*

RICHARD B. MORRIS

If there are difficulties confronting the student of American labor history in the colonial, Revolutionary, and early national periods, there are even greater compensations in the opportunities for original and penetrating insights. Few if any trade union archives for the antebellum years are extant, and the standard published source materials for more recent times, which labor historians have utilized so effectively—trade union proceedings and labor periodicals—are rare and spotty. Instead one needs to turn to unorthodox sources, such as court records and other legal papers, petitions for legislative relief, the records of business firms, and local newspapers. I trust I may be pardoned for citing some specific examples from areas I have explored, but these illustrations come freshest to my mind and I can discuss them with greater authority.

The value of court records for social and labor history was abundantly demonstrated in my *Government and Labor in Early America*. The evidence was in considerable measure drawn from some twenty thousand judicial cases, largely unpublished, which were reviewed in the course of that investigation. These cases were principally from the inferior courts, and were largely unpublished, for litigation involving workers seldom reached the higher courts. My research took me along the Eastern seaboard from the county seats of Wiscasset in

* Reprinted with permission from *Labor History*, I (Fall, 1960), 308–318.

Maine and Woodsville in New Hampshire, as far south as St. Augustine, Florida. Statutes and local ordinances complemented the judicial records, but wherever possible these legal sources were supplemented by contemporary newspapers, accounts of travelers, diaries, letter books, military order books, and business papers.[1]

How much light can court records of the colonial period shed upon the field of labor relations? It must be borne in mind that the courts supervised apprenticeship and served as a forum for the litigation of issues arising out of the master-servant relationship in the old-fashioned common law sense of that term. The seventeenth century courts often required that testimony be offered in the form of written depositions. Hence, the evidence is spread out on the record and the story of what really transpired between employer and employee is there for those able to distinguish truth from fiction. True, these stories are sordid and seamy, for court cases are hospital cases. Satisfied workers did not go into court; contented masters did not bring obedient servants and apprentices before the authorities. Having the right to discipline refractory servants, the masters imposed their own discipline before seeking the aid of the authorities. Court reports, then, give a distorted view of the extent of labor strife, but they also disclose standards of labor relations in any particular period and the extent to which justice is available to the workingman.

Court records, notably those of inferior courts in cases which seldom go up on appeal, also reveal the wide gap between the labor law on the books and the labor law in action. They demonstrate that the statute books and the master-servant and black codes represent little more than a set of standards imposed by legislatures. While the historian must take cognizance of these standards, it is even more important for him to ascertain how they were carried out in practice. There is a rigidity about such codes that is unrealistic. The codes, for example, set penalties for cruel and unfair treatment of servants. But how many servants dared report their masters to the public

---

[1] For the printed legal sources, see E. B. Greene and R. B. Morris, *A Guide to the Principal Sources for Early American History in New York City*, 2d ed. (New York, 1953). In "Early American Court Records: A Publication Program," *Anglo-American Legal History Series*, No. 4 (New York, 1941), I have indicated some of the more significant unpublished court records for the colonial period.

authorities? Many studies of slavery have been based largely on the slave codes, whereas judicial practice and the custom of the plantations recognized the existence of a much less rigid and more diversified set of institutional patterns. Thus, under the codes a slave had no property rights, but in fact the plantation owners allotted their slaves patches and permitted them to sell the products they raised and to keep or spend the proceeds as they wished. Slaves were not entitled to wages, but incentive and bonus wages were frequently paid and other payments in kind or money were customary. I am not trying to paint an attractive picture of what was a sombre system. Rather I want to underscore the fact that we cannot rely on statutes alone but must also examine court records, business accounts, and other relevant materials to ascertain prevailing labor practices.

Court records are especially valuable in shedding light on labor relations on small farms and in small business which kept few if any records. Unless we examine such materials, we risk presenting an unbalanced or distorted picture based on the more systematic records kept by larger farmers and big business corporations. In recent years I have been preparing a sequel to my colonial study. The current study has as its aim an analysis of the coexistence of free and bound labor, chiefly in the period between 1783 and 1861, and attempts to penetrate the shadowland between slavery and freedom that often existed for both Negro and white labor in the slave states; it also reappraises the impact of slave labor upon the free workingman. Several perceptive studies of slavery, notably those of Ulrich B. Phillips[2] and Kenneth M. Stampp,[3] and rather detailed accounts of slavery in a number of the slave states[4] tell the story of slavery under agricultural capitalism, but they focus in the main on the large plantation, and in most cases tell us little or nothing about the small planter as slaveowner, about

[2] *American Negro Slavery* (New York, 1918).

[3] *The Peculiar Institution* (New York, 1956).

[4] James B. Sellers, *Slavery in Alabama* (Montgomery, Ala., 1950); Orville W. Taylor, *Negro Slavery in Arkansas* (Durham, N.C., 1958); Winston J. Coleman, *Slavery Times in Kentucky* (Chapel Hill, N.C., 1940); Charles Sackett Sydnor, *Slavery in Mississippi* (New York, 1933); Anthony Harrison Trexler, *Slavery in Missouri, 1804-1865* (Baltimore, 1914); Emil Oberholzer, "Legal Aspects of Slavery in Missouri," (Master's thesis, Columbia University, 1949); Chase Curran Mooney, *Slavery in Tennessee* (Bloomington, Ind., 1957).

industrial slavery, and about the effect of slavery upon the free white worker.

In examining this unexplored area and in seeking to discover evidences of collective action by free white workers, I have found the court records most suggestive. The higher courts of record have long been recognized as a prime source of information on the enforcement of the slave codes. Helen T. Catterall's abstract of *Judicial Cases Concerning American Slavery and the Negro* constitutes an indispensable guide to the appellate court records on the subject. The light which the law reports shed upon the problems of the free worker in the period, 1800–60, and labor's efforts at organizing trade unions are revealed in volume III and IV of John R. Commons' *Documentary History of American Industrial Society*. These volumes demonstrate the way in which the prosecution for criminal conspiracy was employed to thwart militant trade unionism. They document the attitude of the courts toward the activities of organized labor and provide a remarkable detailed story of the problems and strivings of labor, the objectives, strategy, and tactics of the early unions, and the reactions of employers and nonunion workers to the labor movement. They offer a rich example of the uses to which court reports can be put not only by the legal scholar but also by the social and economic historian.[5]

It is perhaps significant that these labor cases come from the Northern and border states, not from the South, where appellate courts were seldom concerned with the problems of white labor and were ignorant of or indifferent to Northern labor precedents. For example, in the Southern states strikers and labor demonstrators were punished by the courts without regard to the revolutionary position toward trade unionism formulated by Chief Justice Lemuel Shaw of Massachusetts in *Commonwealth v. Hunt*.[6] To determine what the legal authorities considered the limits of legitimate labor activity one must examine local court records, in very large measure unpublished. Included are records of county courts, such as the courts of general sessions and common pleas of South Carolina and Georgia, the findings of grand juries, the records of city courts

[5] See my preface to these volumes in the new edition issued in 1958 by Russell & Russell, New York.

[6] See my "Labor Militancy in the Old South," *Labor and Nation*, IV, No. 3 (May-June, 1948), 32–36.

like the hustings of Richmond, Virginia, or the police reports of New Orleans, or the city jail records of Baltimore.

Some published pilot studies have already shown the value of Southern inferior court records for social history. Guion Griffis Johnson has drawn substantially upon such court records and other legal papers for a superb social history of North Carolina,[7] and Jack K. Williams has analyzed ten thousand South Carolina jury indictments during the ante-bellum period to reveal the high proportion of crimes of violence against the person among all indictments and the relative leniency or ineffectiveness of the criminal machinery compared to the present day.[8] Exploring much the same ground, I have found that inferior court records and grand jury indictments and presentments shed much light on such subjects as pauperism, poor relief, and forced labor,[9] and on problems of controlling the activities of slaves and restraining inhumane slaveowners. The Baltimore city jail records, for example, disclose that the specific performance of labor contracts was enforced long after the legislature had abolished imprisonment for debt. This was done by the simple device of jailing absconding servants, apprentices, and seamen.[10]

One argument against the systematic use of inferior court records is that, while they are generally accessible, they are scattered throughout the county courthouses of the nation. Some centralization has taken place in a few places, however. At Hartford and Annapolis many of the older county court records have been transferred to the state archives. The South Caroliniana Library of the University of South Carolina has a substantial collection of transcripts of the general sessions and common pleas court records of that state made by WPA workers, and Louisiana State University has transcripts of some of the police jury minutes of Louisiana parishes which are available on interlibrary loan.

Aside from court records, other governmental archives are useful to the historian of early American labor. Examination of reports of legislative proceedings and petitions to the legisla-

[7] *Ante-Bellum North Carolina: A Social History* (Chapel Hill, 1937).

[8] *Vogues in Villainy: Crime and Retribution in Ante-Bellum South Carolina* (Columbia, S.C., 1959).

[9] Richard B. Morris, "White Bondage in Ante-Bellum South Carolina," *South Carolina Historical and Genealogical Magazine*, XLIX (1948), 191–207.

[10] Richard B. Morris, "Labor Controls in Maryland in the Nineteenth Century," *Journal of Southern History* (August, 1948), pp. 385–400.

tures can prove most rewarding. At the State Archives at Columbia, South Carolina, and the Virginia State Library at Richmond, petitions to the legislature are systematically arranged. In my own researches I have found that petitions to the legislatures of South Carolina and Delaware provide clues to the survival of white bondage and peonage.[11]

Ideally, the correspondence and proceedings of trade unions should be the central focus of research for a labor historian of the early national and ante-bellum periods, but such material is virtually non-existent. What we do have is the other side of the coin, the records of business firms which often reveal their labor problems and labor policy. Most systematically recorded and preserved are the reports of canal and railroad companies. Among the "Letters Received," of the Chesapeake and Ohio Canal Company, which are now in the National Archives, is a report from a resident engineer of the company under date of January 23, 1834, telling of labor troubles on that line. This clue led me to local newspapers, among them the Hagerstown (Md.) *Torchlight* and the Williamsport *Republican Banner,* which revealed that federal troops had been sent to put down the ensuing labor disturbances. A check of the House of Delegates and Senate Journals at the Hall of Records in Annapolis disclosed that both houses called on the President for military assistance. While no such order was found in the Jackson Papers in the Library of Congress, the records of the War Department in the National Archives revealed that under date of January 29, 1834, Andrew Jackson had ordered Secretary of War Eaton to send "at least two companies of regulars" to "put down the riotous assembly." Thus what seemed like a routine collection of an engineer's reports to the president of his company ultimately led to the discovery of the dispatch of federal troops to a strike area by "Old Hickory" some forty-three years before President Hayes intervened in the railroad strikes of 1877, previously accepted as the "first" instance in American history of the calling out of federal troops in a labor dispute.[12]

The most systematically preserved records of business firms in the ante-bellum period are the printed proceedings of the

[11] See my "White Bondage in Ante-Bellum South Carolina," cited n. 9 supra and "The Course of Peonage in a Slave State," *Political Science Quarterly,* LXV (1950), 238–262.

[12] See my "Andrew Jackson, Strikebreaker," *American Historical Review,* LV (Oct., 1949), 54–68.

annual meetings of the railroads, which report in detail on construction problems and furnish clues to labor difficulties with workers over wages and other conditions of labor. These proceedings can be supplemented by the *American Railroad Journal,* a full file of which is in the Library of Congress. When it is borne in mind that the railroads used imported Irish and later Chinese labor and purchased or hired Negro slaves at times in competition with white labor, it should be obvious that their records constitute a mine of data for the labor historian.

Formal business reports, such as the president's statement to stockholders and the proceedings of annual meetings, cannot be expected to emphasize labor-management difficulties. Interoffice reports and correspondence are likely to be much more revealing. For the ante-bellum period a considerable number of industrial records have been centralized in a few repositories, notably institutions like the McCormick Library in Chicago and the Alderman Library of the University of Virginia. The latter has an unsurpassed collection of iron forge and foundry records. On close inspection they provide illuminating material on white and Negro labor relations, on bonus and incentive payments to slave labor, and on the comparative economic conditions of free whites and Negro slaves who often toiled side by side. Duke University has some important records of tobacco factories, including an invaluable collection of hiring bonds among the Leslie Papers.

John R. Commons' monumental *History of Labour in the United States* demonstrated that in the field of labor history, newspapers can furnish indispensable source material, often indeed the only evidence extant. Applying to one relatively restricted field a technique in which John Bach McMaster has pioneered with such success, William A. Sullivan sampled a great variety of newspapers published in Pennsylvania. In all, he found 135 strikes recorded in Pennsylvania during the years 1799 to 1840 (of which 97 took place during the depression years, 1833–37),[13] a total more than double the number previously uncovered by Commons and his collaborators.[14]

One recent approach to unconventional sources for labor's activities has modified or at least shaken some conventional

13 W. A. Sullivan, *The Industrial Worker in Pennsylvania, 1800–1840* (Harrisburg, 1955), pp. 217–230.
14 *History of Labour in the United States,* I (New York, 1918), 478–484.

views, but not without provoking considerable controversy. To test the generalization of several historians that labor voted for Jackson in 1832, a number of scholars have analyzed the occupations of members of workingmen's committees and conventions and of workingmen's candidates, and have used various devices to determine what relation, if any, existed between property ownership and voting. Such an analysis was feasible where election returns by wards were available and corresponding assessment rolls could be located. Studies in Boston and Philadelphia suggest that the manufacturers and anti-Jacksonians managed to entice the workingmen into the camp of the National Republicans or Anti-Masons, and that it was the small farmer in the back country sections of the Eastern states who supported Jackson far more consistently than did the industrial worker.[15]

My own researches in ante-bellum labor history have been largely confined to the South, and the newspapers I have examined have been largely Southern papers. Any investigator who expects to carry on research in Southern newspapers without leaving the North is in for a severe disappointment, as Northern libraries, with the notable exception of the Library of Congress, have spotty, inadequate, and unrepresentative collections of Southern newspapers. But a thorough combing of the files of the papers of major cities like Richmond, Charleston, and New Orleans will prove most rewarding. They disclose numerous instances of labor unrest and occasional instances of labor organization most often unknown to historians of labor. Our knowledge of the notable Tredegar Iron Works strike of 1847 is largely derived from Richmond newspapers, particularly the *Times and Compiler* and the Richmond *Enquirer*. In that labor dispute white workers struck when Negroes were introduced in certain departments of the mill. Threatened with a criminal prosecution, the workers, on the intervention of the mayor, returned to work. Management had established the principle that slaveowners could employ their property in any way they wished. Richmond newspapers report still other strikes

15 See W. A. Sullivan, "Did Labor Support Andrew Jackson?" *Political Science Quarterly*, LXII, 569–580; E. Pessen, "Did Labor Support Jackson?: The Boston Story," *ibid.*, LXIV, 262–274. For a criticism of the statistical basis of the latter article, see R. T. Bower, "Notes on 'Did Labor Support Jackson?: The Boston Story,'" *ibid.*, LXV (1950). See also Walter Hugins, *Jacksonian Democracy and the Working Class* (Stanford: Stanford University Press, 1960), pp. 201–218.

in the years before the Civil War, but in none of them did the public authorities intervene as the disputes involved normal trade union objectives—higher wages or shorter hours—and did not pose any threat to the South's "peculiar institution." Probably the most highly organized trade unions in the ante-bellum South were the printing trades, and Southern news-papers furnish us with considerable information about the objectives and militancy of the typographical unions.[16]

Finally, researchers uncovering clues to labor issues in the unpublished records of inferior courts should bear in mind that newspapers not infrequently devoted long columns to local news and court gossip. Here testimony taken at magistrate's and other inferior court hearings would be reported, supplementing the relatively arid dockets or minute books. True, these accounts were not infrequently highly spiced, handled in a condescending or sarcastic vein, betraying racial and other tra-ditional biases; but even though we must try to discount their subjectivity, we cannot afford to ignore the material they furnish us.[17]

Ideally, it would have been helpful had early trade unions kept careful and systematic records, had labor leaders preserved their correspondence, or written their memoirs, or tape-re-corded their recollections for some oral history project, and had statesmen, who did preserve their papers, shown a greater preoccupation with branches of labor outside the institution of slavery than they did in fact. But we are dealing with reality. The remote past of our labor history lies buried among thou-sands of trivia, entombed among transient items that we must

[16] See, for example, Richmond *Whig and Public Advertiser*, Feb. 13, 1852; *Louisianian*, April 1, 1823; New Orleans *Commercial Bulletin*, March 16, 1837. For the resolutions of the Augusta, Ga., Typographical Society, see *Southern Banner* (Athens, Ga.), Nov. 19, 1836.

[17] Some of the less obvious newspaper sources I have found informative about labor matters in the ante-bellum period include the Nashville *Republican Banner*, the St. Louis *Republican*, the Frankfort, Ky., *Argus of Western America*, *Brownlow's Knoxville Whig and Independent Journal*, and the Huntsville, Ala., *Southern Advocate and Huntsville Advertiser*, along with several other Alabama papers, all to be found at the Library of Congress.

Several labor papers were published in the slave states, first among them the *Southern Free Press* issued in Charleston in 1825. A few Socialist papers also were issued south of Mason and Dixon's line, notably Adolph Douai's *San Antonio Zeitung, ein Sozial-Demokratisches Blatt für die Deutschen in West Texas*, launched in 1853 and discontinued two years later when its editor fled to the North.

unearth from sources often discrete and seldom obvious. To dig in the right place and then put the pieces together in the right way, we need some of the intuition of the archeologist, some of the techniques of the detective, and all of the sustained enthusiasm of the scholar who knows that his subject is both exciting and significant and finds that it poses a continuing intellectual challenge.

31. The Life and Soul of History*

MERRILL JENSEN, SAMUEL FLAGG BEMIS, AND DAVID DONALD

I

Long after the War for Independence John Adams asked: "Who shall write the history of the American Revolution? Who can write it? Who will ever be able to write it?" Thomas Jefferson replied: "Nobody; except merely its external facts. All its councils, designs, and discussions, having been conducted by Congress with closed doors, and no member, so far as I know, having even made notes of them—these, which are the life and soul of history must forever be unknown."

The two old gentlemen had forgotten that they, among others, had kept at least partial records of the "life and soul of history," and no one had done so more faithfully than John Adams. Portions of the Adams papers have been published from time to time since the 1840's: the *Familiar Letters* (1875), *The Works of John Adams* (1850–1856), *The Warren-Adams Letters* (1917–1925), to mention some of the most important. They are sources no student should do without, and if he does, he should abandon the study of the American Revolution at once. John Adams was one of those rare people who can play a vital part in the history of their times and yet can stand aside and look at those times with a certain degree of detachment. In his generation he was equaled only by a man utterly unlike him, Gouverneur Morris, and Morris, like John Adams' kinsman, Samuel Adams, kept very few of his papers.

* Reprinted with permission from *The New England Quarterly*, XXXIV (March, 1961), 96–105.

The printed Adams material is invaluable but it is but a small portion of the vast treasure revealed by the microfilms of all the Adams papers (the letterpress edition now in progress will also be selective). A mere sampling from among the hundreds of reels is an exciting and a rewarding experience. Charles Francis Adams published large portions of John Adams' diary but he omitted much that is revealing about the diarist and his times: Adams' delight at the purchase of his father's farm and his reflections about it, the earnest discussions among lawyers on circuit about the best way to prepare manure for fields, and so on. Fortunately all of the diary is soon to be published.

Abigail Adams was quite as remarkable as any of the men in her family, but unlike her husband and her son, John Quincy, she was not a diarist. Posterity's loss is great indeed as the brief one she did keep demonstrates. She began it as she prepared to leave for England in June, 1784. Her housewifely horror at the dirt aboard ship and her insistence on a thorough cleaning of her cabin, her comments on seasickness and on the captain who thought more of his sails than his passengers, are a joy to read. The diary stops when she reaches England but she resumes it just three years later. It ends again as she boards ship to return home, and she is glad. She notes that she did not regret the "excursion" because it made her more attached to America than ever. And, she declared, anything further she learned of the world she would be content to learn from history.

The microfilms contain a wealth of legal materials. If combined with other sources such as court records they should make possible the study of John Adams' career as a lawyer and should reveal a good deal about the legal history of the years before 1776. There are invaluable notes on admiralty cases, in addition to the material on John Hancock's trial for smuggling, and some important ones on Chief Justice Thomas Hutchinson's charges to grand juries.

The correspondence, of course, bulks largest and grows in quantity after 1774, and is unbelievably rich for the 1790's. The Adamses wrote to one another constantly and one gets an intimate picture, not only of the family, but of the political history of the times as seen by the family. In addition, the Adamses carried on a vast correspondence with a wide range of people. No less than 133 reels of film are needed to copy the "letters received" until the death of John Adams in 1826. Many of these letters, even from important people, have never been seen before except by the Adamses. Take for example reel 346 which covers the months from May to December, 1776. During May and June, John Adams was in Congress striving to bring about a declaration of independence. Edmund C. Burnett's great edition of the letters of the members of Congress illuminates the activities of that body, but equally important were the events in the various colonies where conventions and congresses were debating the issue of independence, and which had to vote for it before Congress could do so.

The letters to John Adams during these months reveal much of what was going on in some of the colonies and show how closely certain men in them worked with Adams. Such was the case with Richard Henry Lee and Patrick Henry in Virginia. On May 18 Lee sent a copy of the Virginia resolution to Adams, and shortly thereafter, he returned to Congress to move the resolution on June 7. Two days after Lee wrote, Henry wrote Adams and told him that he did not think the resolution was pointed enough but that he had agreed to it to achieve unanimity. He also explained something of the problems of creating a new government for Virginia. He hoped Adams' pamphlet would do good because "there is among most of our opulent families a strong byass to aristocracy." Henry said he hoped to form a "portrait of government" like that of New England, and exclaimed: "Would to God you and Sam Adams were here."

Samuel Chase had left Congress to return to Maryland in an attempt to secure a reversal of the Maryland convention's instructions against independence, and he too kept Adams informed. On June 21 he wrote: "I have not been idle. I have appealed *in writing* to the people. County after county is instructing." At nine in the evening on June 28 he wrote a hasty note. He had just left the convention to secure an "express" to send to Congress with the news that the convention had voted unanimously for independence: "the glorious effects of county instructions. Our people have fire if not smothered." And, he added, *"Now for a government."* On June 15 Jonathan Sergeant in New Jersey wrote even more briefly: "We are passing the Rubicon & our delegates in Congress on the first of July will vote plump."

Such are but a few of the letters on a single reel. Along with them are a wealth of letters about everything from Massachusetts politics to military strategy to the vagaries of military men, about the whole vast complex of things happening in America as it moved from the status of colonies claiming rights to a nation fighting for its independence. Some of the letters reinforce what we already know; some offer new evidence and insights.

The first generation of the Adams family helped bring the United States into being, and thanks be, they kept their records!

MERRILL JENSEN

II

Of the three generations so abundantly recorded in the Adams Manuscripts, the accumulation stemming from John Quincy Adams and his immediate family is the greatest in quantity, perhaps the richest historically. This is not because he was the most important Adams statesman—on this score most scholars would doubtless vote for his father. It is rather because J. Q. A.'s long career of public service, from 1793 when President Washington appointed him as Minister from the United States to The Hague, until his death on the floor of the House of Representatives in 1848, overlaps to a considerable degree in each instance the lives and public activities of his father and his surviving son. Consequently biographers of both these other Adamses, and historians of the period, must consult the J. Q. A. manuscripts for the later decades of John Adams' longer life, and the early decades of Charles Francis Adams. A vast new mine of sources, particularly political material, but also of economic, religious, and intellectual character, is now widely available in these microfilms of the papers of J. Q. A. These documents will engage historians of the whole range of United States history in John Quincy Adams' adult life span: including the establishment of American nationality, the foundations of American foreign policy, the expanding continental republic and the emerging sectional conflict—from the days of George Washington to those of James K. Polk.

The famous diary, of course, runs through all three epochs in the life of J. Q. A. Large portions of the total record have long since been available in print. Charles Francis Adams, Jr., J. Q. A.'s grandson, edited the earliest years of the diary written while the author was a student in Theophilus Parsons' law office in Newburyport in 1787–1788, under the title *Life in a New England Town* (Boston, 1903). Best known is the monumental *Memoirs of John Quincy Adams, 1795–1848,* edited by his son Charles Francis Adams in twelve stout volumes (Philadelphia,

1874–1876). How much of the whole diary did Charles Francis Adams leave out from the dozen massive volumes of the printed record? This could be precisely determined—if someone had the time and patience to make a count of wordage by comparing the original manuscript with the microfilm copy now so widely dispersed. The printed pages can be easily picked out of the original manuscript because Charles Francis Adams marked them with pencil between parentheses.

What was Charles Francis Adams' criterion of selection, his *Auswahlungprinzip?* He conscientiously included everything which he thought was of historical value or interest; the rest, of merely personal character, or trivia, he excluded. Where he had a doubt whether passages were of historical import or not, he included them. The resultant printed *Memoirs* is about as good a rendition of the diary as it would be practical to print without the colossal job of reproducing it in entirety. The editor-son did include a voluminous quantity of personal matter, doubtless considering it of historical import as exhibiting the character of a great statesman. But there is a great quantity of data remaining in the manuscript diary that refines our picture of J. Q. A. and his family, and friends, and much of material importance for the political history of the period: for example, one would never get any true picture of J. Q. A.'s tenacious ambition to be elected again without the unprinted diary. The presidential bee bumbled in his head for at least three national elections following his defeat by Andrew Jackson in 1828.

J. Q. A. did not write this tremendous diary for publication. He labored at the prodigious record, (1) out of a compulsive self-discipline, (2) for his own reference (which he found very useful in many a controversy), (3) for frank and private revelation of himself to his descendants. Perhaps he did think that one of them might some day prepare *selections* for publication, although we do not have any evidence of such an expectation. The style of the diaries is so hurried and unfinished, and the details heaped up in such a rough way as to convince one that the author never expected it to be published completely. It remains for modern scholarship to make a critical examination of the whole diary, now so easily available. Such a study could include a content analysis that would give a wonderful picture of J. Q. A.'s thought and psychology, both of the outer and the inner man.

J. Q. A.'s career as a diplomatist is revealed in much greater detail than the diary affords, in his letterbooks, private and official, for 1794–1801 and 1809–1825, but these should be supplemented with his official dispatches and instructions preserved in the National Archives, Department of State records. These documents have been filmed in the National Archives series of microfilm publications and are available at a moderate cost considering their great bulk. Any library possessing the J. Q. A. microfilms would do well to acquire the supplementary copies of official documents.

The private letters of a diplomatist often throw much more revealing light on his activities than do his official dispatches. J. Q. A. is no exception to this: for instance, his letters to his father the Vice President, from The Hague, warned against the United States being drawn into the "vortex" of European quarrels and wars, were passed on to President Washington, and leave verbal traces in the latter's famous Farewell Address. J. Q. A's private papers are drafts which Worthington C. Ford made use of to show Secretary Adams' close relationship with the formulation of the Monroe Doctrine. Ford's edition of *The Writings of John Quincy Adams* (7 vols., New York, 1913–1917) presents a highly discriminating selection of his letters both public and private, but after all it is only a selection, of less than one-half of the material, and stops in the middle of the year 1823, a victim of publishing stringency during the First World War.

Material for the Presidency is more meager: there are only two private letterbooks for 1825–1829. Most of the public letters and pronouncements, except for drafts, are easily available in print. The manuscript diary and printed *Memoirs* are more revealing.

The circumstances of Adams' election to Congress from the Plymouth district of Massachusetts in 1830, and his long, controversial, and most spectacular career are principally recorded in the diary and in his letters to his son, Charles Francis Adams, although there are many more private letters to and from other people. The problems of nullification and Union, of the anti-Mexican crusade, of Adams as a spokesman on foreign policy, the bitter sectional controversy, the Gag Rule, Texas annexation and the right of partition, Adams' defense of the Africans of the ship *Amistad,* the dramatic defeat in the House of Representatives of a move to censure him, the Oregon Question, the Smithsonian Institution, all these are to be found in great detail in the still unpublished letters, as well as diary. Particular mention should be made of the large mass of incoming letters, from all parts of the country, on all kinds of subjects; perhaps more relating to the sectional controversy than any other single theme. They are an abundant source for historians of this dramatic period and this dramatic personality. Among them will be found several series of sustained correspondence between Adams and such men as Nicholas Biddle, Ward N. Boylston, Henry Clay, Peter Paul Francis DeGrand, Alexander Hill Everett, Edward Everett, the Grimké sisters, Christopher Hughes the "Baltimore wit," Josiah Quincy, Richard Rush, and Benjamin Waterhouse. Above all, his steady correspondence with his father and mother during their lifetimes, and his wife (when absent), and his sons. During the long retirement of the Sage of Quincy, 1801–1826, father and son exchanged ideas on many subjects: politics, economics, literature, religion, philosophy. Here is a theme that needs an author.

Ancillary to the great quantity of J. Q. A. documents suggested above, are the manuscripts of Mrs. John Quincy Adams, their ill-fated son George Washington Adams, and their surviving famous son Charles Francis Adams, together with fragmentary collections of other relatives. These letters and fragmentary diaries reveal among many other things the checkered family relationship of the President in the White House, and the chapter of his life in brief retirement as an American Job.

SAMUEL FLAGG BEMIS

III

"Washington," reads the first diary entry, dated January 1, 1820. "No School. Horace Dawes letter President's drawing room family cold weather dinner, Mr. Forbes." Rarely has a great journal begun so inauspiciously. Fortunately the twelve-year-old diarist was one of the Adams clan, the son of John Quincy Adams and the grandson of John Adams, and he soon showed that he shared the family propensity for detailed introspection. After only a few more brief, cryptic entries the diary of Charles Francis Adams became as full and as revealing as those of his forebears. Ultimately it was, with a few interruptions, to cover sixty years, to fill thirty-six bound volumes, and to occupy nearly eleven thousand pages. Unquestionably it is the most important unpublished journal in the United States today and, together with Adams' letterbooks, incoming correspondence, and miscellaneous records, is a fresh and enormously significant source for the history of the Civil War and Reconstruction eras.

It will be decades before historians are able fully to explore all the treasures contained in this vast collection of Charles Francis Adams' papers. These records offer, first of all, an intimate and revealing picture of one of the most remarkable men America has ever produced, the diarist himself. Charles Francis Adams kept his diary for himself, not for posterity. "It is my intention in commencing this book," he wrote in 1823 as he started a new volume of his journal, "to improve my style of writing by means of it as well as to record one of the most interesting periods of life, for my amusement. . . . I could not help thinking that in case I should live for any space of time, it would be a pleasant thing to me to recollect, by means of this as a refresher of the memory, those scenes which . . . I witnessed and which are about to have a material influence upon this country." Inevitably, therefore, a great part of his diary and of his other papers is taken up with purely personal matters. Here is a full record of the books he read, the sermons he heard, the parties he attended, the opinions he held. Here also is the full, and sometimes painful, record of his relations with his father, who, to the son's dismay, would not settle down in dignified retirement such as befitted an ex-President. Here is the story of Adams' relations with his wife, with his children, with his friends. Adams was occasionally disturbed that so much of his journal should be occupied with these personal matters, feeling "it would be egotism in the greatest degree to trouble any body *but myself* with a minute account of myself." But he speedily came to the sensible conclusion: "In this book made for the amusement of *I*, alone it is fair that I should have that share in its pages to which it is justly entitled."

Fortunately the diaries and papers of Charles Francis Adams also offer a detailed and richly revealing account of the many public movements and events in which he played so prominent a part. Here, for example, is the fullest and best account of the disruption of the Whig oligarchy in Massachusetts, through the rise of the Conscience Whigs and the Free Soilers. Nowhere else can one trace so completely the tangled story of Massachusetts politics in the 1850's, with the election of Charles Sumner to the Senate, the defeat of the Coalition of Democrats and Free Soilers, the machinations of Henry Wilson, and the triumph of nativism and of Henry J. Gardner. After Adams entered the House of Representatives in 1858, his papers and his diaries increasingly became a record of national politics. As an eye-witness and principal participant he recorded the growing conservatism of the Republican party, the 1860 campaign for Lincoln, and the elaborate and unsuccessful maneuvers to keep the peace during the great secession winter of 1860–1861. After Adams was named American minister to Great Britain in 1861, his diary and his papers naturally dealt mostly with his diplomatic career, and they form the most important single source for a study of American efforts to keep England neutral during the Civil War. For the Reconstruction era Adams' papers are equally important, for they record in fresh and exciting detail his services on the Geneva tribunal to arbitrate the *Alabama* claims, and his abortive candidacy for the Liberal Republican nomination in 1872.

Unlike so many men of affairs, Charles Francis Adams had an instinct for keeping the historical record full and straight. He not only kept a diary that is more complete, more detailed, and more objective than that of either his father or his grandfather; he preserved copies of virtually every important letter he ever wrote, and he saved every significant letter he ever received, together with newspaper clippings, copies of speeches, menus of banquets, programs of entertainment, bank books, account book, financial ledgers—and virtually everything else. For hardly any other nineteenth-century American figure is the documentary record so complete.

In his later years Adams permitted himself to doubt the utility of the records he so systematically kept. ". . . it often occurs to me," he wrote in 1876, "whether all my labor will prove of any use. The continuation of families is so uncertain, and the changes of habitation so much depend on the growth of the neighborhood that it is idle to expect permanency." Fortunately, despite many changes in Quincy and in Boston, his fears proved unfounded and his remarkable papers have been preserved intact. Every historian and every serious student of American history will agree that they emphatically were worth keeping. Thanks to the careful and assiduous labors of the staffs of the Massachusetts Historical Society and the Adams Papers, they are now available, on microfilm, in full to scholars, and they form the richest single collection of manuscript material for the study of nineteenth-century American history.

DAVID DONALD

32. *History This Side the Horizon**

ALLAN NEVINS

We have all, at some time or other, wished that *we* had been placed where we might see great epochal events pass before our eyes, and record them in the glowing prose of an excited on-looker or participant. If only *we* had been at Waterloo to see Napoleon's Old Guard falter and retreat before the British squares; if *we* had stood in the Hall of Mirrors at Versailles to witness the German acceptance of the peace treaty painted by Orpen! Henry W. Nevinson in *The Dark Backward* has vividly depicted a series of memorable scenes from history: the ten thousand battered, exhausted warriors of Xenophon reaching the shore of the dark blue Euxine; grim Diocletion at Spalato watching the martyrdom of a group of Christians; Prince Hal's forces on St. Crispin's day in fierce onset against the French knights, the incessant blows on armor sounding like hammers on a thousand anvils; Napoleon at Jena, triumphant as the cuirassiers swept by him. If only, we think, we could have seen such events! Or, better still, if we could have had the chance that John Hay and John G. Nicolay had when they were chosen secretaries to live and work with Lincoln throughout the Civil War. Instead, we seem never to see or hear anything of true historical significance, of dramatically memorable quality; we never talk with the great personages of our time, and know nothing of state secrets.

In this view of the past there lurk two fallacies. The first is our exaggeration of the advantages possessed by men at the heart of great events. It is true that a Winston Churchill does

* Reprinted with permission from *Vermont Quarterly*, XVIII new series (October, 1950), 153–162.

now and then appear, a leader who not only participates in great events, but sees them with the eye of an imaginative historian while they are being enacted. It is true that more frequently a man can play such a role as that of John Hay, who sat with perceptive eye in the White House during the four years of Civil War and wrote about it afterward, or Ray Stannard Baker, who went with Woodrow Wilson to Paris and in due course dealt in historical prose with the events he had witnessed. It is a fact, however, that in general the participants in great historical events or the onlookers at memorable historical scenes know much less about them than those who come afterward. They are too busy and excited to observe, or they see only one facet of a many sided transaction, or they are precluded by their special routine duties from taking note of the activities about them. It was not the men in the front line of Pickett's charge who understood most fully the battle of Gettysburg. When we think enviously of the opportunities that a British or American Cabinet officer has for knowing what is going on, that man may frequently be complaining that he knows less than a newspaper reporter.

It is literally true that some members of Lloyd George's Cabinet (not the inner War Cabinet which directed affairs but the outer general Ministry), working night and day, knew less about World War I than the freely observant man in Regent Street or Pimlico. Nor is this situation unusual. I have lately seen a manuscript letter written by the Secretary of the Treasury in Lincoln's Cabinet, Salmon P. Chase, to Senator Zachary Chandler of Michigan in the late summer of 1862, at the very time that the Emancipation Proclamation was being issued. Chase declared that he knew nothing about public affairs. Day after day he toiled at his Treasury desk over figures of revenue and outgo, over plans for raising money and checks upon expenditures. But a broad picture of the colossal conflict then raging he never obtained. He wrote:

> Maryland has been rescued and Pennsylvania saved from invasion. But the rebel army has suffered far less than our own in the battles of the last two weeks, and has strong positions which it should never have been permitted to win. What now? Who can tell? I, though charged with the responsibility of providing for the enormous expenditures entailed upon the country, have no control over—no voice even—in deciding on the measures by

which the necessity for them is created. In fact, I know about as little of what is being done as any outsider.

Neither credit nor responsibility for what is done or decided outside of the Treasury Department belongs to me. . . . There is . . . at the present time no Cabinet except in name. The heads of Departments come together now and then . . . nominally twice a week; but no reports are made; no regular discussions held; no ascertained conclusions reached. Sometimes weeks pass by and no full meeting is held. One can get some information about military matters if he will make due inquiry at the War Department or about Naval matters at the Naval Department: but full systematic accounts of the progress of the struggle; the purpose entertained; the means and modes of action by or against us, are neither made nor given, nor required.

In short, when Secretary Chase wished to know how the Civil War was being conducted, and what the government in general was doing, he had to send out for a copy of the New York *Herald*.

The secondary fallacy is the idea that we ordinary men and women have no opportunity to observe matters of first-rate historical interest. The fact is that history lies all about us if we have eyes to see it. It lies about us not merely in times of war and crisis, but in everyday humdrum times. Everyone sees immediately that if he had been an English village priest in the days of Crecy and Agincourt, even in a quiet hamlet of Surrey or Norfolk, he would have had matter to record that would greatly interest twentieth century students of history. Everyone realizes that if he or she had been a plain yeoman farmer or a housewife in Revolutionary days, living anywhere—in Virginia, in the Brandywine or Wyoming Valley, in the district between Saratoga and Bennington—and had possessed even a crude use of the pen, a record would have emerged upon which readers of our day would pounce with avidity. But a century hence, five centuries hence, *our* descendants will think of us as living in the most romantic, the most colorful, the most exciting of times; and they will wonder that we did not leave multitudinous records of the fascinating changes, the tremendous innovations, which swept and swirled all about us.

"Just think!" they will say. "Those hardy Vermonters dwelt in the era of the last decades of the railways, with their great express-trains thundering along roads of steel, and first decades of the airplane, then so primitive that people marvelled at airlines that crossed the Atlantic in twelve hours—not twelve minutes, but hours—and at craft that carried a hundred—not a thousand, a pitiful hundred passengers. They dwelt in a time when radio had just lost its novelty, and when in many a humble village people could yet be found who had never seen a television screen. Synthetic fabrics were yet so new that millions still used the quaint cotton and woolen garments of their forbears; and synthetic foods had not yet transformed the old-style grocery stores with their thousand curious and odorous products based on the land. Countless men vividly remembered the uncomprehending awe with which, as a hundred thousand people lay dead in faraway Hiroshima, they heard the epochal announcement of the birth of atomic energy—the announcement that heralded a new era far more distinctly than the fall of Rome or the discovery of a New World by Columbus."

Our extraordinary advantages as observers of living history in this tempestuous year 1950, in the very center of the most terrible and wonderful century mankind has up till this time known, would be perfectly clear to us if we could stand for a moment at the vantage point of (say) the year 2100 A.D. It would be clear because time would give us a perspective which now only imagination can supply—and few of us have very much imagination. Few have even the elementary type of imagination which would enable us to comprehend that the most vital elements of history are not the hey-rub-a-dub events taking place in the Senate in Washington, or at No. 10 Downing Street, or in the offices of the Kremlin; they are instead the humble day-by-day events which register the impact of sweeping economic and social changes upon the masses—the events which exhibit our growing utilization of the air for communication or transportation, of synthetic chemistry for clothing and food, and of the atom for energy. Emerson once congratulated Thomas Carlyle on his imagination as a historian. "I think," he wrote, "you see as pictures every street, church, parliament house, barracks, baker's shop, mutton-stall, forge, wharf, and ship and whatever stands, creeps, rolls, or swims thereabout, and make it all your own." This is a good kind of imagination; but better still is the imagination which sees all these commonplace scenes changing, evolving, taking on new shapes and glowing with fresh life.

Macaulay penned a famous passage upon the nature of history which I have sometimes felt could aptly be turned into modern American phraseology. He was pointing out the inadequacy of the stiff brocaded history which Hume, Gibbon, and Robertson had devoted to wars, monarchs, and state events. This left out the homely life of the plain people, which only the historical novelists had theretofore touched. "A truly great historian," wrote Macaulay, "would reclaim those materials the novelist has appropriated. We should not then have to look for the wars and the votes of the Puritans in Clarendon, and for their phraseology in *Old Mortality,* for one half of King James in Hume and the other half in *The Fortunes of Nigel.* . . . Society would be shown from the highest to the lowest, from the royal cloth of state to the den of the outlaw, from the throne of the legate to the chimney corner where the begging friar regaled himself. Palmers, minstrels, crusaders, the stately monastery with the good cheer of its refectory, and the tournament with its heralds and ladies, and trumpets and the cloth of gold, would give truth and life to the representation."

Convert this passage into terms appropriate to our own time and place, and we can see what an opportunity the townsman of Rutland, the officeholder of Montpelier, and the rude farmer of Windham possesses to record materials for history, or to write history itself. "A truly great historian," we would say, "must reclaim those materials which Dorothy Canfield and Robert Frost have appropriated. We should not then have to look for wars in Parkman and Douglas Freeman, and for the struggles of Republican and Democrat in James Ford Rhodes, while we searched for the customs of the hill farmer in Walter Hard, the speech of the north-country Yankee in Edith Wharton's *Ethan Frome* and *Summer,* and the tricks of the Concord or Montpelier politicians in Churchill's *Coniston.* Society would be shown from the highest to the lowest; from the marble mansions of Manchester and Woodstock to the den of the prohibition hijacker, from the quiet study of the university president to the blaring din of the corner drugstore as teen-agers feed the jukebox, from the college youth on the ski-tow to the lumberjack, from the proud Proctors to the despised summer resident. Palmers, minstrels, crusaders, Fuller brush men, the ornate resort hotel with the good cheer in its cocktail lounge, the State Fair with its heralds, ladies, two-headed pigs, the swing-bands and the nylons, would give truth and life to the representation." For in these terms we define the history that coming generations will cherish.

Too scornful of what is commonplace today, we forget that

in half a century it will begin to seem romantic—"romance draws in with the six-fifteen"—and that in a century much of it will obviously possess transcendent social significance. And we are often misled by a plain, homely, even vulgar exterior into overlooking rich lodes or ore that lurk just under the surface. At Columbia University we have lately made a prolonged, carefully planned, and adequately financed effort to expose and quarry some of the veins of historical material that branch all about us. Our Oral History Project, as it is termed, has undertaken to interview in systematic fashion, according to a well-studied pattern, scores upon scores of men and women whose lives seem of significance to the community. They are asked, before it is too late, to pour out their reminiscences into the faithful ear of a wire recorder; these memoirs are then transcribed; the persons interviewed carefully edit, and if they like, expand their story; and the result, duly signed, is placed in the University Archives under whatever restrictions the donor wishes to impose. Already, within the space of a year and a half, we have obtained the stories of men who have taken their memories into death's dateless night. We rescued from oblivion Burton J. Hendrick's account of how he, Ida Tarbell, Lincoln Steffens, and others made *McClure's Magazine* great in muckraking days. We preserved the late Dr. Joseph Collins's narrative of how he treated Henry James and other distinguished men for mental ailments, and how he founded the Neurological Institute. Some 110 life stories, aggregating more than eleven thousand typed manuscript pages, have now been taken down from the lips of more or less distinguished people. It is obvious that the memoirs of Norman Thomas, for example, or Judge Learned Hand, or Walter Lippmann must have enduring historical value. But it is extraordinary how frequently a person of outwardly ordinary antecedents and appearance, who might seem to have lived an uneventful life, has a record of striking originality and value to relate.

Suppose yourself travelling from Chicago to New York with the author of that shrewdly perceptive but somewhat supercilious volume called *The Man Who Knew Coolidge*. In the smoking car the attention of Mr. Sinclair Lewis and yourself is drawn to a gentleman who might very well have known Coolidge. He looks like the type. He is clearly a prosperous businessman. He is reading not Homer or Shakespeare, but *The Nation's Business*. He is plump, bald, bespectacled; Mr. Lewis would call him pudgy. He looks a bit like Mark Hanna's pictures. His conversation betrays the fact that he is an advertising man; worse still, he has for many years been a Chicago advertising man. As he speaks of his acquaintance with Herbert Hoover, Sinclair Lewis draws back in repulsion.

But Mr. Lewis would be missing one of the many exciting men in our business-minded nation; for the materialistic, obese, ordinary-looking fellow-traveller has played a leading role in several important events and developments. His name, A. D. Lasker, might not mean much to us. His ordinary conversation, while showing wisdom and breadth, might not seem highly impressive. It is only when the lens of Oral History is turned upon him that the significance of his busy life becomes plain. For Mr. Lasker, as head of one of the two or three greatest advertising firms in America (Lord & Thomas), did more than any other man to transform the nature of American advertising. Its guiding principle until he came upon the scene had been "Reiterate the name! Keep the name of the product before the people!" His labors gave it a new guiding principle: "Explain just what your product will do! Educate people in its specific merits!" For senseless iteration ("Mellen's Food: Babies Cry for It") he substituted education ("Ivory Soap: It Floats"). To name but one of Mr. Lasker's feats, he was the man who, more than all others combined, made it permissible and popular for women to smoke cigarettes. And further use of the lens of Oral History showed that Mr. Lasker had other significant pieces of history to reveal. As head of the Shipping Board just after World War I, he was on intimate terms with Warren G. Harding and was able to study shrewdly that President's character. He had encouraged Walter Teagle of Standard Oil to carry to Harding advance information of the dishonesty of Albert B. Fall in the Teapot Dome lease. As an associate of Walter Wrigley in the ownership of the Chicago White Sox, he had been in the midst of the famous Black Sox scandal, and had himself drafted the plan which made Kenesaw Mountain Landis the autocrat of baseball.

Not every community has in its midst an Albert D. Lasker; or a Jackson Reynolds, able to tell at length the history of the founding of the Bank for International Settlements; or a Reuben Lazarus, able to expose (for posterity, not for the present day) the inner workings of Tammany Hall, and to relate how he served as defense counsel for Jimmy Walker at dramatic hearings before Governor Franklin D. Roosevelt which ended in Mayor Walker's resignation. But every community does possess men and women who, though they often do not realize it themselves, have stories to tell which posterity will find significant and engrossing.

One token of our failure to recognize that history lies this side the horizon, and indeed all about us, is found in the excessive preoccupation of Eastern historical societies with the Revolutionary epoch, and of Western historical organizations with the pioneer era. The two greatest and richest historical associations in America, the Massachusetts Historical Society and New York Historical Society, were established one just before and the other just after the year 1800. Their chief founders, Jeremy Belknap and John Pintard, had lived through the Revolutionary period. It was natural that these societies should long devote themselves to the heroic age of the struggle for independence and for a durable Constitution—to the years 1765–1800. In due time the concentration of historical attention upon the late Colonial and Revolutionary epoch was somewhat mitigated by the occurrence of another great heroic era, that of the Civil War, which excited men's imagination and aroused their commemorative instincts. But too much of our organized historical activity still appertains to the infancy and adolescence of the republic. It is too seldom recognized that we have enacted a fuller, prouder, and more complex history in the fifty years from the installation of Theodore Roosevelt to V-E Day than in any other period of American past; that we have made in this fifty years our richest record of martial, political, social, and intellectual achievement; and that our descendants will think us fortunate to have lived in this era as Englishmen hold fortunate those who lived in the age of Elizabeth, and Frenchmen those who shared in the glories of the age of Louis XIV.

In making this plea for a realization that the stuff of history is not something altogether remote in time and distant in place, I do not wish to be misunderstood. No one has a higher respect than I have for the dignity of history. That our best written history requires a perspective which only time can impart; that it is necessarily the fruit of long and wide research; that it is seldom composed except by men who have undergone long and arduous training; that it demands literary talent of a high order; and that it must be invigorated and ennobled by a strong moral impulse—this I fully believe. What is history? Theodore Roosevelt said that history is a vivid and powerful presentation of scientific matter in literary form; and it would be difficult to improve upon this statement. I do not believe that Tom, Dick and Harriet can write history in this sense, or should annoy the world by trying. John Burroughs once remarked that not one man in five hundred can make any observations upon nature that are worth recording. He might have added that not one in five hundred thousand is capable of recording them as Henry Thoreau or Gilbert White of Selborne did. So it is with history conceived in the austerest sense.

But history is a house of many mansions. I do believe that many persons now inert or timid might record historical matter of enduring importance; and that they would do so if they disabused themselves of the notion that history is far away beyond the blue horizon. The fact is that the garments of Clio float about us and by resolutely putting out our hands, anyone of us who is shrewd, observant, and careful can grasp them. Particularly is this true of the great field of social and cultural history—a field in which the village, the provincial town, and the state capital are as important as Washington or London.

Let me quote from another unpublished letter; a letter written almost precisely a hundred years ago by a historical craftsman who believed that history lay all about him—Benson J. Lossing. Mr. Lossing, who belonged to the race of itinerant scholars exemplified by Henry Howe and John W. Barber, wrote three works now too much neglected—his *Pictorial Field Book of the Revolution, Pictorial Field Book of the War of 1812,* and *Pictorial Field Book of the Civil War.* Upon the first-named work Lossing expended more than eleven thousand dollars, then a fortune, before he received a cent of return. He wrote on November 27, 1851, to David L. Swain, president of the University of North Carolina, of his patient, self-sacrificing, laborious efforts to obtain historical materials from the lips of men who had witnessed great events and changes, from traditional family narratives, and from visits to interesting scenes and old buildings:

> The fact is, my dear sir, I visited the various important localities of the Revolution, under the great disadvantage of being an entire stranger in person and name, and "utterly unknown to fame." I sought out the various places with patient perseverance, and the men from whom I might obtain information, I looked for upon

the ground of each event. I know not, personally, a single individual in North Carolina, and I had but one solitary letter of introduction to a gentleman in your state, and that was to the excellent Dr. Wilson of Hillsborough. Even that letter was from a hand, personally unknown to me. Under other peculiar disadvantages, I made the long journey, not the least of which was the claim of the business of my profession, my source of livelihood. Yet, through God's providence, I have accomplished the journeyings, and trust that I have not omitted any place of great general importance. . . . I know that our general histories have given comparatively little of the Revolutionary struggle in the Carolinas, and would lead one to think that they were only the cockpit in which the combatants fought, without furnishing much of the *sentiment* of the Revolution. I have no such appreciation of the matter; on the contrary, I see in the Carolinas, and particularly in the "Old North State," patriotism as deep and abiding, and as early and efficiently manifested as in Boston, Boston the boasted "Cradle of Liberty". . . .

My greatest difficulty has been to discriminate as to what material was most essential to be used and what to omit, so that my work should not be prolix, and too voluminous for popular circulation; for to make the work too large and expensive for the mass of our reading population, would defeat one of the prime objects of my efforts—the placing of a topographical and historical view of our Revolutionary struggle, in a simple manner, before my countrymen. But in this condensation I have not been partial, and my narrative of events in the South will be found quite as minute as of the North.

I like also to think of Henry Howe, the author of the *Historical Collections of New York,* and similar books upon Virginia and above all of Ohio, jogging over a country road in his plain buggy, drawn by his old white horse, pausing at every hamlet and town to talk with the older inhabitants, and record their recollections of historic men and events; collecting newspaper clippings, letters and other materials for the delightful historical grab-bags that he compiled. The methods of such men as Howe and Lossing left much to be desired; the spirit in which they worked was altogether admirable. History to them was not to be found only in remote times and places, beyond the blue horizon; it lay all about them and they gathered it up as eagerly as ever Argonaut gathered a bag of treasure.

Be assured that many of us have a similar opportunity to collect and lay by historical gold. The most difficult part of history to obtain is the record of how plain men and women lived, and how they were affected by the economic, social, and cultural changes of their times; the most fascinating part of history is this same record. The Rev. William Gordon of Roxbury, Massachusetts, struck in 1776 "with the importance of the scenes that were opening upon the world," resolved to write a big bow-wow history of the Revolution. His work is now so dead that few know it exists; but the humble diaries of everyday events by Ezra Stiles, William Bentley, and others of the period are immortal. George Bancroft's biography of Martin Van Buren is utterly forgotten, but Philip Hone's prosaic everyday record of eating, drinking, talking, reading and travelling in Van Buren's time is a perennial joy to readers, and an ever-fresh depiction of life in oldtime New York. We may have many excuses for not setting down historical material, and some of them may be valid. But we do not have the excuse of never seeing matter of enduring historical importance, for it lies around us as the sea lies around the mariner.

33. The Experience of Writing History*

GEORGE F. KENNAN

I just want to make a few very informal observations about the nature of history as a subject and about the condition of the historian. My excuse for doing so is simply that I came to this work unusually late in life, after a quarter of a century, in fact, in a wholly different sort of occupation. The impressions I have gained of these matters have something of the quality of the naïve. And since the naïve is occasionally amusing, whether or not it is instructive, I thought you might just possibly like to hear what these impressions are.

One of the first things that dismayed me, as I tried to put pen to paper with a view to relating historical events, was to discover the hopeless open-endedness of the subject of history itself: its multi-dimensional quality, its lack of tidy beginnings and endings, its stubborn refusal to be packaged in any neat and satisfying manner. I was soon brought to realize that every beginning and ending of every historical work is always in some degree artificial and contrived. No matter what you told, there was always something that had gone before, or came afterward, which you didn't have time to tell about, or which you didn't know about, and which was nevertheless essential to the completeness of the tale.

This open-endedness of the historical subject applied, I was brought to realize, not just to the longitudinal dimension of chronology, but also to the latitudinal dimension of related subjects and related happenings. No matter what field of human activity you selected for treatment, there were always a dozen

* Reprinted with permission from *The Virginia Quarterly Review* XXXVI (Spring, 1960), 205–214.

other fields that had something to do with it, which you couldn't treat. And wherever you tried to draw the boundary between what you could write about and what you couldn't, it was always an artificial boundary, doing violence in some degree to the integrity of the presentation itself.

The perfect historical work, in other words, could not be written. If you were a great enough historian, if you were sufficiently learned in the environment of your subject as well as in its central core, then you might be able to do a good job of concealing from all but the most perceptive of your readers the untidiness of the outer limits of your presentation. But the untidiness would be there, nevertheless. There would always be a border, however well concealed, beyond which the firmness of your knowledge trailed off into the obscurity of your ignorance, or where the obvious limits on the patience of publishers and readers made it impossible for you to tell all you knew.

In addition to this diffuse quality of the subject, I was startled to discover how rigorous, when you stopped to think of it, were the limitations of perspective. History, it seemed, besides being open-ended, partook also of the nature of a sphere. You couldn't see it from all directions at once. You could see it only from some tiny, fixed point in its ample stratosphere. This point was always arbitrary in relation to the subject. An infinite number of other points could conceivably have been selected. Each would have revealed something which you, from the perspective of your particular point, were unable to reveal. Every point was, therefore, severely limited in its possibilities. Not only that, but there was a real question as to what latitude you really had in selecting the point you were going to use—whether, in fact, it was not already substantially selected for you.

This brought up, as you will readily see, the whole perplexing question of subjectivity. I had naïvely supposed, before I tackled this work, that there was a body of unrevealed or unappraised historical fact lying scattered around, like so many archeological fragments, in the archival and bibliographical sediment of the ages, and that the historian's task was only to unearth these fragments, to order them, to catalogue them, and to arrange them in a manner that would permit them to tell their own tale. I was soon to learn that it was not this simple. These fragments were there, all right; but they had, it seemed, no single, definitive tale to tell. They could be arranged in an infinite number of ways, and each had its specific implications. Much was left to the powers of insight of the arranger. He had to do this arranging on the strength of his own good conscience, and to take personal responsibility for the product. This was the task of analysis and interpretation. And this meant that the fixed point from which one viewed history was actually none other than one's own self—one's self in the most intimate personal sense.

The describing of historical events, in other words, was partly an act of the creative imagination of the writer. You might know the bare skeleton of circumstance: that such and such occurred on such and such a day. The fact remains: you weren't there; you didn't see it. To arrive at its true significance—to understand its atmosphere, its meaning for those who experienced it, its relation to other events—you had to put yourself in the place of the people who were there; you had to apply to the historical record something which, however you tried to make it informed and dispassionate, was still an act of the imagination.

But then the question arose: was your imagination not the product of what you yourself had known in life? Of the things you had seen and experienced, as the inhabitant of a specific historical age? And if so, could you really visualize the happenings of another age? Could you conceive of things outside the range of your own experience? If not, then were you not really imposing a distorting lens upon the stuff of history by the very act of attempting to describe it? Was it not history which was serving as a framework for the product of your own imagination, rather than your imagination which was serving to illumine the facts of history?

I recall once seeing a performance of Gogol's Revisor (The Inspector) in one of the leading theatres in Stockholm. It was Gogol's old classic, all right. The words were correctly translated. The script was faithfully followed. Yet what was represented was not Russia but Sweden. Gogol's profound and despairing caricature of bureaucratic life in a Russian provincial administrative center of the early nineteenth century, with all its sad and despairing humor, had been somehow transformed into a jolly, colorful, little Swedish fairy tale, with characters who were like painted dolls—a very creditable performance, a very enjoyable and creative one, in its way; but it was Sweden, not Russia.

One was obliged to wonder whether this was not substantially what one did to any historical subject one touched, no matter how objective one tried to be. I wrote two volumes about certain phases of international life in 1917 and 1918. I did my best to describe things as I thought they looked to the actors in that drama. Sometimes I thought I had succeeded in tolerable degree. But I also had panicky moments of wonder as to whether I had done anything closer to reality than a sort of historical novel. In any case, I was forced to realize, when I looked at the volumes in retrospect, that however revealing they were as a record of the time to which they pertained, they were probably more revealing as a record of our own time—of the outlook and manner of thought of a citizen of the 1950's. I realized then why someone was once caused to remark that all history was contemporary history.

On the other hand, I did see that it was possible to do better or worse in this respect. It was possible to enhance one's capacity for visualizing history by means of the very effort of studying it. One thing supported another. The more you steeped yourself in the environment of your subject—the more, let us say, you supported a study of political events with a parallel study of the art, the religious beliefs, the folklore, the economics, and the manners of the times—the more your imagination could rise to the task. You could, in other words, lift yourself, to a degree, by your own intellectual bootstraps. But this meant that if you really wanted to get near to your subject, it was yourself you had to change. The mere amassing of more data would not do it. To understand a past episode, you had to make yourself to some extent a citizen of the epoch in question. You had to make its spirit, its outlook, its discipline of thought, a part of your own nature.

But this was something which you did only at a certain personal price; and the nature of this price was again one of the things that struck me very strongly about the writing of history. It was something which I can only describe—and I hope the term will not sound too bizarre to you—as its loneliness.

I do not mean to use this term in any self-pitying way. I have enjoyed no less than anyone else the company of my colleagues in the academic life—their company, that is, in the sense of the association one has with them in the odd moments of relaxation: over luncheon tables, and that sort of thing. I even discovered that scholars, so long as they have not constituted themselves a committee to deal with academic-administrative affairs (in which case something very strange indeed happens to them), are the most amusing and companionable of men. I should also like to stress that what I am about to say applies only to the studying and writing of history, not to the teaching of it. But it does appear to me that the studying and writing of history is a relatively lonely occupation.

The historian is lonely, first of all, vis-à-vis the historical personages who are the objects of his study. He lives for long periods among these people. They absorb his attention, his thoughts, sometimes even his sympathies and antipathies. Yet generally speaking, they are not really his companions. They surround him, silently and inscrutably, like figures in a wax museum. He can see them to one extent or another, in the literal sense, depending upon the stage of pictorial or photographic representation in the period when they lived. But they are inanimate. He sees them only frozen in poses—in a series of *tableaux morts*. Sometimes, to be sure, words are to be seen issuing from their mouths, hovering above their heads, so to speak, like the bubbles of utterance that emerge from characters in a comic strip. But one does not actually hear the voices; and one is often not sure whether the words were really theirs or those of the author of the comic strip. In any case, the human context of the utterance: the elusive nuances of circumstances, of feeling, of environment, of intuition and telepathy—the things that made that particular moment unlike any other moment that ever was or will be—all this is seldom to be recaptured. Only, perhaps, in cases of the most profound and selfless and erudite identification of the historian with the period of his study does there occur that intimacy of acquaintance which permits historical personages really to become alive again in their own right—not as products of the arbitrary imagination of the writer, but in reasonable resemblance to what they really were.

But even where such people become real for the historian, he, let us remember, does not become real for them. Their mutual relationship is a one-way street. *He* takes an interest in *them*. He supports them. He becomes their posthumous conscience. He tries to see that justice is done them. He follows their trials and experiences, in many instances, with greater sympathy and detachment than any of their egocentric and jealous contemporaries ever did.

But do *they* support *him?* Not in the least. They couldn't care less. Most of them would snort with contempt if they were to be made aware of the identity of those who would later undertake the effort to interpret their lives and strivings to future generations. Statesmen often conceive themselves to be working for posterity in the abstract, but they have little real respect for individual members of it, in a world where youth is never what age was and where the good old times will never be recaptured. Historical characters would have little solicitude for the brash member of a future generation who takes upon himself so presumptuously the burden of interpreting *their* doings and *their* difficulties.

The historian assists then, like a disembodied spirit, at the activities of his characters. To them, he has a duty, a responsibility, of understanding and of sympathy. But he himself remains unseen, unknown, unaided. This, for my money, is loneliness.

And it is not only vis-à-vis the inhabitants of the past that the historian is lonely. The study of history is something that cuts one off from the age in which one lives. It represents— let us face it—a certain turning of one's back on the interests and preoccupations of one's own age, in favor of those of another. This association with the past cannot occur, if only for reasons of time, otherwise than at the expense of the association with the present.

This is something which one's contemporaries, polite as they may be, rarely really understand or forgive. Every age is egocentric—and fiercely so. Every age thinks itself to be the most important age that ever occurred. Is not the present generation, after all, the occupant of that incomparably most important place in human history—the area between the past and the future? The very idea that one of the members of this generation should turn away from its absorbing and unprecedented concerns to give his attention, professionally and at length, to the affairs of people who suffer from the obvious inferiority of not being alive at all: this, to any normal and full-blooded contemporary, is little short of insulting. It implies that there were people long ago whose lives were so much more important and interesting than our own that the mere contemplation of them from a distance is held preferable to a direct participation in the affairs of our own age, despite all its obvious glories and mysteries. What body of the living, intoxicated by the illusion of progress and the belief in the uniqueness of its own experience, would ever forgive *that?*

The historian too often finds himself, I fear, in the position of the man who has left the noisy and convivial party, to wander alone on cold and lonely paths. The other guests, whom he has left behind, murmur discontentedly among themselves: "Why should he have left? Who does he think he is? Obviously, he doesn't like our company. He thinks us, plainly, a band of frivolous fools. But we are many; he is one of very few. We therefore are clearly right, and he is wrong. The devil take him. Let him sulk." So they say. And so he does.

So much for the historian's loneliness. Let me just mention one more thing that has grown upon me in the course of this work. It is the realization of how deeply one has to dig to find the justification for what one is doing. There are, after all, so many discouragements.

A librarian friend of mine told me the other day that it was most doubtful, in view of the inferior quality of present-day American paper, that anything I, or any of my colleagues, had recently written would still be legible fifty years hence. Since one of the few real consolations of writing history is the faint hope that perhaps one has accomplished something for the ages, this was a shattering thought.

Then, too, there is the atom, with all its grisly implications. I find it hard to forget that we live in an age when all sorts of people who haven't got the faintest concern for history—who don't even know, in fact, what it is—have it already in their power to put an end not only to great portions of the historical record (this, various military characters have done very successfully at frequent intervals in the past), but to both the writers and the readers. It is an uncomfortable reflection that this entire work of the study of the past—its subject, its rationale, its practitioners, its customers, its meaning—that all this is vulnerable, or soon will be, to the whims of brother Khrushchev or brother Mao or even certain of our American brethren that I could name, not to mention others who may, with time, come in to the power of disposition over these apocalyptic weapons.

Even if men manage to avoid, by some unaccountable good fortune, the plunge over this particular abyss, one sees that humanity is now living, anyway, in the midst of some sort of a biological and technological explosion, by which the terms of life are being altered at an ever-increasing pace. A part of this explosive process is the multiplication of the historical record, particularly the recent one. Even the major events of the present century—events which appeared to people at the moment to be of major, headline significance—have accumulated in such volume as to place them quite beyond the apprehension of the layman. It is the rarest of persons who today has any comprehension of the series of events which, just in his own time and that of his father, has brought him where he is today. Even the historian feels increasingly inadequate to this task. He can only wander around, like a man with a tiny flashlight amid vast dark caverns, shining his little beam here and there for a moment on a tiny portion of the whole, but with the darkness always closing up behind him as it recedes ahead. More history is probably written today than at any time in the past; and with respect to distant ages, once largely lost to historical knowledge, we are no doubt making progress. But with respect to the doings of our fathers and grandfathers, or even our elder brothers, we are, I fear, fighting a losing battle. The dizzy pace of change is carrying us into the future faster than we can pay out the delicate thread of historical scholarship that is our only link to the past.

What, then, is the use? Has this pursuit of history become no more than a superfluous habit—something that people assume their children ought to study in school simply because this has always been done within their memory? Are the conditions of our lives being altered with such rapidity that the record of the past would have little to tell us even if we could keep up with the explosive expansion of its volume?

Each of us, I suppose, has to answer these questions for himself. I am personally convinced that they must be answered in the negative. It may be true that it is becoming increasingly difficult ot reconstruct an adequate record of the past. It may be true that there never was a time when history was less susceptible of apprehension, in its entirety, by the layman. It may be true that we are condemned to explore only tiny and seemingly unrelated bits of a pattern already too vast for any of us to encompass, and rapidly becoming more so. All these things, to my mind, merely make the effort of historical scholarship not less urgent but more so.

It is clear that the spectacular mechanical and scientific creations of modern man tend to conceal from him the nature of his own humanity and to encourage him in all sorts of Promethean ambitions and illusions. It is precisely this person who, as he gets carried along on the dizzy pace of technological change, needs most to be reminded of the nature of the species he belongs to, of the limitations that rest on him, of the essential elements, both tragic and helpful, of his own condition. It is these reminders that history, and history alone, can give; for only history can expose the nature of man as revealed in simpler and more natural conditions, where that which was elemental was less concealed by artificialities. And to the supplying of these reminders, which is the historian's task, it is not necessary that one should know or understand the whole unconscionable and spreading panorama of history. A little bit, looked at hard and honestly, will do. In this little bit will be found, in the measure of the devotion applied to it, the compensation for all the essential imperfection of the historical art, for all the struggle with subjectivity, for all the loneliness, for all the questioning as to whether anyone will ever read what you wrote or whether it would do them any good if they did.

Selected titles: revised December, 1966

harper ⚜ torchbooks

HUMANITIES AND SOCIAL SCIENCES

American Studies: General

CARL N. DEGLER, Ed.: Pivotal Interpretations of American History   TB/1240, TB/1241
A. S. EISENSTADT, Ed.: The Craft of American History Vol. I TB/1255; Vol. II TB/1256
CHARLOTTE P. GILMAN: Women and Economics § TB/3073
JOHN HIGHAM, Ed.: The Reconstruction of American History △   TB/1068
JOHN F. KENNEDY: A Nation of Immigrants △ TB/1118
LEONARD W. LEVY, Ed.: American Constitutional Law   TB/1285
ARNOLD ROSE: The Negro in America   TB/3048

American Studies: Colonial

BERNARD BAILYN, Ed.: The Apologia of Robert Keayne: Self-Portrait of a Puritan Merchant   TB/1201
LAWRENCE HENRY GIPSON: The Coming of the Revolution: 1763-1775. † Illus.   TB/3007
PERRY MILLER & T. H. JOHNSON, Eds.: The Puritans: A Sourcebook   Vol. I TB/1093; Vol. II TB/1094
EDMUND S. MORGAN, Ed.: The Diary of Michael Wigglesworth, 1653-1657   TB/1228
EDMUND S. MORGAN: The Puritan Family   TB/1227
RICHARD B. MORRIS: Government and Labor in Early America   TB/1244
WALLACE NOTESTEIN: The English People on the Eve of Colonization: 1603-1630. † Illus.   TB/3006

American Studies: From the Revolution to 1860

RAY A. BILLINGTON: The Far Western Frontier: 1830-1860. † Illus.   TB/3012
W. R. BROCK: An American Crisis: Congress and Reconstruction, 1865-67 ° △   TB/1283
GEORGE DANGERFIELD: The Awakening of American Nationalism: 1815-1828. † Illus.   TB/3061
RICHARD B. MORRIS, Ed.: The Era of the American Revolution   TB/1180
A. F. TYLER: Freedom's Ferment   TB/1074

American Studies: Since the Civil War

MAX BELOFF, Ed.: The Debate on the American Revolution, 1761-1783: A Sourcebook △   TB/1225
EDMUND BURKE: On the American Revolution. † Edited by Elliot Robert Barkan   TB/3068
WHITNEY R. CROSS: The Burned-Over District: The Social and Intellectual History of Enthusiastic Religion in Western New York, 1800-1850   TB/1242
W. A. DUNNING: Reconstruction, Political and Economic: 1865-1877   TB/1073
FRANCIS GRIERSON: The Valley of Shadows   TB/1246
SIDNEY HOOK: Reason, Social Myths, and Democracy   TB/1237

WILLIAM E. LEUCHTENBURG: Franklin D. Roosevelt and the New Deal: 1932-1940. † Illus.   TB/3025
ARTHUR S. LINK: Woodrow Wilson and the Progressive Era: 1910-1917. † Illus.   TB/3023
JAMES MADISON: The Forging of American Federalism. Edited by Saul K. Padover   TB/1226
ROBERT GREEN MC CLOSKEY: American Conservatism in the Age of Enterprise: 1865-1910   TB/1137
ARTHUR MANN: Yankee Reformers in the Urban Age   TB/1247
GEORGE E. MOWRY: The Era of Theodore Roosevelt and the Birth of Modern America: 1900-1912. † TB/3022
R. B. NYE: Midwestern Progressive Politics TB/1202
FRANCIS S. PHILBRICK: The Rise of the West, 1754-1830. † Illus.   TB/3067
WILLIAM PRESTON, JR.: Aliens and Dissenters TB/1287
JACOB RIIS: The Making of an American ‡   TB/3070
PHILIP SELZNICK: TVA and the Grass Roots: A Study in the Sociology of Formal Organization TB/1230
TIMOTHY L. SMITH: Revivalism and Social Reform: American Protestantism on the Eve of the Civil War   TB/1229
IDA M. TARBELL: The History of the Standard Oil Company. Briefer Version. ‡ Edited by David M. Chalmers   TB/3071
GEORGE B. TINDALL, Ed.: A Populist Reader ‡ TB/3069
ALBION W. TOURGÉE: A Fool's Errand   TB/3074
VERNON LANE WHARTON: The Negro in Mississippi: 1865-1890   TB/1178

Anthropology

JACQUES BARZUN: Race: A Study in Superstition. Revised Edition   TB/1172
JOSEPH B. CASAGRANDE, Ed.: In the Company of Man: Portraits of Anthropological Informants. TB/3047
DAVID LANDY: Tropical Childhood: Cultural Transmission and Learning in a Puerto Rican Village ¶ TB/1235
EDWARD BURNETT TYLOR: The Origins of Culture. Part I of "Primitive Culture." § Intro. by Paul Radin TB/33
EDWARD BURNETT TYLOR: Religion in Primitive Culture. Part II of "Primitive Culture" §   TB/34
W. LLOYD WARNER: A Black Civilization: A Study of an Australian Tribe. ¶ Illus.   TB/3056

Art and Art History

EMILE MÂLE: The Gothic Image: Religious Art in France of the Thirteenth Century. § △ 190 illus. TB/44
ERICH NEUMANN: The Archetypal World of Henry Moore. △ 107 illus.   TB/2020
DORA & ERWIN PANOFSKY: Pandora's Box: The Changing Aspects of a Mythical Symbol   TB/2021

Business, Economics & Economic History

GILBERT BURCK & EDITORS OF FORTUNE: The Computer Age: And Its Potential for Management   TB/1179

---

† The New American Nation Series, edited by Henry Steele Commager and Richard B. Morris.
‡ American Perspectives series, edited by Bernard Wishy and William E. Leuchtenburg.
* The Rise of Modern Europe series, edited by William L. Langer.
¶ Researches in the Social, Cultural, and Behavioral Sciences, edited by Benjamin Nelson.
§ The Library of Religion and Culture, edited by Benjamin Nelson.
Σ Harper Modern Science Series, edited by James R. Newman.
° Not for sale in Canada.
△ Not for sale in the U. K.

1

NATURAL SCIENCES
AND MATHEMATICS

DATE DUE